MODERN LANGUAGE PERFORMANCE OBJECTIVES AND INDIVIDUALIZATION

A HANDBOOK

MODERN LANGUAGE PERFORMANCE OBJECTIVES AND INDIVIDUALIZATION
A HANDBOOK

REBECCA M. VALETTE
Boston College

RENEE S. DISICK
Valley Stream Central High School

HARCOURT BRACE JOVANOVICH, INC.
New York / Chicago / San Francisco / Atlanta

To **J.-P. V.** *and* **D. M. D.**

ISBN: 0-15-561893-8

Library of Congress Catalog Card Number: 75-176359

Printed in the United States of America

FOREWORD

Over the past several years, much has been said and written in support of and in attempted refutation of the concept of performance objectives. This book, long needed in the field, provides not only a sensible rationale for the use of behavioral objectives, but also leads the reader systematically through the steps necessary for implementation. The concept of behavioral objectives is given perspective through the relationship which is established with individualized instruction. The taxonomies provide the final component which enables the reader to refine objectives and place them into the spectrum of the total teaching situation.

The book's thoroughness, practicality, and usability make it must reading for foreign-language teachers concerned with the demands for a dynamic curriculum in our schools.

C. Edward Scebold

Executive Secretary of the American Council on the Teaching of Foreign Languages

PREFACE

In the 1960's, foreign-language teachers felt that students would acquire a second language readily once the appropriate materials were available. This emphasis on means of presentation led to the development of new programs, the dissemination of language laboratories, and government subsidies for teacher training.

A decade later, however, foreign-language teachers are realizing that despite innovative methods and new media many students have failed to learn a second language and, in fact, that foreign-language enrollments are declining. The new concern, in foreign languages as well as in other subject-matter areas, is with the outcome of instruction: What has the student learned? What can he do with what he has learned? How does he feel about his learning experience? Have his attitudes and self-image changed as a result of this experience?

This concern on the part of teachers and administrators is now frequently leading to the preparation of performance objectives—carefully worded statements describing the desired outcome of instruction in terms of student behavior. Within the classroom, an attempt is also being made to individualize instruction, that is, to reorganize the learning activities in such a way as to meet the needs of each individual student.

Part One of this handbook provides practical guidelines for writing performance objectives and for implementing them in the classroom. Part Two contains sample performance objectives classified in increasing order of difficulty. The Appendix contains a sample performance contract with its learning steps, a sample report card, and sample guidelines for teacher training. The selected bibliography lists some sources on specific topics that readers desiring further information will find helpful. The glossary defines terms that may be unfamiliar to some readers. Finally, a comprehensive index enables the reader to refer easily to specific sections and examples.

In the preparation of this handbook, we have incurred obligations to many people. We should like to thank F. André Paquette, Jerald R. Green, C. Edward Scebold, and Joan Robert who commented on parts of the manuscript. Gerald Logan was so generous as to allow us to reproduce some of his materials in the Appendix. To these, and especially to our students at Boston College and Valley Stream Central High School, we wish to express our sincere gratitude.

R. M. V.
R. S. D.

CONTENTS

PART TWO   CLASSIFYING STUDENT BEHAVIORS

MODERN
LANGUAGE
PERFORMANCE
OBJECTIVES
AND
INDIVIDUALIZATION
A HANDBOOK

HOW TO USE
THIS HANDBOOK

To obtain maximum assistance from this handbook, the user should be familiar with its organization.

Part One defines performance objectives, explains the taxonomies for subject-matter and affective goals, and offers suggestions for the application of these ideas in the individualization of foreign-language instruction. Self-tests provide practice in recognizing valid performance objectives and in writing them.

Part Two presents a taxonomy of affective behaviors and test items as well as taxonomies for subject-matter behaviors and test items in listening, speaking, reading, writing, gestures, way-of-life culture, civilization, and literature. At the end of each chapter, self-tests enable the reader to practice classifying student behaviors and test items in that particular area. The items included in the taxonomical listings are intended to represent most of the current foreign-language teaching practices. The lists, however, are not comprehensive, nor can the inclusion of certain objectives and test items be considered as an endorsement by the authors of the teaching strategies they may represent.

The second part of the book can be a useful reference for teachers seeking to establish performance objectives and measures for their courses, as well as for teachers who wish to check the taxonomical classification of the behaviors and test items they have already developed.

INTRODUCTION

In "the good old days," it seems that students were docile, passive, and accepting; if their teacher commanded, "Jump," their response was likely to be, "How high?" Today, however, students seem to be obstreperous, demanding, and challenging; if a teacher commands, "Jump," their response is likely to be, "Why?"

This is certainly a reasonable question that both students and teachers should ask. If learning is to occur in school, all those involved in this process should be aware of exactly what they are doing and why they are doing it. One means of accomplishing this is to state instructional goals in terms of performance objectives.

Performance objectives can give each learning activity a purpose. They enable the student to see exactly what he is expected to do and to understand why he is asked to do it. They are equally important for teachers, for unless a teacher knows exactly where he is going, it is impossible to tell how much progress his classes are making and when, if ever, they achieve the goals set for them. Furthermore, without clearly stated objectives, it is impossible to construct valid tests to measure whether the desired learning has actually taken place.

Performance objectives are also essential components of individualized instruction. Students can be freed to learn at their own pace and in their own way only if the behaviors they are to produce at the end of the instructional period are clearly specified.

4

In addition, performance objectives are important for supervisors of teachers. It is difficult to evaluate a teacher's work accurately unless the supervisor knows what goals have been established for a particular lesson and how this lesson fits into the general unit and course goals. The supervisor also needs to know whether or not students have achieved the performance objectives set for them.

Finally, performance objectives are useful in communicating clearly to parents, administrators, and other interested members of the community the results of the instruction offered in school. In a time when support for foreign-language education is vitally needed, it is essential that teachers hold themselves accountable for providing rewarding experiences to all their students.

In many ways, then, performance objectives offer the possibility of improving the quality of learning. It must be added, however, that performance objectives have their limitations. They do not of themselves provide a panacea for the problems related to language teaching. If they are to contribute substantially to the improvement of instruction, they must be used wisely. Therefore, it is the purpose of this book to present ways in which performance objectives may serve to increase the effectiveness of foreign-language teaching. To this end, several performance objectives have been set.

Mastery of the material in this book should enable the reader to accomplish the following goals.

KNOWLEDGE

a. List the four parts of a formal performance objective and distinguish it from an expressive performance objective.

b. List the five stages of the subject-matter taxonomy and at least the first three stages of the affective taxonomy.

TRANSFER

c. Classify the student behaviors and test items given according to their position in the subject-matter or affective taxonomy.

COMMUNICATION

d. Write an original formal or expressive performance objective, as appropriate, for each stage of the subject-matter taxonomy and for the first three stages of the affective taxonomy.

It is also hoped that the reader will demonstrate achievement of the following affective goals.

APPRECIATION

a. Establish performance objectives for the subject-matter and affective goals of his courses and communicate them to his students.

b. Bring his students, insofar as possible, to **Stage 4: Communication** and **Stage 3: Appreciation** behaviors.

c. Individualize his instruction by teaching for mastery of performance objectives, by employing group-work techniques, or by implementing a system of student contracts.

d. Evaluate the results of his instruction in terms of the objectives set and seek ways to improve it.

PART ONE
PERFORMANCE OBJECTIVES

CHAPTER ONE
DEFINITION OF A PERFORMANCE OBJECTIVE

1.1 GENERAL CONSIDERATIONS

During the 1960's, educators sought to improve the quality of education by total curriculum revision. This effort resulted in the NDEA language institutes and the audio-lingual approach, the New Math, the introduction of linguistics into English textbooks, and innovative science curricula. Since these revised curricula in themselves failed to bring about the anticipated educational utopia, the 1970's are witnessing a new direction of inquiry. Research has shifted away from the inputs of instruction—curricula, textbooks, methodology—and has focused on the outcomes of instruction—changes in behavior and attitude in the student.

This concern with the outcomes of education takes two different forms. The first is *accountability:* Are students really learning what the teachers profess to be teaching them? In foreign-language teaching, this means: Are the students able to understand conversations at the end of two years of instruction? What can they write? What kinds of materials can they read? In other words, what will students be able to do with the language as a result of the instruction they receive? Many educators feel that these outcomes can be most precisely communicated to parents, administrators, and to the students themselves if instructional goals are stated in terms of observable student behavior.

The other current educational concern focuses not only on the acquisition of subject-matter competence, but also on *affective goals*—the individual student's attitudes, feelings, and values concerning learning in general. Is the instruction organized so that each student experiences success and satisfaction in his learning activities? Are students eager to continue with their study of foreign languages? Do they try to use the foreign language once they leave the classroom? Affective goals of this sort may also be stated in terms of observable student behavior.

Goals that specify the observable outcomes of instruction are called *performance objectives*. Performance objectives are also frequently referred to as *behavioral* or *instructional objectives*. For the sake of simplicity, we shall use *performance objectives*. The term "goal" will be used when referring to broad, general objectives of a course or of language teaching.

1.2 OUTPUT RATHER THAN INPUT

All learning requires activity of some sort on the part of the learner. In foreign-language classes, these activities take many forms: listening to tapes, repeating sentences, writing exercises, and so forth; such activities may be termed input. Performance objectives emphasize what the student can do, once he has finished the specified activities. In other words, they emphasize student output.

1.2.1 *An Illustration: the Case of Igor Beever*

Igor Beever was about to begin the study of his first foreign language. His father, a hydraulics engineer, would have preferred that his son take a course in dam building. "You should learn to do something constructive," he always said, but Igor persisted, since he had hopes of becoming a diplomat.

On the first day of school, his teacher, Miss Bea Wilder, spent the period talking about the course. She said she would teach the class how to understand, speak, read, and write the language and would present its grammar and culture. She then handed out the textbook, *Overcoming Language*, and said the students were responsible for knowing it. Igor didn't understand exactly what he would have to do to succeed in the course, but he was very impressed with his teacher's presentation and decided to wait and see.

He waited until the end of the first quarter and saw that no matter how hard he tried, he was unable to pass. Mr. Beever, concerned over Igor's low grades, asked his son what he was supposed to do in order to pass. Igor didn't know what to say, so Mr. Beever arranged a parent-teacher conference. Miss Wilder said Igor would have to listen harder in class and put forth more effort at home in order to know the book. Mr. Beever thanked her politely for her good advice and went home to tell this to his son. Igor tearfully informed his father that he listened to every word that came from Miss Wilder's mouth and that he spent many hours studying at home. This was certainly very perplexing. "I just don't know what to do," wailed Igor. Mr. Beever promised his son a summer trip abroad if he earned passing language grades.

Anxious to be rewarded, Igor applied himself with renewed fervor to his studies. He realized he had to "know" the book, but he didn't really understand what this meant and exactly what he had to do in order to accomplish it. He continued to fail.

Toward the end of the winter, Mr. Beever thought he finally had an answer to the problem. "You know what you have to put into the course—time in class and time with the book at home—but not what you have to put out, what you have to produce." Igor told his father that this analysis was brillant but that it was too late because he was hopelessly lost and had decided to drop the language.

Epilogue

The local elections came, and a campaign of concerned citizens succeeded in defeating the new tax levy to support education. The leader of the movement was Mr. Beever.

Several dejected teachers were discussing the defeat of the levy. "How could this happen?" said Bea Wilder in disbelief. "The parents and students simply don't understand what we are doing."

Miss Wilder had gotten to the heart of the matter. Unfortunately, she was totally unaware of it.

1.2.2 Stating Student Output

According to Igor and his father, the problem in language class was caused by Igor's not knowing what he had to do. Miss Wilder thought she had communicated this information on the first day of class when she told the students what she intended to do. Students, however, need to understand exactly what behaviors are expected of them, and they need to know whether or not they have been successful in attaining them. Knowing what the teacher's behavior will be is of little value in helping them produce the desired performance.

Defining student output consists of letting the student know what he is expected to do at the end of the period of instruction and how well he must do it. Vague instructions, such as "study the chapter," are of limited value because they are open to so many different interpretations.

1.2.3 *Student Behavior or Teacher Behavior: a Self-Test*

The following are examples of either student or teacher behaviors. Identify the four student behaviors by marking *S* next to them.

_____ 1. To present rules of subject-verb agreement.

_____ 2. To explain the differences between direct and indirect object pronouns.

_____ 3. To write answers to questions on a reading selection.

_____ 4. To model the pronunciation of dialog sentences.

_____ 5. To repeat after the speakers on a tape.

_____ 6. To mark whether a statement heard is true or false.

_____ 7. To introduce cultural material into the lesson.

_____ 8. To review the numbers from one to one hundred.

_____ 9. To describe in German a picture cut from a magazine.

_____10. To go over material taught in Unit Five and answer questions on it.

Answers: 3, 5, 6, and 9.

1.2.4 *Input or Output: a Self-Test*

The following are examples of student input and output behaviors. Write an *O* next to the four output behaviors.

_____ 1. To pay attention in class.

_____ 2. To recite a dialog from memory.

_____ 3. To study Lesson Twelve.

_____ 4. To learn the rules for the agreement of the past participle.

_____ 5. To look at foreign magazines.

_____ 6. To attend a make-up lab period.

_____ 7. To write a brief composition about a picture.

_____ 8. To read a paragraph aloud with no mistakes.

_____ 9. To watch a movie on Spain.

_____10. To answer questions about a taped conversation.

Answers: 2, 7, 8, and 10.

1.3 SPECIFYING STUDENT OUTPUT IN TERMS OF PERFORMANCE

It is not enough to specify output rather than input. Each student must be made aware of precisely what type of performance is expected of him.

1.3.1 *An Illustration: the Case of Frank O'Filia*

Mr. Frank O'Filia is a diligent and conscientious language teacher who prides himself in meticulous preparation and the high standards of his classes. "The students who are able to pass my course have *really* learned something," he always says. Today Mr. O'Filia is giving a homework assignment.

"Study your list of vocabulary words for a test on them tomorrow." General groans are heard; then several students raise their hands to ask questions.

Minnie Effort: Do we have to know *all* fifty words?

Mr. O'Filia (to class) : Of course. (To himself) I'm only testing the twenty most common words, but if I say so, they won't study the whole list.

Simon Simpul: Will we have multiple choice questions?

Mr. O'Filia (to class) : Perhaps. (To himself) I don't believe in guessing-game questions, but why say so?

A. Fazic: Will we have to write out the words?

Mr. O'Filia (to class): Perhaps. You just study hard and do your best.

Della Gent: How many questions will there be?

Mr. O'Filia (to class) : Now I think we've wasted enough time on silly questions today. You'll find out all you need to know on the test tomorrow. (To himself) Students these days are so lazy; they are only willing to do the minimum of work.

Since this was their very first test of the year, Mr. O'Filia's students wanted to make a good impression on him. Each one studied according to what he thought Mr. O'Filia would ask.

Minnie Effort thought she had to know all the words on the list. This is her idea of the test:

Was this word on the list?

　　　　　Yes　　　No

1. Maison ＿＿＿　　＿＿＿

Simon Simpul decided this test would be like the ones he had the year before:

Write the letter of the English meaning that best suits the underlined word.

1. Voici ma voiture (a) garage (b) car (c) barge (d) wagon (e) train.

A. Fazic thought the test would look like this:

Translate the following words:

1. dog _____
2. teacher _____
3. bite _____

Della Gent was sure there would be fifty matching questions on the test:

Match each word with its English meaning. Write the letter of the meaning in the blank.

<u>X</u> 50. bête   X. stupid

What was Mr. O'Filia's test actually like? It looked like this:

Fill in the appropriate word according to the definitions given. There are twenty items at five points each. Any misspelled word is wrong. Passing is 65 percent correct.

1. Mon frère n'est pas intelligent. Il est _____

Mr. O'Filia's students were *very* surprised, among other things.

Minnie was miffed. "I can remember if a word was on the list, but I certainly can't write it down!" So, she turned in a blank paper.

Simon was stunned. "All I know is the English for every word on the list." He answered in English hoping to get some credit at least.

A. Fazic was appalled. "I didn't know spelling counted!" The words he had written sounded correct if read aloud, but the spelling system was his own invention, so he received no credit.

Della was disgruntled. "Only twenty questions! I thought we would be tested on all fifty words. I'll never study this long again." She was so annoyed that all the words became jumbled in her mind, and she wrote the right answers in the wrong places.

The next day Mr. O'Filia handed back the tests and gave a lecture. "Your test grades show that you obviously did not study enough at home. You will have to put forth more effort if you don't want to fail." (To himself) "How could their teachers have possibly passed them last year? I certainly have a lot of weeding out to do."

Then, trying to be more positive, he added, "I am happy to see that Ray Peters has done very well. In fact, he is the only student who passed." (Since Ray had failed Mr. O'Filia's course the year before, he knew what kind of test to expect.) "Keep up the good work, Ray. You have certainly learned some language." ("And," he might have added, "some Mr. O'Filia, too!")

There are many teachers like Mr. O'Filia. They test not only on the subject, but on the ability of their students to figure them out. A restatement of Mr. O'Filia's assignment might be:

In order to learn vocabulary words, study them somehow at home so that you can succeed to some unspecified degree on a test of indeterminate nature tomorrow in class.

Had Mr. O'Filia stated his objectives more clearly, could his students have come to four different (and incorrect) conclusions about the nature of the vocabulary test?

1.3.2 *Describing Student Behavior*

A performance objective must describe the student behavior, or "performance," that is desired. In the illustration above, Mr. O'Filia was looking for the following behavior:

Write out and spell correctly the foreign-language word that corresponds to a given foreign-language definition.

However, he simply told the students to "know" the words on the list, an instruction open to several interpretations:

1. Identify which words are included on a particular list.

2. Produce an English equivalent of a foreign-language word.

3. Write the foreign-language word that corresponds to an English definition.

4. Match each word with its definition.

Not all terms are equally useful in describing student behavior. Certain instructions tend to be ambiguous—know, understand, become aware, comprehend, grasp, appreciate, gain insight into. Since such terms fail to indicate exactly what a student should *do* to show that he knows or is aware or understands, they should either be avoided or further clarified when used in performance objectives.

The following terms communicate more clearly to the learner what he is to do: spell correctly, pronounce, write a sentence, read aloud, complete, match, define, analyze, list, answer orally, translate from . . . into . . . , demonstrate listening comprehension by . . . , demonstrate reading comprehension by. . . . Instructions such as these promote clarity when used in descriptions of desired student behavior. Frequently, however, some additional explanation will still be needed. The word "pronounce," for example, is open to several interpretations. What is to be pronounced? A memorized dialog, a reading of a familiar dialog, a reading of unfamiliar material, a repetition of a teacher's statement, an oral response to a question?

The following guideline may be useful: The desired student behavior must be stated so clearly that even an outside observer can understand precisely what type of performance is called for.

1.3.3   *Ambiguous or Clearly Stated Assignments: a Self-Test*

The following assignments are stated in terms of student behavior. Mark with an *X* the five assignments that are stated with the least ambiguity.

_____ 1. Study pages 53 to 55 and be ready to discuss them in class tomorrow.

_____ 2. Write the sentences in Exercise A on page 69 in the past tense.

_____ 3. Answer questions 1 to 10 on page 75 in writing.

_____ 4. Listen to the sentences on the practice record and imitate the speakers as accurately as you can during the pauses provided.

_____ 5. Go over the exercises on page 35.

_____ 6. Review the reading selection on pages 100 to 101.

_____ 7. Write in the blanks on page 44 the correct form of the verbs given in parentheses.

_____ 8. Prepare yourself for an oral quiz on the basic dialog.

_____ 9. Cut out a magazine picture for each line of the dialog and write the corresponding line under each picture.

_____10. Understand the difference between the two past tenses used in the story on page 67.

The assignments in items 2, 3, 4, 7, and 9 are stated in performance terms. In each case the learner knows exactly what he has to do in order to accomplish the work assigned.

Let us examine the assignments that are *not* stated in performance terms. In these cases the instructions do not indicate to the student what he has to produce in order to meet the requirements of the assignment. Study and be ready (1), go over (5), review (6), prepare yourself (7), and understand the difference (10) are ambiguous and can admit many interpretations of what activities actually fulfill the assignment. To determine whether an assignment is stated in performance terms, ask yourself whether the assignment clearly states what observable behavior the learner must exhibit while doing the assignment.

On the following test, check which assignment of each pair is stated in behavioral terms.

_____1a. Appreciate the beauty of the description on page 55.

_____1b. List five words or expressions that you think contribute to a vivid description of the action taking place.

_____2a. Learn the vocabulary words on page 65.

_____2b. Show you understand the meaning of the words on page 65 by using them correctly in written sentences.

_____3a. On the outline map supplied, fill in the names of all the countries in South America. Refer to the map on page 52 of your text if necessary.

_____3b. Familiarize yourself with the map of South America on page 52 of your text.

_____4a. Know when French meals are normally served.

_____4b. List in French the name of each meal and the times at which it is normally served in France.

_____5a. Look over the reading selection on pages 88 to 90 and be ready to ask questions in class about what you do not understand.

_____5b. Read pages 88 to 90 carefully to make sure you understand the story. Write the page and line number of any sentences or paragraphs you do not understand. Ask for an explanation of them in class tomorrow.

Answers: 1b, 2b, 3a, 4b, and 5b.

1.4   THE FOUR PARTS OF A FORMAL PERFORMANCE OBJECTIVE

A formal performance objective is more complete than an assignment. A formal performance objective not only describes what the student is to do, but also explains the purpose for that behavior, the conditions under which it will occur, and how it will be evaluated.

The formal performance objective that Mr. O'Filia had mentally set for his class but failed to communicate to the students would read:

To demonstrate knowledge of twenty out of fifty vocabulary words (list attached), write out and spell correctly the word that corresponds to each of the twenty definitions given on a twenty-minute classroom test. At least thirteen of the twenty items must be entirely correct in order to pass.

This formal performance objective contains four parts:

1. **PURPOSE:** To demonstrate knowledge of twenty vocabulary words.

2. **STUDENT BEHAVIOR:** Write out and spell correctly the word that corresponds to each of the twenty definitions given.

3. **CONDITIONS:** On a twenty-minute classroom test.

4. **CRITERION:** At least thirteen of the twenty items must be entirely correct in order to pass.

In addition, a sample test item may be included.

1.4.1 *A Self-Test on Part One of a Formal Performance Objective: the Purpose*

In each of the following performance objectives, the purpose is missing. Complete the objective by devising an appropriate purpose for each.

1. Answer the following five questions so that your responses form a coherent composition. You have thirty minutes in which to respond. No more than five grammatical errors are allowed in order to pass.

2. Read the short story (pp. 90–101) at home and answer the ten questions on page 102. You may use a dictionary to help you understand the text. The answers to the questions are to serve as the basis for your participation in the discussion of the story in class. You will be graded on factual accuracy, literary insight, and comprehensibility of your answers.

3. Fill in the following outline map with all the rivers, mountains, and cities indicated. Check your accuracy against the map in your text on page 59. Make any corrections necessary.

4. Give a two-minute speech on a topic of your choice. You may use no notes during your classroom presentation and will be graded on pronunciation, fluency, and grammatical accuracy. No more than five major errors in grammar or pronunciation will be allowed in order to pass.

5. Listen to the following story, which will be repeated twice. Then answer the ten true/false questions that you will hear afterwards. To pass, 70 percent accuracy is required.

Some sample answers:

1. To develop writing skill, to practice new grammatical structures, to learn to write guided compositions.

2. To develop reading skill, to develop understanding of foreign-language literature, to learn to read with the help of a dictionary, to develop speaking skill.

3. To become acquainted with major geographic features of the country being studied.

4. To develop speaking skill, to learn to speak without using notes, to develop accurate pronunciation, to apply grammatical knowledge in communication.

5. To develop listening comprehension, to develop skill in retaining material heard.

1.4.2 *A Self-Test on Part Two of a Formal Performance Objective: the Student Behavior*

In each of the following formal performance objectives, the student behavior is missing or is inadequately explained. Complete the objective by devising an appropriate behavior for each.

1. To develop ability in literary analysis, read the selection on pages 201 to 235 and write a paper analyzing an element of your choice. Your work will be judged according to whether or not your conclusions are substantiated by the text.

2. To develop skill at speaking extemporaneously, act out the situations written on these index cards. Only fluency and comprehensibility will be evaluated. Grammatical errors will not be counted insofar as they do not interfere with the listener's understanding.

3. To gain background knowledge of the foreign culture, read the following chapter in your textbook. Fulfillment of this assignment will be checked in class.

4. To demonstrate skill in writing from dictation, write a passage dictated to you. In order to pass, 90 percent of the words should be spelled correctly.

5. To demonstrate the ability to pronounce correctly, read a given passage aloud. Pronunciation accuracy as well as intonation, stress, and rhythm will be evaluated. You will be tested individually by the teacher.

Some sample answers:

1. Specify the length of the paper and what elements are to be analyzed.

2. Indicate how long the skit should last and if any rehearsal or thinking time is allowed.

3. Indicate if the student should take notes, answer questions, outline reading, and so forth.

4. Indicate the length of the dictation, the material it will be based on, and whether the material is familiar or recombined.

5. Indicate the length of the reading and whether the material is to be familiar or not.

1.4.3 *A Self-Test on Part Three of a Formal Performance Objective: the Conditions*

In each of the following performance objectives the conditions are missing. Complete the objective by devising appropriate conditions for each.

1. To demonstrate reading fluency, read a newspaper article as rapidly as you can. The required accuracy on the ten multiple choice questions that follow the article is 80 percent.

2. To demonstrate the ability to use appropriate body gestures, participate in a simulation of one of the situations listed. Appropriateness of all gestures will be the criterion for passing.

3. To show the ability to analyze works of art, compare and contrast two of the works selected from among those on this list. Appropriateness of the contrasts will be the criterion for passing.

4. To display knowledge of an important historical event, write an essay on it based on class notes and information gained from the textbook. Clarity of organization, appropriateness of material selected, and factual accuracy will be used in evaluation.

5. To demonstrate writing ability, write a composition of three hundred words with no more than ten errors in grammar or spelling.

Some sample answers:

1. Specify the length of the article, the time allotted for reading, where reading is to take place, and whether or not dictionaries may be consulted.

2. Specify the length of the simulation and where it is to occur.

3. Indicate the length of the presentation, the elements to be contrasted, the time limit if any, whether the presentation is to be oral or written, and whether (if a paper) it is to be written at home or in class.

4. Specify the length of the essay, where it is to be written, and whether notes may be used at the time of writing.

5. Indicate what aids will be available to the student (dictionary, grammar

textbooks), where the composition is to be written, the time limit if any, and the topic limitations if any.

1.4.4 *A Self-Test on Part Four of a Formal Performance Objective: the Criterion*

In each of the following performance objectives, the criterion is missing. Complete the objective by devising an appropriate criterion for each.

1. To demonstrate knowledge of specialized literary terminology, match the following ten terms with their definitions on a classroom test.

2. To demonstrate the ability to form literary judgments, evaluate a book you have read outside of class. State the purposes of the book and whether or not the author was effective in achieving them. Then justify your position with illustrations from the textbook. Write your evaluation in the foreign language, outside of class, using any dictionaries or grammar textbooks that might be helpful to you. The paper should be about five hundred words long.

3. In order to show your ability to carry out independent research, propose a plan of original research into an area of interest to you. Describe the techniques you intend to use as well as the sources you intend to consult.

4. To show the ability to control foreign-language pronounciation, repeat each of the following five sentences after the tape model. The test will be administered in class on an individual basis with the teacher making the evaluation.

5. In order to demonstrate native-like competence in listening comprehension, listen to the following passages to be played once each in class. Circle the choices on the answer sheet that best describe the speaker's socio-economic class, his mood, the region he comes from, or his standard of speech.

Some sample answers:

1. The minimum percentage of correct answers or the minimum number of correct answers.

2. A statement about the appropriateness of the arguments or the organization of the paper.

3. A statement about the clarity, completeness, and comprehensibility of the research plan.

4. Indicate which sounds are to be tested or whether general accuracy of pronunciation will be evaluated; indicate whether stress, rhythm, and intonation are evaluated. Specify the minimum satisfactory performance.

5. Indicate the minimum percentage or number of right answers required to pass.

1.5 INTERNAL CONSISTENCY IN FORMAL PERFORMANCE OBJECTIVES

As we have said, formal performance objectives consist of four parts: purpose, student behavior, conditions, and criterion. The mere presence of these four parts, however, does not automatically guarantee a valid performance objective. The four parts must be consistent with each other in that they all refer to the same type of behavior.

1.5.1 *Inappropriate Purpose*

Study the following performance objective:

To demonstrate an understanding of cultural patterns, list six Mexican cultural themes and an appropriate example of each. On a classroom test, nine correct responses out of twelve (six themes and six examples) will be considered a passing grade.

In the example above, the purpose, student behavior, conditions, and criterion are all clearly stated and are interrelated. However, is the student really demonstrating understanding of cultural patterns when he exhibits the desired behavior? If we assume the students have been taught the predominant cultural themes of Mexico and have been given many examples of these themes in class, the test does not measure understanding, but simply memory.

The revised—and internally consistent—performance objective would read:

To demonstrate a *knowledge of* cultural patterns, list six. . . .

1.5.2 *Inappropriate Student Behavior*

Let us assume that the teacher really wanted to test *understanding* of cultural patterns. In the example above, the student-behavior part of the performance objective might be modified so that the student would be presented with unfamiliar illustrations of cultural patterns and be required to identify the themes they exemplify. The revised performance objective would read:

To demonstrate an understanding of cultural themes, study closely the twelve brief videoclips of typical Mexican situations that you have never seen before. Indicate which cultural themes are illustrated in each videoclip. On this thirty-minute classroom test, nine out of twelve correct responses will be considered a passing score.

1.5.3 *Inappropriate Conditions*

Here is another inconsistent performance objective:

To demonstrate the ability to use written forms of the demonstrative adjectives *ce, cet, cette,* and *ces* appropriately, complete fifteen items of the following type on a twenty-minute classroom quiz:

Regarde _____ maison. (Look at this house.)

You will not be allowed to use a dictionary. You may make no more than three mistakes in order to pass.

Here, all the parts are consistent except the dictionary clause. The students must know the gender of the nouns in order to use the appropriate demonstrative adjective. With a dictionary, textbook, or other guide, the student can check the gender of nouns about which he is unsure. Without a dictionary he might make several mistakes because he has forgotten the gender of the nouns or because some of the words are unfamiliar to him. Thus, although the teacher intends to test only control of grammar, the condition clause introduces an additional factor: the student must know the genders of the nouns that appear on the test.

The performance objective may be made internally consistent by stating that the students may use a dictionary. Alternatively, the need for a dictionary might be eliminated by cuing the gender of the noun in the item itself (Regarde _____ vieille maison.) or by listing the gender of each noun at the bottom of the test (la maison).

1.5.4 *Inappropriate Criterion Measure*

Consider the following performance objective:

To apply a knowledge of German prosody, analyze in German on a classroom test the versification pattern (meter, rhyme scheme, and so on) of an unfamiliar poem of Heinrich Heine. You may make no more than five grammatical mistakes in this essay in order to pass.

Again, all four parts are present. Yet, while the purpose, the student behavior, and the conditions are all related to each other (the student will *apply* what he has learned to a new literary work that he has not studied in class), the criterion measure is totally inappropriate. The presence or absence of grammatical mistakes has absolutely no bearing on the stated goal of instruction. This is not to say that the teacher should be unconcerned with grammatical mistakes and accurate written expression in the foreign language, but rather that the goal of literary analysis and the goal of fluent written communication are distinct from each other: the criteria for one are not applicable to the other.

Perhaps the teacher will wish to set two performance objectives for his students.

1. (Literary) To apply a knowledge of German prosody, analyze the versification pattern (meter, rhyme scheme, type of poem) of a brief, unfamiliar poem of Heinrich Heine's on a ten-minute classroom test. You may answer in German or English. No more than one mistake in describing prosody will be allowed in order to pass.

2. (Written expression) To write German fluently, write in German on a half-hour classroom test a ten- to fifteen-line résumé of the poem above. A dictionary may be used. You may make no more than five grammatical mistakes in order to pass.

1.5.5 *Internal Consistency: a Self-Test*

Read the following formal performance objectives carefully. Only one is internally consistent. For each of the remaining four performance objectives, indicate which part is inconsistent and suggest a modification to improve its validity.

1. To demonstrate the ability to order food in an Italian restaurant, recite in pairs the basic dialog of Lesson Five (books closed). To pass, you must recite your role without prompting.

2. To demonstrate the ability to communicate in Spanish with the aid of gestures, perform gestures to communicate the idea expressed in English on a card that you draw. (Example: you are hungry and want to eat.) Each of you will come before the class and perform according to the directions on three cards. You pass if your classmates understand all three gestures and can tell you what was on each slip.

3. To demonstrate the ability to understand a story written in German, write a brief German résumé of "Die Küchenuhr" (which the class has just finished studying), with your book closed. The essays are to be written in class during half an hour. You must write the five main events in their proper sequence in order to pass. Mistakes in grammar and spelling will not be counted.

4. To demonstrate the ability to make sound-symbol associations, read aloud a familiar dialog. This reading will be recorded in the language laboratory. Six mistakes or less (that is, the wrong sound assigned to a written symbol) will be considered passing.

5. To communicate in spoken French, describe five different foods to your classmates. You will stand behind a screen so that you may only communicate verbally without recourse to gestures. Your classmates will write down the five foods described. You may not make more than ten pronunciation or grammatical mistakes while speaking.

Some sample answers:

1. Inconsistent purpose, since the ability to recite a memorized dialog does not at all guarantee that the material would be applied to a real-life situation. A suggested modification: To demonstrate that the lesson dialog has been memorized. . . .

2. Internally consistent performance objective.

3. Inconsistent student behavior, since the use of a familiar story demonstrates knowledge of previously learned material rather than understanding of new material. A suggested modification: . . . you will be given a short *un*familiar story comparable in difficulty to those you have been studying and will write a brief résumé in German (or in English).

4. Inconsistent student behavior, since the purpose requires an application of knowledge to new, not familiar, situations. Suggested modifications: . . . you will read aloud an *un*familiar dialog; . . . you will read aloud an *un*familiar passage.

5. Inconsistent criterion, since the purpose of the assignment is comprehensibility, not accuracy. Suggested modifications: The class must identify at least four out of five objects correctly; at least 75 percent of the class must identify all five objects correctly.

1.6 FORMAL PERFORMANCE OBJECTIVES AND EXPRESSIVE PERFORMANCE OBJECTIVES

Formal performance objectives, as we have seen, are stated in four parts: purpose, student behavior, conditions, and criterion. They focus on student output, described in terms of observable and predictable student performance.

In foreign-language learning, the outcomes of certain types of activities may be specified very precisely: recitation of memorized materials, counting, directed dialogs, conjugations of verbs, declensions of nouns, naming objects in the foreign language, manipulation of sentence patterns, and so on. These types of goals, which represent the simpler or more elementary aspects of language learning, lend themselves readily to the mold of the formal performance objective.

It is much more difficult, however, to specify with precision the outcomes of activities involving free composition or conversation, analysis, and evaluation. These higher goals of language learning resist statement as formal performance objectives, because the teacher cannot always predict what the student behavior will be like. For example, all students may be told to write a brief composition about a picture, but the teacher cannot know in advance which sentences the students will write, which vocabulary they will use, which structures they will select.

An open-ended *expressive performance objective* is needed. It contains a purpose and a statement of student behavior in terms of performance. However, the conditions may be less precise. There may be no specific time limits, and the length may be limited to a range—for example, three to six pages for a paper or one to three minutes for a talk, and so on. The criterion also tends to be somewhat more subjective. In fact, the criterion might be simply whether or not the desired behavior has occurred.

The objective of one lesson in a third-year Spanish class, for example, might be to pick out dominant themes in a short story that has been read as homework. The teacher might offer some guidance in the class discussion, but the actual listing of themes would reflect the student's suggestions. Another class, given the same assignment, might develop a different list. The aim of the class activity is not to elicit a specific list, but rather to have students read a text carefully with an eye to uncovering themes. The teacher has a specific behavior in mind but not a specific outcome.

Expressive, or open-ended, performance objectives are appropriate for the higher aims of language instruction. Although such objectives do not require specific conditions or criteria, it is nonetheless useful for the teacher to indicate general conditions and a general criterion. The conditions might include a description of the types of materials to be used, nature of resources permitted, approximate length of paper or talk, and so on. The criterion might also be sketched in: it may describe how the performance will be judged and whether some aspects of the performance will be considered more important than others. In oral and written free communication assignments the criterion can be stated simply in pass/fail terms: Is the student's work generally comprehensible or not?

The classification of student behaviors into simpler ones and more complex ones helps the teacher determine which behaviors lend themselves to formal performance objectives and which are more appropriately described in expressive objectives. Such a classification is presented in Chapter Two.

CHAPTER TWO
SUBJECT-MATTER AND AFFECTIVE TAXONOMIES

Learning a second language is a cumulative experience. Students learn basic sentences before they learn how to recombine them. They learn the present tense of auxiliary verbs before they learn how to use them in forming compound tenses. They learn to read recombinations of familiar material before they are presented with more difficult selections.

Student behaviors in the realm of attitudes, feelings, and values are also the result of cumulative experience. The student's initial attitude toward foreign languages and foreign-language study might be simply the awareness that foreign languages exist. As he begins to learn a new language, he may experience satisfaction in his accomplishment. He may become so interested in language study that he will begin to look for additional opportunities to practice the language and to learn more about the country where that language is spoken.

Performance objectives must therefore be written for the more complex and more advanced student behaviors and attitudes as well as for simpler ones. This chapter proposes a classification system for both subject-matter goals and affective goals in foreign-language education. Examples of student behaviors and test items that may measure the goals are found in Part Two of this handbook.

2.1   GENERAL CONSIDERATIONS

There is no single correct way to classify the goals set in foreign-language learning. The system described in the following pages represents a modification of one method of classification, the Bloom taxonomy.[1] The categories defined by Bloom and his coauthors were designed primarily for the physical and social sciences, history, and literature, rather than for second-language acquisition. For this reason, it has often been difficult in the past to classify foreign-language goals within the Bloom framework. The system described in this chapter has been modified and developed specifically to allow foreign-language teachers to classify their goals in a meaningful way.

2.1.1   *Subject-Matter Goals and Affective Goals*

The goals of foreign-language instruction can be divided into two general groupings: subject-matter goals and affective goals.

Subject-matter goals refer to what is being taught: the language skills, the grammar and vocabulary, the culture, the literature. Can the student recognize verb tenses? Can he understand a conversation in the foreign language? Can he identify cultural patterns typical of the foreign country? Can he analyze a poem? These behaviors fall into the area of subject matter. In foreign languages, these subject-matter goals cut across two domains of the Bloom taxonomy: the cognitive domain and the psychomotor domain. The *cognitive domain* includes behaviors which require knowledge, understanding, and intellectual skills. The *psychomotor domain* includes behaviors which require physical activity, such as sound discrimination, sound production, gestures, etc. A foreign-language student may recite sentences which he does not understand and thus be acting only in the psychomotor domain. He might also be able to translate sentences from German to English, without being able to pronounce German properly, and thus be acting only in the cognitive domain. Usually, however, in language teaching the cognitive and psychomotor domains are closely interrelated.

Affective goals, mentioned in Chapter One, refer to the student's attitudes and feelings. Does the student pay attention in class? Does he participate in discussions? Does he want to speak the foreign language, or is he afraid to try? Does he engage in outside activities related to foreign-language learning? Is he eager to travel abroad? Is he tolerant of other peoples? These are considered affective behaviors.

---

[1] The Bloom taxonomies are described in Benjamin S. Bloom et al., *Taxonomy of Educational Objectives: The Classification of Educational Goals, Handbook I: Cognitive Domain* (New York: David McKay, 1956); and David R. Kratwohl, Benjamin S. Bloom, and Bertram Masia, *Taxonomy of Educational Objectives, Handbook II: Affective Domain* (New York: David McKay, 1964). A preliminary adaptation of the Bloom categories to foreign-language learning appeared in Rebecca M. Valette, *Directions in Foreign Language Testing* (New York: MLA/ERIC, 1969).

2.1.2 *A Definition of the Term "Taxonomy"*

A *taxonomy* is a classification system that begins with the simplest behaviors and proceeds to the most complex. This hierarchical system is easily adapted to the classification of performance objectives in foreign-language learning. Knowing the meaning of individual words is much simpler than using these words correctly in an original sentence. Producing sentences in a guided drill is simpler than expressing one's personal ideas. Reading a letter is simpler than writing a similar letter.

Each of the taxonomies presented in this chapter is divided into five *stages*, or levels, Stage 1 being the simplest and Stage 5 being the most complex.[2]

Furthermore, the behaviors at each stage of the subject-matter taxonomy are subdivided into two components: *internal behavior* and *external behavior*. Behavior is considered internal when the teacher is most concerned with what is going on in the student's mind. Does he hear the difference between two sounds? Does he understand what he has just read? Does he think foreign-language study is valuable? Although the behavior is internal, the student must exhibit it through some sort of external activity so that the teacher can tell whether the desired internal behavior has taken place. Thus the behavior is measured indirectly. For example, the student indicates whether two sounds are the same or not, he answers questions about a reading, he gives his opinion of foreign-language study. Behavior is considered external when the teacher is most concerned with what the student produces, with the activity in which he engages. Does he imitate a sentence with the correct accent? Can he write a short paragraph about what he did last weekend? Does he often listen to foreign radio broadcasts on his own initiative? Generally, the foreign-language skills of listening and reading involve internal behavior, while the skills of speaking and writing involve external behavior.

2.2 CLASSIFYING SUBJECT-MATTER GOALS

The attainment of subject-matter goals is the primary concern of most language teachers. In foreign languages, the subject matter might consist of speaking, reading, and writing the language itself; or it might consist of a study of the foreign culture, an introduction to the foreign literature, or a combination of all the above.

2.2.1 *An Illustration: the Case of Gunne Academy*

The committee on instruction had decided that high-caliber teaching should be encouraged at their school. So, faculty members were asked to define what this meant in their subject area. At the language department meeting, each teacher presented his ideas on what he thought were his highest goals.

---

[2] The word "stage" is preferred to "level," since the latter term has come to refer to the amount of language students are to learn in one year.

Mr. Otto Mattick began: "Communication is what counts. I believe in lots of repetition and memorization. Students should build strong response habits that become as natural as their native language habits. In my classes we concentrate on perfect pronunciation and perfect dialog recitation."

Next, Mrs. Rhea Cawl spoke: "Students have to remember certain important facts about language in order to communicate effectively. They have to know what individual words mean and how to write appropriate forms. If students can understand and remember the basic facts, they will be well along the road toward language proficiency."

Miss Carrie Over then presented her ideas: "The most important skill we can teach students is how to apply what they have learned to new communication situations. In class we spend a great deal of time doing exercises with recombinations of familiar material."

She was followed by Mr. Hi Thayer: "Using the foreign language for communicating should be our primary goal. Expressing ideas so that other people understand them is more important than strict grammatical accuracy. The mistakes can be eliminated eventually through practice. That is why we have lots of skits and speeches and role-playing in my classes."

Finally Mr. Rhett Oricks gave his views: "True language competence involves the ability to communicate by using the type of language required by the particular situation. My students develop sensitivity to words and their appropriate uses. I teach them how to distinguish slang from formal language and how to recognize a speaker's social class and regional origins from the way he talks."

In the heated discussion that followed, each teacher felt *he* was the most effective in achieving the goal of communication. There was little agreement on which emphases represented the highest caliber of teaching. There was agreement, however, on the area of disagreement:

1. Students who perform by rote memory do not necessarily understand what they are saying.

2. Students who remember certain specific facts do not necessarily know how to use them.

3. Students who can use what they have learned when presented with recombinations of familiar material may not be able to express their own original thoughts.

4. Students who communicate easily may make many grammatical mistakes and do not necessarily tend to correct these mistakes.

5. Sensitivity to the differences between formal and informal language may be too difficult or too specialized a goal for the majority of the students.

Somehow, no one teacher's approach seemed all right or all wrong; rather, the five approaches seemed complementary. But in what order should they be arranged? Also, which emphases might be most appropriate to language students with low, average, and high aptitudes? Which might be best used at the beginning, intermediate, and advanced levels of language learning?

The department chairman decided to discuss the problem with the principal.

"Why don't you adapt the approach of the biology department?" suggested the principal.

The chairman looked puzzled.

"You know what a taxonomy is, don't you?"

The chairman looked perplexed.

"Sure you do. That's a classification system of all the animals in the world, which ranks them from the lowest to the highest. You know, you start with an amoeba and you wind up with a man."

The chairman looked bewildered.

"Well, you go through intermediate steps of insects, fish, amphibians, reptiles, birds, and mammals, of course. You see, the taxonomy lists all creatures from the simplest to the most complex."

"So what does that have to do . . ." the chairman began dubiously.

"Well, the biology department listed the behaviors it expected of its students from the most elementary to the most advanced. You could do the same with foreign-language behaviors."

"But, I wouldn't know where to start . . ."

"Why not just think about it?"

The chairman thought about it and started by presenting the idea at the next department meeting. It made sense, the teachers became enthusiastic, and they decided to classify student behaviors. Here is the order they developed:

1. Mechanical skills   (Mr. Otto Mattick)
2. Knowledge   (Mrs. Rhea Cawl)
3. Transfer   (Miss Carrie Over)
4. Communication   (Mr. Hi Thayer)
5. Criticism   (Mr. Rhett Oricks)

What an amazing discovery! Each of the five teachers had been under the impression that he was teaching his students how to communicate, when actually he was presenting only one stage of the general goal.

"From now on," they firmly resolved, "we will classify the behaviors we expect from our students to see if they achieve our departmental goal of communication."

Thus high-caliber teaching was achieved at Gunne Academy.

2.2.2   *Reasons to Classify Objectives Taxonomically*

By classifying student behaviors according to a taxonomy, a teacher can gain a better perspective on his instruction. He can see whether his course emphasizes simpler or more complex language behaviors. He can determine the stage of behavior at which his students perform and can then create activities that will lead them to higher stages of achievement. He can also classify his test items taxonomically to determine whether they actually measure the behaviors being developed. In these ways, a taxonomy provides a teacher with a precise instrument for rigorous self-evaluation.

A taxonomy is equally useful in designing a foreign-language curriculum. By establishing a hierarchy of language behaviors, a taxonomy can help determine an appropriate sequence of instruction. Furthermore, it can facilitate more accurate communication among teachers by clarifying ambiguous statements such as "I teach my students how to speak." The objectivity of the categories in a taxonomy can promote meaningful evaluations of classroom objectives and learning outcomes, since imprecise and emotionally charged terms such as "good teaching" and "bad teaching" are never employed. Finally, taxonomically classified performance objectives can serve to increase articulation of language learning between different schools as well as between different courses in one school.

2.2.3 *Taxonomy of Subject-Matter Goals*

A taxonomy of subject-matter goals in foreign-language instruction is presented in Figure 2-1. The five basic stages are indicated on the left. The first stage of the taxonomy represents the simplest type of language-learning behavior; the fifth stage represents the most advanced type of behavior. Each stage is divided into two substages: internal and external behaviors. The internal category comprises behaviors such as listening and reading; the external category comprises behaviors such as speaking and writing.

FIGURE 2-1

STAGES OF THE SUBJECT-MATTER TAXONOMY

Stage	Internal Behavior	External Behavior
1. **Mechanical Skills**	*Perception*	*Reproduction*
2. **Knowledge**	*Recognition*	*Recall*
3. **Transfer**	*Reception*	*Application*
4. **Communication**	*Comprehension*	*Self-Expression*
5. **Criticism**	*Analysis* *Evaluation*	*Synthesis*

Stage 1: Mechanical Skills

The first stage of behavior is **Mechanical Skills.** Here the student performs very simple tasks of perception, discrimination, or differentiation. This stage of behavior also includes performance based on mimicry and rote memorization.

Perception (internal) is the subcategory that deals with listening and reading skills. The student is called on to discriminate between sounds or letters. He can tell the difference between foreign-language and native-language sounds. He indicates whether two words or sentences he has heard or seen are the same or different. He makes sound-symbol relationships and can identify the stress and intonation patterns he hears. On request, he can listen selectively for specified elements, such as the negative *pas* in French or *dem* as a sign of the German dative. He can distinguish between native and foreign gestures when these are presented to him.

Reproduction (external) is the subcategory that includes speaking and writing. Here the student functions like a robot: whatever is put in comes out unchanged. He memorizes dialogs, songs, poems, sayings, or lists (numbers, days of the week, months of the year). He is also capable of mimicking sentences uttered by the teacher or by a tape, and he can mimic gestures typical of foreign-language speakers that are modeled for him. He copies sentences accurately and can write from dictation material he has memorized.

At this first stage, it is important to note that the student performs mechanically and may not necessarily understand the meaning of what he is hearing or saying or doing. He may indicate that two words are the same without the faintest idea of what the words mean. He may indicate which gender is used in a sentence but be incapable of understanding the sentence. He may relate sounds and symbols but not be aware of their meanings. He may recite a memorized dialog or mimic faithfully the teacher's pronunciation with no comprehension of the words he has uttered. He may be able to reel off the days of the week with lightning speed yet find himself incapable of producing on request the foreign-language word for "Thursday."

Of course, it is probable that the student does understand at times what he is hearing or saying. The point is, however, that understanding is not required for the simple behavior of the first stage. (Conceivably parrots could equal, if not surpass, the speaking skills of students performing at this stage.)

Stage 2: Knowledge

The second stage of behavior is **Knowledge.** Here the student shows that he can recognize and recall familiar facts. In language learning, these "facts" might be the spelling of words, the meaning of vocabulary items, grammatical forms, the meaning of entire sentences, responses to familiar questions (greetings, weather, and so on). The teaching of culture, civilization, and literature involves the following types of "facts": identification of authors, painters, composers, scientists; meaning of cultural patterns and specialized terms; knowledge of important dates and events; the description of trends, themes, styles, ideas.

Recognition (internal) is the subcategory that requires the student to identify facts that are presented to him. He may answer true-false, matching, or multiple-choice questions. He may give the English equivalent of a word or phrase or gesture.

Recall (external) is the more demanding subcategory. Here the student must produce the fact. He may answer a question, fill in a blank, make identifications, or supply definitions. When given an English word or sentence, he may provide the foreign-language equivalent that he has learned in class.

In Stage 2 behaviors, understanding is required for satisfactory performance, but originality is not. The student shows that he has assimilated the material presented in class. Nothing unfamiliar is presented to him. He does not interact with or change the material in any way; he simply demonstrates his knowledge by producing on request the information desired. In a language class, this demonstration may consist of writing the dialog lines that correspond to visual cues. In a culture class, it may consist of listing predominant cultural themes. In a literature class, it may consist of writing down the insights gained from class discussions or of presenting a critic's analysis of a poem.

Stage 3: Transfer

The third stage of behavior in the taxonomy is **Transfer.** Students demonstrate that they can use the knowledge acquired in Stage 2 in new combinations and in unfamiliar situations. Although the elements, or facts, are familiar, their arrangement is different. Most language exercises and pattern drills fall into this category, as do recombined narratives and dialogs.

Reception (internal) is the first subcategory. The student understands contrived speech samples when he hears them spoken or played on tape. This type of activity, which involves only familiar structure and vocabulary, is guided listening comprehension. The student can also identify gender, number, tense signals, and so on, in unfamiliar sentences. He understands reading passages that recombine known structures and vocabulary in new sequences. The student may demonstrate his understanding by answering questions, by choosing among multiple-choice items, or by giving an English equivalent. In the area of literature and civilization, the student may be asked to explain an unfamiliar quotation in terms of other ideas expressed by the same author or with reference to known historical trends. An unfamiliar custom or convention of daily life may be explained in relation to known patterns of living.

Application (external) is the second subcategory. Under guidance the student applies his knowledge of the elements and patterns of the language to produce new statements. He uses known grammatical rules to transform unfamiliar sentences, according to directions, into singular or plural, past or future, masculine or feminine, and so on. He may ask and answer questions as requested by the teacher. He may rewrite a passage in another tense or mood. He may expand dehydrated sentences or fill in blanks. In the area of culture, he is able to play the role of a native of the country being studied. In literature, he may describe the rhyme scheme of an unfamiliar poem.

Certain characteristics of this stage of behavior are particularly significant. First, all the elements of the test material are known, but their order or sequence of presentation is new. Second, the situations are considerably structured. The student acts because he has received precise directions regarding what is expected of him. He is instructed to give an English equivalent, classify a statement as true or false, perform a grammatical transformation, or play a specified role. At this stage, student behavior is subject to teacher control and is evaluated in terms of accuracy of response.

Stage 4: Communication

Communication is the next stage in the taxonomy. Student behavior differs here from that of Stage 3 in two ways. First, the listening and reading materials are now examples of authentic language. They may be edited or controlled, but they have not been contrived to incorporate only known vocabulary and structure. Second, the student's performance in speaking and writing is relatively unstructured by the teacher. The student himself determines what he wants to say and how he will express himself. For this stage of behavior, fluency and comprehensibility are more important performance criteria than the accuracy required in the first three stages.

Comprehension (internal) is the first subcategory. The student listens to or reads material in the foreign language. The nature of the material may range from very simple to quite complex, but no matter what its degree of difficulty, it sounds natural to speakers of the language. If the material contains unfamiliar structures and vocabulary, the student may be instructed to read with or without the aid of a dictionary. The teacher may wish to evaluate ease of comprehension or speed of reading at this point. Understanding major ideas may be given more importance here than the ability to comprehend each word or phrase. In the area of civilization, students may be asked to explain the main historical or literary ideas or positions evidenced in an essay or speech. In the realm of culture, students might have to explain the significance of cultural patterns they observe in a foreign film.

Self-Expression (external) refers to the speaking and writing behaviors of the communication stage. The student expresses his own ideas orally or in writing. Although the teacher may give direction to student responses by assigning a speech, a skit, or a composition, in which he is to use certain grammatical structures, the student is not told precisely what to say or write. Beyond the minimum requirements of the assignments, the ideas a student expresses are his own. At this stage in the taxonomy, fluency and ease of expression are given more importance than strict grammatical accuracy. Behavior in the area of culture may involve the use of behavioral patterns, gestures, and reactions in communication with native speakers of the language.

In a very rudimentary way, behavior at Stage 4 may actually begin on the first day of language instruction when the student learns to react to, or comprehend, the foreign-language commands of "listen" and "repeat." He is functioning at the *Self-Expression* behavior when he uses the foreign language to say he has not understood or when he asks for clarification. At the other extreme, when the communication stage reaches its highest development, the student performs like a bilingual.

Stage 5: Criticism

The most complex behavior in the taxonomy is **Criticism.** The main concern is with manner of expression. Does the speech convey regional differences, social differences, levels of formality and informality, emotion, irony? Can the student vary his expression to convey nuances in meaning?

Analysis (internal) is the first subcategory of Stage 5. The student, listening to a speech sample or reading a passage, can explain its connotations and implications. Artistic translation from the foreign language into English falls in this area. In literature the student can perform an *explication de texte* and can analyze plots, themes, structures, techniques, and character development. The use of a semiotic approach to culture[3] would also be classified here.

Synthesis (external) is the second subcategory in Stage 5. The student can speak or write the language with a conscious personal style. He can vary his manner of expression to convey specific implied meanings. He can create a literary work or develop a critical essay. He can translate literature from English into the foreign language.

Evaluation (internal) is the highest subcategory in this stage. The student judges, orally or in writing, a speech, a film, a piece of literature, either according to internal criteria (Does the work attain the goal it sets for itself? Is it internally consistent?) or external criteria (Does it meet the requirements of a specific set of critical guidelines? Does it meet the student's personal standards?). Here, the content of the student's work is of prime importance, although another grade may also be assigned to his form and expression.

---

[3] Michel Beaujour and Jacques Ehrmann, "A Semiotic Approach to Culture," *Foreign Language Annals*, vol. 1 (1967), pp. 152–63. The semiotic approach is based on the analysis of cultural "signs" and symbols.

The behaviors in Stage 5 may be applied to either students of the foreign language or to native speakers of that language. That is, while all native speakers of a language attain Stage 4 behaviors (**Communication**), many never become sensitive to nuances of literary tone. Many never develop a personal written style, nor do they learn to evaluate what they see, hear, or read. Consequently, behaviors at this stage in the taxonomy are appropriate only for advanced students and are usually not stressed in secondary school programs.

2.2.4 *Guidelines for Using the Subject-Matter Taxonomy*

For the subject-matter taxonomy to be useful to the teacher, he must be able to determine readily how to classify the performance objectives he is preparing for his students. The taxonomy helps the teacher visualize the interrelationship between different types of student behavior by assigning to each behavior a stage, ranging from simple (Stage 1) to complex (Stage 5). Furthermore, at each stage the internal behavior is generally acquired before the corresponding external behavior.

In this section we propose several questions that the teacher might ask himself when classifying a performance objective. By answering each question about a specific performance objective, the teacher may gradually classify the objective in its appropriate category in the taxonomy.

Question 1: Is the student's actual performance, or behavior, important in itself, or is it mainly thought of as an outward reflection of an inner mental process? What is being measured? The student's actual behavior or his mental processes as reflected in his performance?

When the student mimics a gesture or gives an oral exposé or writes a composition, the teacher is interested in the student's observable behavior and in the product of that behavior. Did the student imitate the movements accurately? Did he speak so that his classmates understood him? Did he express himself well in writing? Behaviors of this type are considered external; the teacher is primarily concerned with the outward form of what the student says or does.

On the other hand, when the student is asked to listen to a recording or to read a short story or to watch a foreign film, the teacher is concerned with the mental processes that are going on within the student. Did he understand what the speaker was trying to say? Did he understand what happened in the story? Did he notice specific examples of cultural patterns in the film? Behaviors of this type are considered internal; they are hidden from the view of the observer. Since the teacher cannot enter into the mind of his student, the student must do something to show what is happening within. He may pick out appropriate pictures, answer true-false questions, give an English equivalent, prepare a résumé, and so on. The teacher is concerned with the form of the student's outward response (Did he put his check precisely in the middle of the box as he was instructed? Did he spell the words correctly in his résumé?) only to the extent that it helps the teacher evaluate the nature of the student's inward response.

When a student learns a foreign language, he learns to understand the spoken and written language (internal behavior) and to express himself in speech and writing (external behavior). Thus, in a general way, one might say that internal behavior equals listening and reading comprehension while external behavior equals speaking and writing. However, the fact that a student writes something in the foreign language does not necessarily classify his behavior as external, nor does the fact that he does not write make his behavior internal.

Example A: The student listens to a dialog and writes a brief summary in the foreign language of what he heard. The teacher is mainly interested in finding out whether the student understood what was being said. He grades the written summary on content rather than form. This objective is an example of internal behavior.

Example B: The student reads a brief recombined narrative. The teacher asks oral questions about the reading. Students answer in the foreign language. The teacher is primarily concerned with whether the students understood what they were reading. He listens to *what* the students are saying, rather than how they are saying it. Although he may correct speaking errors, he is again focusing on *internal* behavior.

Example C: The student sees three written words and indicates which two rhyme. The teacher is indirectly measuring whether the student knows how to pronounce the words—an external behavior.

Example D: The student answers multiple-choice questions of the type:

Je n'ai rien_____faire.   A. à   B. de   C. pour

The teacher is interested in whether or not the student knows which preposition to use in the sentence and not whether he knows what the sentence means. The teacher's concern is with *external* behavior.

Example E: The student hears the sentence: "Quelle moisson!" On an answer sheet he indicates which sentence he heard:

A. Quel maçon!   B. Quelle moisson!   C. Quelle maison!

If the student knows all the words, their pronunciations and their spellings (this having been checked before), and if the teacher wants to know if the student understands the meaning of "Quelle moisson!" when he hears it spoken, then the item is testing internal behavior.[4] However, such an item is

---

[4] In this case, the option might be: A. a picture of a brick mason; B. a picture of a harvest; C. a picture of a house.

usually used to test whether the student knows how written words are pronounced, or conversely, how spoken words are spelled; in such cases, it would be testing external behavior.

Example F: In a literature class, the student analyzes a play. If the teacher grades the paper solely on content ("fond"), he is judging internal behavior. If he grades it solely on how well it is written ("forme"), he is judging external behavior. He may grade it on both content and form, assigning one grade for internal behavior and another for external behavior.

Question 2: Is student behavior characterized by rote performance, or is understanding necessary?

If the student can perform without necessarily knowing the meaning of what he hears, says, sees, or writes, then his behavior is at the **Mechanical Skills** stage. If understanding is essential to proper performance, then the student is at Stage 2 or higher on the taxonomy.

Example G: The student recites a dialog or plays a role in a skit. If he is merely judged on his fluency and pronunciation, he is performing at Stage 1. If he must recite lines that correspond to visual or English cues that give the meaning of the sentences, he is performing at Stage 2.

Question 3: Is the student behavior that is tested identical to that of the teaching situation, or is novel behavior called for?

If student behavior in the testing situation is identical to that practiced in the learning situation, the performance belongs at Stage 2. If novel behavior is called for, the student performance would be classified at Stage 3 or higher.

Example H: The student tells time in the foreign language. If all the "times" being tested have been previously practiced in class, this behavior is classified as Stage 2. However, if the class has practiced "3:10" and "4:10" and the test asks the student to give the foreign-language equivalent of "5:10," the student behavior is classified as Stage 3. If the teacher thinks the classroom clock might be wrong and asks the student to give the exact time according to his own watch, the student behavior is classified at Stage 4.

Question 4: Is student behavior guided or is it relatively unstructured?

Student behavior is guided and controlled by the teacher and is therefore judged as "right" or "wrong" in the first three stages of the taxonomy. At Stages 4 and 5, student behavior is either partially or totally unstructured by the teacher. The student's responses may take a variety of forms. His performance (external behavior) is judged on fluency, appropriateness, originality, organization, comprehensibility, and so on. In internal behavior the student may exhibit a variety of interpretations (internal behavior), all of which may be considered acceptable.

Example I: The student writes a composition that maintains a specific point of view. If the teacher gave the students a composition and told them to rewrite it sentence for sentence as if it were written by a student of the opposite sex, the student behavior falls in Stage 3. (If the entire exercise had already been done in class and if students could use their notes, the behavior would be classified at Stage 2.) However, if the students have read a short story and the teacher asks the class to write the opening scene from the point of view of another character in the story (and if sentences are not to be transposed verbatim), the student behavior is classified as Stage 4. If, in addition, the students are to imitate the style of the original author in their point-of-view compositions, then the student behavior is classified as Stage 5.

Question 5: Is the student behavior judged as to whether or not the message is communicated clearly, or is style of primary importance?

If the main concern of the student is communicating a message accurately, then the behavior is classified as Stage 3, if the message is structured, or Stage 4, if the teacher does not dictate the precise content of the message. However, if the focus is on the style or tone of the message, the behavior belongs at Stage 5.

Example J: The student expresses his regret at being unable to accept an invitation. If this is a directed dialog, the behavior is classified at Stage 3. If the student chooses his own words and structures, the behavior is classified at Stage 4. If the student must first express his regret as if he were talking to a school friend and then as if he were talking to the wife of his boss, his behavior would be classified at Stage 5.

Figures 2-2 and 2-3 show the interrelationship between the stages of the subject-matter taxonomy and various areas of foreign-language learning.

2.2.5   *Competence and Performance*

In Noam Chomsky's now classical dichotomy between competence and performance,[5] a distinction is made between the individual's potential for communication (his *competence*) and actual examples of communication acts, such as the comprehension of specific sentences and the speaking or writing of them (his *performance*).

Performance, not competence, is the concern of performance objectives. Can performance, however, be thought of as an accurate indicator of the

[5] Noam Chomsky, *Aspects of the Theory of Syntax* (Cambridge, Mass.: M.I.T. Press, 1965).

FIGURE 2-2

SUMMARY OF THE SUBJECT-MATTER TAXONOMY

Stage	Internal Behavior	External Behavior
1. **Mechanical Skills:** The student performs via rote memory, rather than by understanding.	*Perception:* The student perceives differences between two or more sounds or letters or gestures and makes distinctions between them.	*Reproduction:* The student imitates foreign-language speech, writing, gestures, songs, and proverbs.
2. **Knowledge:** The student demonstrates knowledge of facts, rules, and data related to foreign-language learning.	*Recognition:* The student shows he recognizes facts he has learned by answering true-false and multiple-choice questions.	*Recall:* The student demonstrates he remembers the information taught by answering fill-in or short-answer questions.
3. **Transfer:** The student uses his knowledge in new situations.	*Reception:* The student understands recombined oral or written passages or quotations not encountered previously.	*Application:* The student speaks or writes in a guided drill situation or participates in cultural simulations.
4. **Communication:** The student uses the foreign language and culture as natural vehicles for communication.	*Comprehension:* The student understands a foreign-language message or a cultural signal containing unfamiliar material in an unfamiliar situation.	*Self-Expression:* The student uses the foreign language to express his personal thoughts orally or in writing. He uses gestures as part of his expression.
5. **Criticism:** The student analyzes or evaluates the foreign language or carries out original research.	*Analysis:* The student breaks down language or a literary passage to its essential elements of style, tone, theme, and so forth. *Evaluation:* The student evaluates and judges the appropriateness and effectiveness of a language sample or literary passage.	*Synthesis:* The student carries out original research or individual study or creates a plan for such a project.

FIGURE 2-3

INTERRELATIONSHIPS BETWEEN FOREIGN-LANGUAGE TEACHING AREAS AND
STAGES OF SUBJECT-MATTER TAXONOMY

	Stage 1: Mechanical Skills: Perception (Internal)	Stage 1: Mechanical Skills: Reproduction (External)	Stage 2: Knowledge: Recognition (Internal)	Stage 2: Knowledge: Recall (External)	Stage 3: Transfer: Reception (Internal)	Stage 3: Transfer: Application (External)	Stage 4: Communication: Comprehension (Internal)	Stage 4: Communication: Self-Expression (External)	Stage 5: Criticism: Analysis (Internal)	Stage 5: Criticism: Synthesis (External)	Stage 5: Criticism: Evaluation (Internal)
Listening	X		X		X		X		X		X
Speaking		X		X		X		X		X	
Reading	X		X		X		X		X		X
Writing		X		X		X		X		X	
Gestures	X	X	X	X	X	X	X	X	X	X	X
Way-of-Life Culture	X	X	X	X	X	X	X	X	X	X	X
Civilization	X		X	X	X		X		X		X
Literature		X	X	X	X		X		X		X

student's newly acquired competence? Frequently this is the case. But it is obvious to all teachers that a student's performance, especially under test conditions, does not always reflect his real competence. In this sense, researchers sometimes classify student mistakes as either slips or errors. A slip is a mistake that the student himself would correct if given the opportunity to do so. An error is a mistake that the student would not be likely to correct. Errors indicate deficiencies in the student's competence, whereas slips do not.[6]

The goal of language instruction is the development within the student of a new type of competence. Performance objectives are of value because they specify how this competence is to be demonstrated and because they define the types of performance that this competence may lead to. They provide an objective measure of success for both student and teacher. They define the observable outcomes of instruction in terms both student and teacher can recognize.[7]

2.3 CLASSIFYING AFFECTIVE GOALS

The language-teaching profession has devoted much energy to reassessing the language skills, to defining the role of culture, and to devising ways of presenting the foreign literature. This activity has centered primarily on subject-matter goals—what information students should know and what skills and understanding they should possess as a result of foreign-language study.

By contrast, goals relating to student attitudes and feelings have been largely neglected. It is ironic that these affective goals have not been thoroughly examined, since attitudes and feelings that students develop as a result of language study are often among the reasons presented by the profession to justify foreign-language instruction: the foreign language student is supposed to experience feelings of accomplishment and enjoyment in the use of a foreign language; he is expected to become more tolerant of other peoples and more appreciative of other cultures. Some teachers even state that as a result of foreign-language instruction, the student will later seek to promote international peace and understanding.

In view of the importance of these objectives, it is necessary to define them more clearly than has been the case in the past.

2.3.1 *Taxonomy of Affective Goals*

Affective goals may be classified according to five stages of feeling with each stage subdivided into two categories of behavior. The basic progression of the classification system is from the student's neutrality toward foreign lan-

---

[6] For a deeper investigation of this matter, see Alan Davies, "Language Testing" in Heinrich Schrand, ed., *Leistungsmessung im Sprachunterricht* (Marburg/Lahn: Informationszentrum für Fremdsprachenforschung, 1969), pp. 27–51.

[7] There are other ways of measuring competence besides performance objectives. Bernard Spolsky, for example, is experimenting with sensitivity to redundancy as a factor correlating with communicative competence. He finds that the ability to understand recorded sentences heavily masked with static reflects language competence. See Bernard Spolsky et al., "Preliminary Studies in the Development of Techniques for Testing Overall Second Language Proficiency," in John A. Upshur and Julia Fata, eds., *Problems in Foreign Language Testing*, published as special issue no. 3, *Language Learning* (Aug. 1968), pp. 79–98.

guages, culture, and literature to his voluntarily seeking them out. It moves from teacher-directed activities to student self-direction. It progresses from values existing outside the student to his internalization of those values.

The taxonomy of affective goals is shown in Figure 2-4. The categories and their sequencing have been adapted from the Krathwohl-Bloom taxonomy for the affective domain.[8]

Stage 1: Receptivity

At Stage 1 the learning process is stimulated and directed by the teacher. The student obeys the instructions he is given and is at least neutral in his attitude toward language study. He is cooperative, does not resist learning, and is willing to acquire the knowledge and skills presented. This stage is typical of a beginning language student or a student at the beginning of an academic year.

Awareness is the first subcategory. The student becomes aware of the existence of other languages, cultures, and civilizations. He notices when people around him are speaking a foreign language. He is especially aware when he hears people using the foreign language he is studying. He notices foreign phrases in advertisements and foreign products in stores.

The second subcategory is *Attentiveness*. The student pays attention in class and carries out directions and assignments with care. At this first stage, he does not yet exhibit a personal interest in the foreign language or culture, but agrees to do what is asked of him.

FIGURE 2-4

STAGES OF THE AFFECTIVE TAXONOMY

Stage

1. **Receptivity**	*Awareness*	*Attentiveness*
2. **Responsiveness**	*Tolerance*	*Interest and Enjoyment*
3. **Appreciation**	*Valuing*	*Involvement*
4. **Internalization**	*Conceptualization*	*Commitment*
5. **Characterization**	*Integration*	*Leadership*

[8] See Krathwohl, Bloom, and Masia, *Taxonomy of Educational Objectives, Handbook II: Affective Domain* (New York: David McKay, 1964).

Stage 2: Responsiveness

At Stage 2, the student has a generally favorable attitude toward the learning activities planned by the teacher. He displays no hostility toward the foreign language and has no overpowering feelings of frustration in his attempts to perform the activities desired. He generally enjoys the work connected with language study and has a sense of accomplishment and satisfaction with his progress. This stage characterizes the beginning or intermediate student who intends to continue his study of the language.

The first subcategory is *Tolerance*. The student is open to learning about other ways of linguistic expression and other cultural patterns. He does not reject or ridicule foreign languages or their speakers and is generally considerate of other people.

The second subcategory is *Interest and Enjoyment*. The student is interested in activities of his foreign-language class. He enjoys the activities he is asked to engage in and gains satisfaction from participating in them. The student does not, at this stage, look for available foreign-language activities on his own, but rather finds enjoyment in doing what is proposed to him.

Stage 3: Appreciation

The third stage of the affective taxonomy is **Appreciation.** Here the student, of his own volition, attaches value and worth to the study of foreign language, culture, and literature. He seeks out extracurricular opportunities to involve himself in language learning and cultural activities. The student performs voluntarily; he engages in activities because he wants to and because he enjoys them, not because he is overtly or covertly forced into doing so. Stage 3 activities are student initiated and student directed. Behavior at this stage characterizes those students who are active in the foreign-language or world-affairs clubs and those who voluntarily attend foreign-language cultural events, such as talks, films, exhibits, and so on. It also applies to students who take out or buy foreign-language books, who subscribe to or read foreign-language magazines or newspapers or who correspond with foreign pen pal.

Valuing is the first subcategory. The student views the study of foreign language and culture as valuable, worthwhile, and important. He believes that he is benefiting from his experiences in and out of class and feels that all students should have the chance to study at least one foreign language.

Involvement is the second subcategory. The student voluntarily participates in activities that might improve his language skills or increase his knowledge of foreign peoples, their culture, and their civilization. His interest in the foreign language may carry over into his leisure time activities, such as stamp collecting, baking, music, art, science, and so on.

Stage 4: Internalization

The fourth stage of the taxonomy is **Internalization.** The student begins to shape his own attitudes, values, and philosophy in relation to his foreign-language experiences. These concepts result in his strong preference for learning foreign languages and his decision to devote a major portion of his available time and energy to additional study. This stage characterizes the high school student or college undergraduate who decides to major in foreign languages, literature, linguistics, or education.

The first subcategory is *Conceptualization.* Here the student develops a personal system of values relating to foreign-language study. If the student is challenged to defend the values of foreign-language study, he will at least be able to explain that he himself found this study rewarding and stimulating.

The second subcategory is *Commitment.* Here the student is willing to make a major investment of time and energy in order to perfect his foreign-language skills and to increase his knowledge of the foreign culture. He may engage in part-time work to earn enough money to travel abroad. Once in the foreign country, he will actively try to meet the people and learn more about their way of life. He may also decide to master other languages or to delve more deeply into areas of interest, such as art, literature, sociology, or geography. He may work actively for organizations promoting world peace and harmony among peoples.

Stage 5: Characterization

The fifth and highest stage of the affective taxonomy is **Characterization.** The student engages in advanced studies or chooses a career related to foreign-language study. A considerable portion of his time is devoted to promoting the study of foreign language, literature, or culture. Alternatively, he may be engaged in promoting harmonious relations between nations with differing languages and cultures. The major decisions and judgments he makes in regard to his life are so strongly influenced by his foreign-language background, interests, and values that he is known as a linguist, a language teacher, or a diplomat. This stage characterizes those persons who are active in one of these professions.

The first subcategory is *Integration.* At this point the student has integrated foreign-language values into his personal value system. In fact, time spent in activities related to those aspects of foreign-language learning that the student has found most valuable (language, linguistics, literature, culture, sociology, and so on) is no longer considered work but in a special way pleasure.

The second subcategory is *Leadership.* The student (now a leader or teacher) takes a major role in promoting those activities that he himself has come to value: language learning, cross-cultural study and understanding, literature and the arts.

2.3.2 *Guidelines for Using the Affective Taxonomy*

The classification of behaviors in the affective area is rather straightforward, since the categories are self-explanatory. Generally, only the first three stages apply to high school students. Stage 1 is essential to any learning whatever, for it is necessary that the student be in class and remain awake. At Stage 2 the student not only pays attention to what is going on, but also responds willingly. He may even enjoy foreign-language activities the teacher suggests. Students who reach Stage 3 behaviors value foreign-language study and look for additional knowledge and experiences on their own.

In view of the high degree of student initiative involved at Stages 4 and 5, these affective behaviors are generally not considered appropriate goals for typical beginning or intermediate language students. Setting performance expectations at these stages is unrealistic, since the number of students in a class who choose to make a career in foreign languages or in related fields is necessarily restricted. Stage 3 is a desirable goal toward which all teachers should aim. If language learning is to continue once the student leaves the classroom, then he must be taught to seek additional knowledge independently of teacher guidance. If the language-teaching profession is to remain strong, there must be a citizenry that values foreign languages, that encourages students to enroll in these courses, and that lends support to school language programs.

Nevertheless, it should be recognized that Stage 3 may not be a realistic goal in all teaching situations. A host of negative factors over which the teacher may have no control can at times preclude the possibility of reaching even Stage 2. In some cases, minimal Stage 1 behavior might even be difficult to achieve. In these situations, the teacher may have to set more limited affective goals. He might specify that student attitudes at the end of the year will at least be no less positive than they were at the beginning of the year. Or he might aim for Stage 2 if students display only Stage 1 behaviors (for example, absence of major discipline problems). Suggestions for developing and measuring affective behaviors are offered in Chapter Five. Figure 2-5 summarizes the various stages of the affective taxonomy.

The following questions may help in the classification of affective behaviors.

Question 1: Does the student do the bare minimum, or does he take a more active interest in class activities?

If the student simply pays attention, his behavior is at Stage 1. If he participates willingly in class and enjoys what he is doing, his behavior is at Stage 2.

FIGURE 2-5

SUMMARY OF THE AFFECTIVE TAXONOMY

Stage

1. **Receptivity:** The student is open to learning about a foreign language and culture.	*Awareness:* The student is aware of the existence of languages and cultures other than his own and of the fact that differences exist between them.	*Attentiveness:* The student attends to information about foreign language and culture both in and out of class. He pays attention to the careful preparation of his assignments.
2. **Responsiveness:** The student responds positively to learning about a foreign language and culture.	*Tolerance:* The student is tolerant of the differences in foreign-language expression and in foreign patterns of living. He does not reject or make fun of foreign ways.	*Interest and Enjoyment:* The student is interested in activities related to foreign-language study, enjoys the activities presented to him, and gains satisfaction from participation in them.
3. **Appreciation:** The student of his own accord attaches value to language and cultural experiences.	*Valuing:* The student views the study of foreign language and culture as valuable, worthwhile, and important.	*Involvement:* The student voluntarily participates from time to time in activities designed to improve his language skills or increase his knowledge of the foreign language and culture.
4. **Internalization:** The student forms his own ideas and values based on foreign-language learning experiences.	*Conceptualization:* The student develops a personal system of values relating to foreign-language study.	*Commitment:* The student makes a major investment of time and energy in the pursuit of further learning.
5. **Characterization:** Foreign language and culture have become an integral part of the student's life to the extent that he is characterized by activities in this area.	*Integration:* The student integrates foreign-language values into his personal value system.	*Leadership:* The student takes a major role in promoting language learning and instruction.

Question 2: Who initiates the language-learning activities or the study of cultural topics, the student or the teacher?

If the teacher initiates the learning activities, the student behavior is at Stage 1 (if the student is rather neutral in his attitude) or at Stage 2 (if the student shows that he is interested). If the student initiates the learning activities, whether in class or outside of school, his behavior is at Stage 3 or higher.

Question 3: Is the student's extracurricular involvement in foreign languages one of many similar activities, or does he devote a major portion of his time to foreign-language activities to the exclusion of most other interests?

If the student's demonstrated involvement in foreign-language activities is simply one of many interests, his behavior falls in Stage 3. If the student has singled out foreign languages for predominant attention, his behavior is classified in Stage 4.

Question 4: Does the student's commitment to foreign-language study affect mainly his personal life or does it affect others?

If foreign-language study is mainly a hobby or a personal field of endeavor, the student behavior is classified at Stage 4. If the commitment is social and proselytizing in nature, the student behavior falls in Stage 5.

2.4 THE RELATIONSHIP BETWEEN SUBJECT-MATTER GOALS AND AFFECTIVE GOALS

The five stages of behavior of the taxonomy of subject-matter goals coincide roughly with the five stages of behavior in the affective taxonomy. This interrelationship is depicted in Figure 2-6. The student's progress in mastering the foreign language is frequently, although not necessarily, accompanied by a growing positive attitude toward foreign-language instruction and the values of knowing another language. Conversely, if a student experiences frustration in his efforts to learn another language, he loses interest, he becomes less tolerant (especially of the teacher, if he feels the fault lies with the method of instruction), and he exhibits little attentiveness.

The second part of Figure 2-6 presents the same interrelationship between subject-matter goals and affective goals, but with more descriptive detail.

FIGURE 2-6

INTERRELATIONSHIPS BETWEEN SUBJECT-MATTER AND AFFECTIVE TAXONOMIES

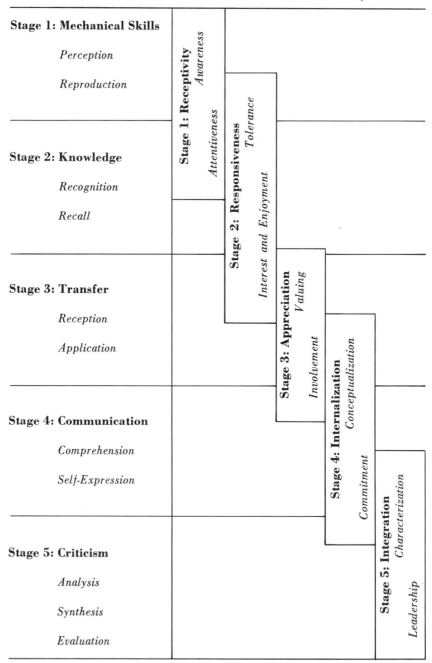

Subject-Matter Taxonomy   Affective Taxonomy

FIGURE 2-7

INTERRELATIONSHIPS BETWEEN SUBJECT-MATTER AND AFFECTIVE TAXONOMIES

Subject-Matter Taxonomy		Affective Taxonomy
1. **Mechanical Skills** *Perception* *(internal)*	The student becomes aware of differences between the foreign language pronunciation, grammar, syntax, and writing system and the corresponding elements in his native language. He also becomes aware of foreign culture, gestures, and way of life as well as instances of foreign language and its culture in his own daily life. He is attentive to the presentation of material in class and performs willingly the tasks required of him.	1. **Receptivity:** *Awareness* *Attentiveness*
Reproduction *(external)*	The student does not reject the foreign language and culture because of its strangeness to him. He maintains an attitude of acceptance and tolerance of new foreign-language ways.	2. **Responsiveness:** *Tolerance*
2. **Knowledge** *Recognition* *(internal)* *Recall* *(external)*	The student enjoys learning the material presented to him, he has a sense of satisfaction with his accomplishments in language class, and he expresses an interest in knowing more about the subject.	*Interest and Enjoyment*
	The student values the language, literature, or culture he is studying.	3. **Appreciation:** *Valuing*

FIGURE 2-7 (CONTINUED)

INTERRELATIONSHIPS BETWEEN SUBJECT-MATTER AND AFFECTIVE TAXONOMIES

Subject-Matter Taxonomy		Affective Taxonomy
3. **Transfer** *Reception* *(internal)* *Application* *(external)*	He considers it worth- while to use his knowl- edge in new situations.	
4. **Communication** *Comprehension* *(internal)* *Self-Expression* *(external)*	The student seeks on his own additional opportuni- ties to learn about the language and culture and to use the knowledge he possesses. He communi- cates freely and volun- tarily in relatively un- structured situations. He engages in out-of-class language activities inde- pendently of teacher su- pervision and evaluation. He travels to the foreign country.	*Involvement*
	The student's communi- cation skills progress to the degree that the for- eign language becomes a natural part of him, and he approaches the ability of a native speaker of the language. He may re- side in the foreign country.	4. **Internalization:** *Conceptualization*
5. **Criticism** *Analysis* *(internal)*	Thus he is capable of analyzing the foreign lan- guage, literature, and cul- ture. He consciously as- similates foreign-language ideas and values into his personal philosophy and his general outlook on life.	

FIGURE 2-7 (CONTINUED)

INTERRELATIONSHIPS BETWEEN SUBJECT-MATTER AND AFFECTIVE TAXONOMIES

Subject-Matter Taxonomy		Affective Taxonomy
	The student is committed to spending a significant portion of his time and effort in acquiring greater proficiency in the language or in furthering his knowledge of its literature and culture.	*Commitment*
Synthesis (external)	The student develops the sensitivity of a native speaker of the language and can demonstrate this by commanding subtle nuances of foreign-language style.	
	The student is considered bilingual and bicultural.	5. **Characterization:** *Integration*
Evaluation (external)	The student is capable of judging the foreign language, literature, and/or culture.	
	The student chooses as his vocation the evaluation of the foreign language, literature, and/or culture. He is committed to further instruction in this field and to the promotion of cross-cultural understanding and cultural enrichment.	*Leadership*

2.5 FORMAL AND EXPRESSIVE PERFORMANCE OBJECTIVES AND THE TAXONOMIES

Formal performance objectives may be written for the first three stages of the subject-matter taxonomy. At these stages it is possible to establish conditions and criteria with high precision. Programed instruction may be used effectively in achieving goals at these stages. It is also possible to write formal performance objectives for the first stage of the affective taxonomy, since the student is responding to activities and suggestions he has not initiated.

Expressive or open-ended performance objectives apply to Stages 4 and 5 of the subject-matter taxonomy and to Stages 2, 3, 4, and 5 of the affective taxonomy. Here the type of student behavior can be carefully specified, but the actual form such student behavior will assume is not as readily predictable.

The relationship between the taxonomies and these two types of performance objectives is shown in Figure 2-8.

FIGURE 2-8

FORMAL PERFORMANCE OBJECTIVES AND EXPRESSIVE PERFORMANCE OBJECTIVES

Subject-Matter Taxonomy	Affective Taxonomy
Stage 1: Mechanical Skills	**Stage 1: Receptivity**
Stage 2: Knowledge	**Stage 2: Responsiveness**
Stage 3: Transfer	**Stage 3: Appreciation**
Stage 4: Communication	**Stage 4: Internalization**
Stage 5: Criticism	**Stage 5: Characterization**

Formal Performance Objectives ☐

Expressive Performance Objectives ▨

CHAPTER THREE
SETTING
PERFORMANCE
OBJECTIVES

The use of performance objectives in the classroom is governed by one principal consideration: making instruction more effective and more meaningful to the students. The time and energy that go into the preparation of performance objectives and the development of appropriate tests are well spent if they lead to greater student learning.

3.1   GENERAL CONSIDERATIONS

Many schools are moving toward the adoption of some sort of performance objectives for their classes. Language teachers throughout the country are beginning to view their teaching with an eye to evaluating the results of their instruction.

3.1.1   *An Illustration: the Case of Mainstream High School*

One sunny September morning a tidal wave engulfed Mainstream High School. It fragmented the faculty and terrorized each teacher. In its wake it left whirlpools of controversy, undercurrents of dissent, and ripples of anguish.

This shattering event was the arrival of a terse directive from the school board. It read:

"All tenure in this system has been suspended. A teacher will be rehired only if his students give evidence of achieving the goals he has established for them."

The directive resulted from the fact that the preceding year the board members had engaged in conversations such as these with their children:

Mrs. Hedda Board: What did you do in school today?
Ima Board: Oh, nothing ever happens in school.
Mrs. Board: Oh, come now, you must have done *something*.
Ima: Well . . . I tried to pass a note in class, but my teacher caught me.
Mrs. Board: But you should have been listening to your teacher.
Ima: Why? She wasn't saying anything important.

Mr. Seymour Clearly: What did you learn in school today?
Les Clearly: Nothing. We just messed around.
Mr. Clearly: But certainly you must know something today that you didn't know yesterday.
Les: Well, maybe.
Mr. Clearly: And what's that?
Les: My French teacher had a real groovy time in Paris.

And there were other disquieting incidents.

Mr. Schreiber wanted his daughter to write a letter in German to her grandfather, but he abandoned the project when he learned that all she knew how to write was five hundred nouns in their singular and plural forms.

Mrs. Mamamia had her son speak Italian to his grandmother. He proceeded to recite all three roles of a dialog he had memorized. His grandmother realized that he couldn't understand what he was saying but said that his pronunciation was excellent. It was unfortunate she could not have a conversation with him, though.

Eventually, such individual incidents of dissatisfaction added up to a mass expression of discontent: "Our schools are not effective!"

Parents gathered together to discuss the problem. Phrases such as these rent the charged air: ". . . hard-earned money . . . produce or get out . . . down the drain . . . responsible for doing their job . . . measure their output . . . accountable to taxpayers. . . ." All this resulted in the terse directive, which in turn resulted in emergency meetings of each department in the school. We turn now to the language department.

Someone had finally dug up a yellowed copy of the department course catalog, which had been moldering beneath a pile of tapes.

"Well, here are the goals we're responsible for," said Eve Plurabus. "Let's have a look at them."

Essie Pagnol began to read. "'To create enthusiasm for language study.'" She shifted in her seat uncomfortably. "'To make students better world citizens by encouraging them to develop better relations with people in other lands.'" She was barely able to suppress her giggle.

Mauro Lesso continued. "'To expose students, as a result of personal experience, to new and pleasant vistas, and simultaneously to instill in them a real feeling of accomplishment.' Say, I don't understand what this means!" Apparently, no one else did either, so the discussion ended there.

"Here's one," said Jean D'Arme. "'To develop in students a broader understanding and appreciation of people whose language and way of life are different from theirs.' Now, that's not really such a bad goal, but I couldn't prove that my students had achieved it."

"I think you're going about it wrong," interrupted Anne Howe. "We need to get down to the more specific goals and not these abstract generalities. Let's see. . . . Here we have Level One goals: 'Development of audio-lingual skills, Introduction to reading and writing, Development of relationships between language and culture, Development of sense of personal satisfaction through the use of language.' Hmm . . . well, let's look at Level Two goals. 'Continued development of audio-lingual skills, Intensive development of reading ability, Additional emphasis on writing ability, Continued emphasis on language as culture. . . .'" She didn't have the heart to go on. Everyone looked glum and wondered how much their unemployment checks would come to.

"Well," said Eve, "either these goals go or we do".

"But they sounded so nice," sighed Essie. "Maybe we can still write pretty ones in terms of student performance. Then we'll be able to show that our students have accomplished them.

3.1.2 *Accountability in Foreign Languages*

When the teachers at Mainstream High discovered that keeping their jobs depended on their effectiveness in attaining specific performance objectives, they looked at their catalog of course descriptions more realistically.

What are foreign-language students able to *do* after one year of instruction? Can they just recite memorized dialogs? Can they merely perform pattern drills they have practiced in the laboratory and in class? Can they read with comprehension only familiar texts? Can they understand orally only conversations they have already heard? What can they write—only the dialogs and drills they have been taught? Can *all* the students reach even the minimal level just described?

How do foreign-language students *feel* after one year of instruction? Are they proud of their achievements? Are they eager to continue on to their second year? Do they correspond with foreign pen pals (even if only in English)? Do they hope to travel abroad?

Teacher accountability obliges teachers to be more realistic and more precise in their statements of course goals. This may lead to the development of different sets of performance objectives for different classes. Perhaps one set of goals may be established for the fast sections and another for the slow sections. Maybe listening and speaking will be stressed in one section, while reading goals will be emphasized in another. Such precision can be achieved if goals are stated in terms of observable or measurable student performance.

3.2 SELECTING PERFORMANCE OBJECTIVES FOR A COURSE

Usually it is the foreign-language department that decides on performance objectives for its courses, but the individual teacher may determine which objectives will be stressed in his classes. The following guidelines should be considered in the selection of performance objectives for a specific course.

3.2.1 *Guideline 1: Find Out What the Students Are Like*

How old are the students? Have they had other experiences with foreign languages? Are any aptitude measures available? Have the students experienced success in other school subjects?

Younger students may be more willing to memorize dialogs or plays than older students. Students with previous foreign-language experience may learn a third language more rapidly than other students for whom the foreign language represents a new second language. Students with high audio-lingual aptitude may do better in a course that stresses the spoken language; conversely, students who are low in listening-speaking aptitude but high in grammar sensitivity may perform better orally if at first they see the written language and receive grammar instruction. Students with records of success in school may do best in a slightly competitive atmosphere where they can advance at their own pace, whereas students with poorer records may perform better if testing is informal and praise frequent.

If the students have already had one or more years of foreign-language study, the class will contain students of varying degrees of proficiency. The middle and lower students might feel that the situation is rigged against them, for no matter how hard they work, the better prepared students will always receive the best grades. The following case shows how one teacher used performance objectives to minimize the effect of previous training on current learning.

A college teacher of second-year French found that his students exhibited a broad range of abilities in French pronunciation. He wanted them to improve their accents but felt it unfair to assign high grades to those who already spoke rather well and would have to make the least effort. He set the following performance objective: students would be given two months during which they were to correct two of their pronunciation errors. The students each recorded twenty French sentences for diagnostic purposes and the instructor assigned two errors to each student for correction. The students were positively motivated by the fairness of the assignment. As the semester progressed, the instructor noted that the students were helping each other with their assigned pronunciation problems. When the final recorded test was given, the instructor was delighted to note that not only did nearly everyone attain the performance objective, but that all students exhibited a general improvement in pronunciation. The poorer students not only corrected the two assigned sounds but managed to correct many other errors as well.

A similar approach might be tried with written compositions in intermediate and advanced classes. The teacher might analyze an initial writing sample and assign each student two or three errors to work on.

3.2.2   *Guideline 2: Determine the Conditions of Instruction*

How much time is allowed for learning? How big are the classes? What basic materials are being used? What other aids are available? How flexible is the school system?

Performance objectives must be realistic. If a class meets twenty minutes a day three times a week, the goals must be more modest than they would be for a similar class meeting fifty minutes a day five times a week. Class size itself may not limit the instructional goals, but it may well call for the selection of different instructional techniques in order to attain the goals. The textbook and materials will at least determine the subject-matter content of the performance objectives. Many cultural objectives, however, become difficult to reach if the teacher does not also have access to appropriate films, film strips, realia, and so forth. The rigidity or flexibility of school administrations and policies are major factors in determining the types of goals a teacher can set.

3.2.3   *Guideline 3: Discover Which Performance Objectives Students Think Are Appropriate*

Do they want to speak and understand the language? Do they mainly want to read? Are they more interested in certain aspects of culture? Is their main concern how well they will do on a specific standard test? Do they have specific vocational goals?

The suggestion that students be consulted in no way implies that they should have the final say in determining the nature of the foreign-language program. On the other hand, however, total lack of consideration for student desires will probably lead to failure in attaining the affective goals of the language program. It is difficult to develop positive student attitudes in a course that fails to take into account the students' own interests.

If the entire class, for example, is eager to perform well on a standard test that has a heavy vocabulary bias and if the teacher feels that appropriate objectives for the course involve development of communication skills and not cramming vocabulary, then perhaps a compromise is advisable: the last ten minutes of every period might be devoted to intensive vocabulary practice.

If a few students wish to do more reading and if the class performance objectives stress the audio-lingual skills, then separate objectives could be set for a reading group. Perhaps this group could do a reading assignment while the others in the class practice conversation in small groups.

Specific vocational goals can also be worked into the classroom objectives. In one California town, the teacher decided to offer a "diploma" to students who demonstrated that they could guide a monolingual Spanish speaker through a store and help her with her shopping. The tests were carried out in local stores. Students possessing this "diploma" found that they could get part-time jobs working as interpreters and sales personnel for local businessmen.

3.2.4   *Guideline 4: Be Sure to Establish Performance Objectives for Affective Goals*

Though affective outcomes—that is, the attitudes, feelings, and values that students develop—have long been used to justify the study of foreign languages, little has been done to specify affective goals, create teaching activities that develop them, or devise ways of measuring student attitudes and feelings. For too long language teachers have hoped that by some osmotic miracle, attainment of subject-matter goals would lead automatically to commensurate achievement in affective areas. All too often this has not occurred, though the converse is true: failure to attain subject-matter goals usually leads to an unfavorable attitude toward foreign languages. In view of the long-term importance of student attitudes and feelings, it is imperative that all teachers specify the student behaviors that demonstrate achievement of affective goals. Ways of accomplishing this will be offered in Chapter Five.

3.3   ESTABLISHING PERFORMANCE OBJECTIVES FOR A UNIT OR LESSON

When setting performance objectives, it is important that they be relevant to the needs of the students enrolled. Unless students find foreign-language study rewarding and interesting at the beginning stages, they will not continue toward higher, more advanced learning.

3.3.1   *An Illustration: The Case of Jigsaw Junction*

Jigsaw Junction, for centuries unsurpassed in puzzle producing, suddenly found the future of its primary industry gravely imperiled. Scores of puzzle apprentices were dropping out of the profession.

"Perhaps the problem's pedagogical," volunteered a well-known puzzle-maker.

"These young apprentices are certainly perplexing," said another.

"Perhaps we should investigate our schools," suggested a third puzzle producer.

So off they went. First they visited Mr. Percy Verence. "If you just keep at it long enough," he told his classes, "some day you too will reach the Grand Design." (The Grand Design, for those of you unfamiliar with puzzle terminology, is the pinnacle of creation: a beautiful picture incorporating all types of pieces in all sorts of combinations. Every serious puzzle-maker aspires to reach the Grand Design stage of achievement.)

"Of course, since you are just beginners," Percy Verence continued, "you can't hope to reach the Grand Design right away. You'll have to stick to your studies for many years before being able to create a Grand Design of your own.

"Until then, you will learn all about the types of pieces there are: projectors, recessors, ingressors, and egressors. You will also learn what to call the various sides of the pieces: obverse, reverse, converse, or transverse. You will also use several modes of putting pieces together: conjunctive, disjunctive, pre-emptive, and corruptive.

"If you master all these terms, then you will eventually become skillful enough to make a Grand Design."

Unfortunately, Percy Verence's apprentices were in a hurry to learn their trade. They were not willing to work every day for some far-off goal, and many of them never completed the course.

Next, the puzzle producers visited Otto Matton. This teacher tried to eliminate as much puzzling terminology as possible. He simply taught the theory of Frames and Slots and called all the pieces either functors or descriptors. The main activity of the class was trying to match pieces selected at random. If any of them fit, a bell rang to announce this success.

Otto Matton told his students that with daily practice they would eventually be able to create a Grand Design. So his students diligently began the exercise. Some of them, in fact, showed unusual talent for matching pieces quite rapidly. Proudly they showed the teacher their work. Mr. Matton heaped lavish praise on their efforts, then quietly, efficiently, swept the matched pieces back into the unsorted pile.

And so it went. The more pieces the students matched, the more pieces they were given to put back together. It wasn't long before they realized that finishing one assignment just meant they would have to do another of the same kind. So the students slowed down, and as they did, dreams of the Grand Design faded from their minds.

The three investigators pursued their research. Everywhere they went conditions were puzzlingly similar. Students were making little progress toward achieving the Grand Design and puzzle apprenticeships remained unfilled.

Then one day they found something extraordinary. Students in Vince

Relev's classes were happy, alert, and hard-working. What could have produced this unusual situation? The investigators entered the classroom to find out.

Vince Relev told his students he knew that they were all very eager to create a Grand Design. Of course, if would take quite a bit of time to acquire this skill—perhaps more time than they were willing to spend in preparation. So, he had an idea. After learning each new puzzle combination, the students would be allowed to create a Mini-Design. True, this puzzle would not be as large as the Grand Design in all its magnificent complexity, but at least it would be a complete picture. And so it was. Puzzle apprentices rushed through their preliminary drills in order to see what Mini-Design they would be able to create with their newly acquired skills.

The three investigators smiled broadly. They had found a solution to their perplexing problem. The puzzle-producing industry could be saved! Now all they had to do was convince the pedagogues to adopt the approach of Vince Relev. Still the big questions remained: Could the teachers change their ways? Would they offer their students meaningful and worthwhile experiences?

Foreign-language students resemble the puzzle apprentices of Jigsaw Junction. They want to use the new language to understand others and to express their own thoughts. They want to see how classroom exercises fit into the general goal of language acquisition. It is in this area that performance objectives and taxonomical classification can make a most significant contribution by clarifying the aims of instruction and by placing the learning activities in proper perspective.

There are two basic ways of going about the establishment of performance objectives for a unit or lesson. The teacher can look at the content of the lesson and then begin setting his goals; this might be termed working from the bottom up. Or he can look at the highest-level goal he intends to attain in the lesson and then see what intermediate steps are needed; this might be called working from the top down.

In establishing performance objectives, teachers need to work both from the bottom up as well as from the top down. That is, teachers must provide for student mastery of the basic material as well as for opportunities to use what the students have learned in communication situations. Since these approaches are complementary, teachers will find opportunities to use both during the course of the year.

3.3.2   *Working From the Bottom Up: Teaching for Mastery*

The early stages of language acquisition are highly dependent on cumulative learning. If a student has not learned the gender of a noun, he cannot use the appropriate adjective form with it. If a student is unsure of the accusative forms of nouns, he will have difficulty with accusative pronouns. If the student does not control the simple tenses of the auxiliary verbs, he will be unable to form the compound tenses requiring those auxiliary verbs.

Performance objectives at these early stages must stress the need for student mastery of the basic or core features of the new language. These are the lexical and structural elements that cannot be forgotten if students are to continue language study successfully.

The level of mastery for these basic or core features is usually set around 80 or 90 percent rather than 65 percent. This means that on a test that covers these features, students must answer at least four-fifths of the items correctly in order to pass. Failure to pass, however, is not considered a stigma. The student who scores below 80 percent is like the prospective Little League fielder who misses too many balls: he needs more practice in order to perform better. Each student has an individual mode of learning and an individual learning rate. The considerable differences among students in language-learning ability can be lessened by allowing slow learners more time to master the material presented.

Setting the mastery level at 100 percent is not recommended, however. The small portion of the lesson that was not mastered will be gradually assimilated in subsequent lessons, especially if the teacher or teaching materials systematically reintroduce previously taught vocabulary and structures.

When a teacher requires his students to demonstrate a high level of control over basic lesson material (Stages 1, 2, and 3) before proceeding to his communication objective (Stage 4) or to the next lesson, he is *teaching for mastery*. When he sets these objectives, he works from the bottom up.

3.3.3 *Working From the Top Down: Teaching for Communication*

The teacher is working from the top down, when he looks over the contents of the lesson and sets his highest objectives first. Those belonging to lower stages may be explicit or may remain implicit. When teachers use this approach they generally set goals at Stage 4. Within this framework, the vocabulary, structures, and patterns of the lesson are all subsumed in the ultimate goal.

For example, if an intermediate lesson focuses on the house, its rooms, the layout, and so on, the lesson goal might be: "The student will orally describe a house for which he is given a floor plan. He will describe the rooms and their location relative to each other." In preparation for this final goal, students may be expected to master vocabulary (Stage 2) that relates to houses, as well as patterns that indicate direction and spatial relationships.

Communication goals may even be set for elementary language classes. For example, if the beginning lesson has food as its theme, the lesson goal might be: "Given four pictures showing four different menus, the student will be able to describe one of these to his classmates so that they will know which one he is talking about." In this type of goal, both the student performing and his classmates are participating in the communication situation. Mastery of needed vocabulary and structures acquires meaning within the framework of the higher goal.

The teacher who adopts communication goals for more advanced classes will have to stress interaction among students and reserve for himself the role of observer and reference source. He may then introduce grammatical points as errors occur and as certain topics seem appropriate.

If a teacher emphasizes communication objectives, whether they are in the area of spoken or written language, the teaching of vocabulary and structure becomes subservient to the communication goal. This type of emphasis is especially important once the student has a foundation in the foreign language, even if the foundation is rather weak in some places and perhaps nonexistent in others.

Communication objectives are important, for if a foreign-language student never progresses beyond the first three stages of the taxonomy, the language remains for him a series of sterile exercises rather than a vehicle for live self-expression. It matters little whether these exercises take the form of vocabulary lists and translations or dialogs and oral drills. The student whose behavior does not progress beyond the **Transfer** stage has reached a plateau.[1] While it is necessary to bring the students to this plateau, the strength of a language program lies precisely in its ability to lead the students to the next higher stage of behavior: **Communication.**

Communication takes place when a person uses the foreign language to express his own thoughts or when he clearly understands what others have said or written. Here, the emphasis is placed on the message, the fluency with which it is transmitted, and the ease with which it is understood.

Just because **Communication** is the fourth behavioral stage of the taxonomy does not mean that the student must master all the technical aspects of the preceding three—an undertaking of many years' duration—before being allowed to communicate independently. Even in the early phases of language learning, students use the new language as a means of communication when they open their books to the right page according to the teacher's instructions. From the very beginning, some communication objectives should be included in every lesson. Remember, the emphasis is not on accuracy, but on success in communicating. Students will learn to communicate only if strongly encouraged to do so by the teacher.

3.3.4 *Avoiding Pitfalls in Setting Performance Objectives*

Performance objectives in themselves do not automatically guarantee success in foreign-language teaching. If they are to help promote learning, they must be used wisely. Since there are pitfalls inherent in using these objectives, this section will offer suggestions on how to write effective ones.

[1] See Simon Belasco, "The Plateau, or the Case for Comprehension: The 'Concept' Approach," *Modern Language Journal*, vol. 51, no. 2 (Feb. 1967), pp. 82–86.

3.3.4a ANALYZE THE CONTENT OF THE LESSON

Before setting performance objectives for a lesson or unit, the teacher must first analyze that lesson. Some of its elements, such as high-frequency vocabulary items, idioms, and common structures, are essential to subsequent lessons and necessary for basic communication. These parts of the lesson constitute its *core*. Often, lessons also include some lower-frequency words or special idioms that fit in nicely with the theme of the lesson but rarely, if ever, reappear in the course. These parts of the lesson should be considered as *non-core*. While the student may have to recognize the meaning of the non-core material in order to handle the lesson, he should be expected first to master the core material. Consequently, performance objectives should specify which parts of the lesson are considered core material and stress the mastery of those features. It does not make sense to stress irregularities and exceptions when the students have not yet demonstrated their mastery of the basic structures.

3.3.4b SPECIFY THE SUBJECT-MATTER GOALS

For a beginning or intermediate lesson, these goals will include behaviors in the categories of **Mechanical Skills** (correct pronunciation, demonstrated through a memorized dialog or set of sentences), **Knowledge** (knowledge of new vocabulary, new grammatical forms, new drill patterns), and **Transfer** (ability to use these new elements in unfamiliar combinations).

However, unless performance objectives go beyond the ability to recite a dialog with a specified degree of fluency and the ability to perform language drills with a specified degree of accuracy, the students (and hopefully the teacher) will begin to question the relevance of a language course having such objectives. Students should at least be expected to understand recombinations of the lesson material (**Stage 3: Transfer:** *Reception*). For beginning students the following represents a meaningful goal: "At the end of this unit you will be able to understand sentences you have never heard before on the topic of. . . ." If such a short dialog or passage is played for the students, their understanding may be classified as **Stage 4: Communication:** *Comprehension.*

Once students have grasped the fundamentals of the foreign language, they will want to practice expressing themselves. If they are provided with ample opportunities for free communication, they will be more willing to accept the necessity of learning new vocabulary and grammar and of manipulating patterns with a given degree of accuracy.

3.3.4c AVOID MAKING THE OBJECTIVES TOO NARROW

Consider the following performance objective: In class the student will be able to give the correct responses to pattern drill B on page thirty-five; the student will have his book closed; no more than five seconds may elapse between the question and the answer.

Although this statement meets the specifications of a performance objective, and although the teacher may indeed wish to have the students perform certain drills rapidly and accurately, the objective is trivial. The preparation of dozens of such highly detailed, specific performance objectives for a single lesson is self-defeating.

The cumulative learning effect of a series of practice drills might be expressed in a single broad performance objective: The student will answer affirmative and negative sentences in the present tense, replacing the expressed direct object with the appropriate pronoun. Core vocabulary from lessons one, three, and five will be used in the sentences. The student must answer four out of five questions correctly, with no more than five seconds' hestitation.

3.3.4d AVOID LIMITING OBJECTIVES TO THE LOWER STAGES OF BEHAVIOR

Without more advanced communication behaviors that give meaning to the simpler ones, students tend to find themselves caught up in a never-ending procession of exercises and drills. They have the feeling that once they have mastered one set of exercises they will simply progress to a slightly more difficult set, and they begin to question their learning activities.

Performance objectives for the simplest behaviors on the subject-matter and affective taxonomies are the least complicated to write—and to teach. In contrast, objectives for the more advanced behaviors are often open-ended, unpredictable, and, consequently, more difficult to prepare. For this reason, there is a natural tendency to avoid them, and teachers who set performance objectives for a language course should therefore classify them according to the appropriate taxonomy. This will enable them to verify that the higher learning goals as well as the simpler ones are included.

3.3.4e AVOID OVERLY SPECIFIC OBJECTIVES

It is impractical to write performance objectives that are so specific that applying the criterion would take an inordinate amount of the teacher's time. For example:

> In his three-minute speech on a prepared topic, the student shall not make more than five phonemic errors. He shall not hesitate more than five seconds between sentences. He shall not make more than two errors in subject-verb agreement, nor shall he make more than four errors in gender.

The performance objective has a most precise criterion, but it would take hours to evaluate the speeches of a class of thirty students. In fact, the speeches would have to be recorded because the teacher would need to listen to each one several times in order to check off the various types of possible errors.

3.4 TESTS

All tests used to measure whether or not performance objectives have been attained are called *criterion-referenced tests*. Student scores on such tests let the teacher and student know whether a certain body of knowledge has been learned or whether a specific set of tasks has been properly accomplished. Students are not ranked in relation to each other (for example, Sam is better than Susie), but simply in reference to the criterion (for example, Sam can use the present tense of *to have* in unfamiliar sentences, whereas Susie is not yet capable of this performance).[2]

3.4.1 *Pretests and Posttests*

In its most refined form, the use of performance objectives implies that the teacher will administer both a *pretest* and one or more *posttests* for each unit and segment of instruction.

The pretest is given prior to instruction—for example, at the beginning of a new unit. This pretest is an alternate form of the posttest (or, in the case of recorded tests, the pretest and the posttest may be the same). The pretest serves two functions. First, it communicates the performance objectives of the unit. Second, it lets the teacher know whether some students already possess the behaviors that the unit aims to develop. In the latter case, these students may be given individual projects or may be enlisted to help teach the new behaviors to their classmates. Note: For those students who can demonstrate the terminal, or end, behavior at the beginning of the unit, it is evident that the performance objective is inappropriate. Only those students who do not obtain a perfect score on the pretest will be able to exhibit a positive change in behavior on the posttest as a result of the instruction they have received.

The posttest is given at the end of the instruction. In the classroom situation, the posttest is given when the teacher feels that the students have "finished" the unit. If the results of the posttest show that the students have indeed acquired the desired new behaviors, the class will proceed to the next unit. However, if the class, or part of the class, does poorly on the posttest, (fails to reach 80 percent accuracy), additional instruction will be necessary and a second posttest must be scheduled.

[2] Tests used to rank students and give grades are called *norm-referenced tests*.

3.4.2   *Formative and Summative Evaluation*

Formative tests are tests that are given in the course of instruction. The pretests and posttests discussed in the preceding section are examples of formative tests. The aim of formative evaluation is not to grade the student, but to determine the degree to which a learner has mastered a learning task and to determine what precisely remains to be mastered.

Summative tests cover all the material taught during the semester or year. Summative tests can also be extramural tests, such as the commonly used commercial standardized tests. Summative evaluation is used to make a general assessment of the outcomes of a course of instruction and is used to grade the students.

Formative tests are given frequently in the course of instruction, whereas summative tests are given once or twice a year. Teacher-made quizzes and unit tests are formative tests. Standardized achievement tests are summative tests. Teacher-made tests given at the end of the semester or the end of the year with the purpose of grading and ranking students ressemble summative tests rather than formative tests.

When teaching to specific performance objectives the teacher should be interested in both formative and summative evaluation. At the lower stages of the subject-matter taxonomy, he stresses mastery of specific elements; the use of formative tests lets him know where each student stands. There are times, however, where it is necessary to compare student performance in one program to that of another program. At this point, the teacher must use summative evaluation.[3]

3.5   FACING SETBACKS

Once a teacher sets certain performance objectives for a class, he must be ready to face the possibility that those objectives may not be achieved. The implementation of a set of performance objectives is not of itself a guarantee of success.

3.5.1   *Setbacks in Subject-Matter Objectives*

What if, at the end of the time allotted for a unit, the students (or many of the students, or even several of the students) have not attained the unit objectives? The teacher must review the objectives carefully and ask himself some pertinent questions:

1. Could the students attain the objectives if a little more time were allotted?

---

[3] For more on this, see Benjamin S. Bloom, J. Thomas Hastings, and George F. Madaus, *Handbook on Formative and Summative Evaluation of Student Learning* (New York: McGraw-Hill, 1971).

2. Might the students have been able to attain the objectives under different instructional conditions (more laboratory time, more small-group work, and so forth)?

3. Were the standards too high? Were the objectives too ambitious? Perhaps this class needs modified objectives: more oral work, if they handle it easily, and less written—or vice versa, if the written work is easier; more practice in manipulating structures and less emphasis on formal grammar, or vice versa; greater stress on passive objectives such as listening and reading.

4. Were the objectives inappropriate? An analytical, book-oriented class might find a strict audio-lingual presentation irrelevant, artificial, or monotonous. The same class might advance much more rapidly in the acquisition of both spoken and written skills if the course contained explicit presentations of grammar and vocabulary. Conversely, a group of students who equate books and reading with academic failure might successfully meet the objectives of an audio-visual language program.

5. Were the materials appropriate to the interests of the class? Perhaps the class found the materials too babyish or too adult. Maybe sports-minded students would develop their Spanish reading skills more rapidly if the material described baseball in Puerto Rico or the biography of some Puerto Rican baseball star rather than the story of a Mexican boy and his donkey.

A setback encountered with one performance objective, consequently, should become the starting point for new experiments in improving the instruction and, if appropriate, for the modification of other performance objectives.

3.5.2 *Setbacks in Affective Objectives*

The inability to meet affective performance objectives is a more serious matter than are temporary setbacks in subject-matter objectives. It is evident that students cannot master a second language in a couple of years of classroom exposure. Yet, if their interest in another language or another culture is aroused, they may continue language study later in life, they may travel to the country where the second language is spoken, or they may use the language in other ways. If, however, after a year or two of instruction students feel that language study is a painful waste of time or simply an unpleasant hurdle blocking the way to some desired goal, the teacher has created citizens who will be uninterested in (or actively opposed to) supporting language instruction in the future. If the percentage of the student body enrolled in foreign languages does not increase, the entire foreign-language staff should search for ways of making their courses more meaningful and more attractive to greater numbers of students.

3.5.2a   AN EXPERIMENT IN OXON HILL, MARYLAND

Oxon Hill High School was faced with the problem of attrition. Only 65 percent of the students in first-year language courses were enrolling in the second-year courses. Only 20 percent of these students continued to the third year. Such a dropout rate indicated that the foreign-language program was not developing positive attitudes toward language and culture. An attitude test did in fact corroborate the fact that most students held a neutral-to-negative attitude toward the program.

The school decided on the goal of improving the foreign-language program so as to reduce the attrition rate. (A smaller attrition rate could be taken as objective proof that the school program was increasing in effectiveness and that student attitudes were improving.)

The foreign-language department, with the support of the principal made the following changes. Students finishing Level I with A's or B's continued into the regular (on-level) Level II course. Students finishing Level I with C's or D's were placed in a below-level Level II course. Similarly, on-level and below-level courses were established for the third and fourth years. Furthermore, as much as possible, all courses in the same level were offered at the same hour. Consequently, a student could be easily moved either from a below-level to an on-level course if his work improved, or from an on-level course to a below-level course if he was having difficulties or if he had been absent for an extended period. These changes in section did not entail any other changes in the student's schedule and could be handled by the teachers involved. As a result of the establishment of this program, the attrition rate declined. Furthermore, student attitude became more favorable and enrollments in foreign languages increased.

There was no stigma attached to being in a below-level section. An A earned in a below-level section was recorded on the student's transcript and carried the same credit as an A earned in an on-level section.[4] The transcript indicates whether a course is on-level or below-level.

3.5.2b   DISCUSSION

Given the school objective, the foreign-language department might have selected other remedies, such as the selection of new materials or the development of a new pattern of courses. The objective only specified that the measure of success would be a decline in the attrition rate. Perhaps it is not too farfetched to say that a student will continue any course sequence in which he is experiencing success in meeting new challenges. Language requirement or no language requirement, if foreign-language study offers the student a positive learning experience, enrollments will increase.

[4] Michael Hernick and Dora Kennedy, "Multi-Level Grouping of Students in the Modern Foreign Language Program," *Foreign Language Annals*, vol. 2, no. 2 (Dec. 1968), pp. 200–04.

CHAPTER FOUR

USING
PERFORMANCE
OBJECTIVES

4.1 GENERAL CONSIDERATIONS

Once performance objectives have been developed, there remains the question of how to use them to improve instruction. Performance objectives can be employed in a variety of ways with no one approach considered the only right one. The way a teacher chooses to use performance objectives depends on a number of factors, such as age of students, size of classes, level of language taught, and individual preferences in regard to class organization.

The following sections will describe various methods of employing performance objectives. They range from methods appropriate in formal teacher-centered classrooms to those that involve individualization of instruction and an open, learner-centered classroom.

4.2 COMMUNICATING PERFORMANCE OBJECTIVES TO STUDENTS

The least complex way of using performance objectives is simply to let students know what they are. Then, at the end of a unit of study, students can see the progress they have made.

4.2.1 *Reasons to Communicate Objectives to Students*

There are several justifications for communicating performance objectives to students. A clear statement of purpose is essential to today's students who ask why they must learn seemingly irrelevant material. When students understand what behaviors they must demonstrate and under what conditions these behaviors are to be produced, there is a much greater likelihood of their fulfilling teacher expectations. If students are aware of how their work will be evaluated, their chances of success are greatly increased. Improved performance on tests results in feelings of greater accomplishment and satisfaction on the part of both teachers and students. This, in turn, exerts a positive influence on teacher-student relations and creates a pleasant class atmosphere that is conducive to learning.

Performance objectives serve to eliminate much student uncertainty regarding what material they must master and how that material will be tested. Psychologists have shown that known or familiar situations produce far less anxiety than those that are unknown and unfamiliar. By reducing student anxiety related to success on tests, performance objectives can promote interest in learning and can reduce pressures that may result in student cheating.

Performance objectives can also increase each student's responsibility for his own success and failure. No longer can students blame their low grades on factors beyond their control. No longer can they offer excuses such as, "I didn't know what would be on the test;" "I had bad luck;" "The teacher doesn't like me, so I got a bad grade;" "The questions weren't the way I expected them to be."

4.2.2 *Communicating Objectives Informally*

With younger students, performance objectives may be communicated informally. The teacher may tell his third-grade class, for example, "At the end of the day (or week), you will have learned how to play 'Simon Says' in Spanish." With beginning students at all levels the teacher may informally describe the objectives of the class period: "Today you will learn how to tell time in Italian."

At beginning and intermediate levels, unit objectives might also be communicated informally. For example, the teacher might play a new tape recording of a couple ordering food in a restaurant and assure the students that by the end of the week they will be able to understand the entire conversation. Or the teacher might tell the students that by the end of the unit they will be able to express in French their reactions to statements (using sentences like "I doubt that . . . ," "I am afraid that . . .") and to use a new verb form called the subjunctive.

4.2.3 *Communicating Objectives Formally*

With older students, teachers may wish to communicate performance objectives in a more formal manner. In an oral or written statement, the teacher specifies the objectives of the unit to be studied. Usually, this means describing material to be covered, tests to be given, and conditions of testing, bases for test evaluation. The teacher may also list expressive objectives in the area of affective behaviors that he hopes his students will achieve by the end of the year.

4.3 TEACHER RESPONSIBILITY FOR MASTERY OF PERFORMANCE OBJECTIVES

The major responsibility for attaining a particular set of performance objectives may be placed either on the teacher, on the students, or on both teacher and students.

If the teacher assumes specific responsibility for the progress of his class, it is he who determines the pace of instruction. Typically, he sets minimum objectives for each lesson or unit and does not proceed to the following lesson or unit until a predetermined degree of mastery has been demonstrated. This approach is most often used with younger students but may also be used with older students.

4.3.1 *An Experiment in Modesto, California*

Recent research had shown that most students were not mastering the material presented in foreign-language classes. Would the students be more successful in attaining course objectives if the teachers were not allowed to begin a new unit until 90 percent of the students had attained the following listening comprehension objective.

Purpose: To understand aurally the vocabulary and structures contained in the basic dialog sentences of the unit (**Stage 2: Knowledge:** *Recognition*).

Desired behavior: Given a series of familiar Spanish sentences, each spoken twice, the student will select the appropriate English equivalent among three printed choices.

Conditions: The test tape will be recorded at slow conversational speed. The sentences will occur in random order. A single sentence may be used several times to test different points of vocabulary or structure. The test tape will be played once.

Criterion: Students must answer 80 percent of the items correctly.

Sample item: (tape) Damelo! Damelo!

(answer book) 1. Give it to me!
2. Tell it to me!
3. Dim it for me!
4. (I don't know.)

The sixth-grade Spanish classes participating in this research project were divided into three groups. A pretest was administered to all classes before beginning each unit, and all classes were given a posttest upon completing the unit. In Group I (specific responsibility) the teacher was not permitted to continue until 90 percent of the students had answered 80 percent of the items correctly. In Group II (informed but not responsible) the teacher was given the test results, but was allowed to continue to the next unit. In Group III (not informed) the teacher was not given the test results. By the end of the year, Groups II and III had finished the prescribed three units in the first edition A-LM materials. Group I had done only two and one-half units. All classes were given the final Unit III test. The students in Group I (specific responsibility) scored significantly higher on the final test than the students in Groups II and III. Students in Group I also showed greater gains between pretests and posttests. The study concludes: "Teachers who are held responsible for specific objectives can be, at least, 1.6 times more effective in their teaching than teachers who are not held responsible." [1]

4.3.2 *Discussion of Modesto Experiment*

In teaching a foreign language via an audio-lingual approach, the teacher must set as the very minimum objective that the students understand the meaning of the basic dialog sentences (**Stage 2: Knowledge:** *Recognition*). It is also to be hoped that the students might become capable of understanding variations of the basic sentences using the vocabulary and structures of the lesson (**Stage 3: Transfer:** *Reception*). At the end of the Modesto study, the students were all given precisely such a listening comprehension transfer test. It was similiar to the basic dialog comprehension test, except that certain known words were substituted in the basic sentences. Of all three groups, the highest individual score was fifteen correct out of twenty-three, or roughly 65 percent!

The language teachers participating in this study had blithely assumed that their students were "learning" Spanish until the definition and measurement of a minimal performance objective demonstrated the limited extent of this "learning." Only when the teachers taught a specific objective as their goal and were *held accountable* for reaching that objective did their instruction begin to increase in effectiveness. As a result of this research project, all teachers in the Stanislaus County schools are being trained to teach with an aim toward specific performance objectives. In view of the cumulative nature of foreign-language learning, this approach is highly recommended as a means of improving the effectiveness of elementary (initial) language instruction.

[1] Melvin I. Smith, *Teaching to Specific Objectives* (Modesto, Calif.: Stanislaus County Schools Office, 1968).

4.3.3 *Use of Group Work in Teaching for Mastery*

It is evident that if a teacher decides not to begin new work until the majority of his students have mastered the current material, the lock-stepped nature of traditional classroom teaching must be broken. Since various students in one class will differ widely in the time they need for mastery, the same lesson will no longer be appropriate for every member of the class. The teacher is then confronted with the problem of what to do with students who have already mastered the material and will be bored if they are required to sit through the lesson once again.

One solution is to divide the class in half. While the teacher works with students who need additional help, the students not requiring this instruction may be free to engage in a variety of enrichment activities. They may read books or magazines kept in class for this purpose. They may be allowed to do independent library research on a topic of interest to them. The most able students might even work with some of the slower students.

A different application of this technique involves the incorporation of group work into the daily lesson plan. Here the entire class is divided into small groups to perform any number of activities: oral drillwork in pairs, discussion of a reading selection according to a list of questions, performing of skits or writing of original compositions.

In this situation, the teacher can visit each group and help students with individual problems. Alternatively, the teacher can lead the group of students who need the most help. Since student-formed groups tend to be fairly homogeneous, wide variations in time required to complete a given assignment may be expected. Here, too, groups that finish far ahead of others can be assigned enrichment reading or composition work, or they may be allowed to relax for a few minutes at the end of class as a reward for their diligence.

The individual attention that students receive in groups as well as the display of the teacher's personal concern for their success can contribute significantly to student mastery of performance objectives.

4.4 STUDENT RESPONSIBILITY FOR MASTERY OF PERFORMANCE OBJECTIVES

Absolute teacher accountability for student performance is a realistic expectation only if the time allowed for learning is flexible. In most schools, however, teachers are required to cover completely the curriculum established for one school year. The effectiveness of these teachers' instruction is judged according to the quantity of material presented, rather than by the quality of student performance. In these inflexible, tradition-bound schools, arguments relating to the necessity for student mastery often fall on deaf ears. How, then, can teachers reconcile their desire for improving student performance with the administrative necessity of moving on to new material before all students have gained full command of the old? To some extent this can be accomplished by assigning to students some of the specific responsibility for their foreign-language progress.

4.4.1   *The Retest Approach*

The retest approach involves providing each student with a detailed description of the forthcoming test. He may even be given an alternate form of the actual test as a practice exercise. Those students who attain the minimum performance level on the first test—for example, 85 percent—are considered to have mastered the material. Students who fail to attain the mastery level have the privilege of retaking a similar test before or after school or during a free period. In the intervening time, extra help is offered to those needing it. Students who attain the mastery level on the second test are graded accordingly, and no penalty is attached to their having taken the test twice. If necessary, a third test may be offered. In all cases, the highest grade the student achieves is the only one recorded.

A similar approach may be used for mid-term and semester final examinations. The first and second forms of the final exam (or of four-fifths of the final exam if additional material is still to be taught) are given toward the end of the semester. Students who attain mastery are dispensed from taking the exam during the examination period (or must take only one-fifth of the exam—that is, the part that represents the additional matter not covered on previous tests). An advantage of the retest approach lies in its psychological value: students no longer feel that the academic system is working against them. The teacher wants them to learn the second language well and is willing to help. Given the opportunity to take a test two or three times without penalty, students will spend more time studying and will actually strive harder to meet the performance objectives set by the teacher.

4.4.2   *An Application of the Retest Approach*

The retest approach is unusually effective as a means of reviewing the work of a year or even of several years. The teacher of a high-school French III class felt that her students did not display sufficient mastery of the present tense forms of irregular verbs. Consequently, she wrote the following performance objective:

"In order to demonstrate mastery of present tense irregular verbs, you will write the appropriate forms of the following verbs (list of verb forms attached) on a test consisting of fifty questions such as this: (être) Nous _____ ici. Each verb must be entirely correct for it to be counted correct. In order to pass, you must demonstrate accuracy on 90 percent of the items. Failure to reach this score will be counted as zero. You may retake the same test as many times as needed in order to achieve this standard. One month's time will be allowed."

Though some students had to take as many as six or eight tests before reaching 90 percent accuracy, every student in the class eventually passed within the time allowed. Thus encouraged, the teacher wrote similar performance objectives for the past, future, and subjunctive tenses. Here, too, the results were the same.

In attempting to explain why all students in this average class worked so hard to achieve very high performance standards, the teacher concluded that the prospect of a zero was intolerable to the students, while the reward of a ninety served as considerable motivation. More important, perhaps, the students had accepted the value of the objectives set for them. They agreed when their teacher pointed out that after six years of French, it was certainly justifiable to expect that they master their irregular verbs. They also knew there was no excuse for not reaching the 90 percent mastery level.

4.4.3 *Contract Teaching*

In contract teaching, students receive a written list of the behaviors they must demonstrate in order to prove that they have mastered a particular unit of study. Both the material to be covered on tests as well as the criteria used in evaluating student performance are clearly communicated in writing. In addition, the learning steps a student must follow to prepare himself for each test are specified. They include both classwork and homework, such as vocabulary lists and exercises, reading assignments, oral tape drills, and written exercises and compositions. In some cases, the elements of the contract may be negotiated between the teacher and individual students. An example of a contract and an explanation to students may be found on pages 222–30 of the Appendix.

4.5 INDIVIDUALIZING INSTRUCTION: DESCRIPTION

While contracts can be used in full-class, teacher-centered situations, their full potential is realized when they are employed to break the lock-step and free students to work at their own rates and in their own ways. In this way, contracts can serve as the basis for individualized instruction. Ways of using performance contracts to vary the method, pace, content, and goals of instruction will be described in the following sections.

4.5.1 *Individualizing Method of Instruction*

It is well known that all students do not learn in the same way. Some prefer oral explanations, while others choose written ones. Certain students enjoy finding out information for themselves; other students prefer being spoon-fed.

While some students work best with their peers, their classmates might bene-fit more from the personal attention of their teacher. These differences can be provided for if the teacher creates a classroom environment rich in supple-mentary books, tapes, cassettes, language masters, and other learning aids. In addition, the learning steps should allow students to choose the way they prefer to achieve mastery of the material in the unit.

4.5.2   *Individualizing Pace of Instruction*

Once each student has received his contract, he may proceed to work at his own pace, consulting his teacher only when he encounters difficulty. Students may work alone or in small groups, and explanations of new material are offered to them when they are needed and as many times as they are needed. Students take tests whenever they are ready for them. If their performance is not satisfactory, the test paper serves as the basis for individual remedial instruction. Mastery can then be demonstrated on a subsequent retest.

Another way of individualizing pace involves the use of pretests. Conceiv-ably, some intermediate or advanced students in a class may already know some of the material in a new unit. In this case, they may demonstrate their knowledge on tests without going through the learning steps leading up to them. Thus, student boredom can be avoided while opportunities for further learning are offered.

4.5.3   *Individualizing Content of Instruction*

Contracts can enable the teacher to vary course content according to individ-ual needs and interests. One way of accomplishing this is by establishing a fixed core of tests based on the new material of the unit that all learners must pass. After mastering these tests, each student is then free to choose additional activities he would most enjoy. These activities might include outside read-ing, oral speeches or skits, written compositions or skits, or any idea the student may have, subject to teacher approval.

Optional extra tests at Stage 4 might be graded as "pass" or "not yet pass-ing" in order to encourage students to try for higher stages of language be-havior without fearing the consequences of low grades.

A further development of this idea could involve teaching the core grammar through the use of different materials. For example, the grammar of the new unit is the present subjunctive tense. One set of materials may present the topic via a recorded dialog between a parent and child. A second set of ma-terials may present it in a reading selection about a coach instructing his team. Students could select the materials that hold the most appeal for them.

4.5.4   *Individualizing Objectives of Instruction*

Students enter foreign-language courses with different goals in mind. Some want to develop oral fluency, while others are more interested in reading the language. For some students, limited passive recognition of foreign-language material is sufficient. On the other hand, certain students may intend to major in the foreign language and may therefore wish to gain an active control of it. Students also differ in the language skills they want to develop and may express strong preferences for one or several language skills to the exclusion of others. These different needs may be met, in part, by allowing students to choose the type of tests they take covering basic material. For example, after having read a short story, some students might elect to prepare for a multiple-choice reading test, while others might prefer to take a listening test or to summarize the story orally or in writing. In this way, each student can concentrate on the skill or skills he considers most relevant to his particular needs.

4.5.5 *Continuous Progress Instruction*

Continuous progress permits students to advance in a course at their own pace. In the case of high aptitude and well-motivated students, the learning rate may be increased by one and one-half times or even more! Similarly, slow learners are allowed to continue their foreign-language study over a period of three or even four years in order to master one or two levels. No penalty is attached to a slower rate of progress. The enrichment provided by continuous progress is vertical rather than lateral. In other words, students move on to the new unit as soon as they have mastered the old, rather than spend their extra time unnecessarily on applications of the material just learned.

4.6 INDIVIDUALIZING INSTRUCTION: CASE STUDIES

There are many ways of individualizing foreign-language instruction. The case studies presented on the following pages are examples of the approach of one classroom teacher.[2]

4.6.1 *Contract Teaching in a High School French II Class*

Problem: The teacher was dissatisfied with her lock-stepped teaching method. Although her classes were ability-grouped, she was aware that lessons taught to the whole class bored the fast learners and confused the slow ones. As a

---

[2] Nancyanne Fitzgibbons presents another description of individualized instruction in *1971 Northeast Conference Reports*, Working Committee III, "The Open Classroom: A Case-Study," pp. 97–107. See also Gerald R. Logan, "Curricula for Individualized Instruction," in Dale L. Lange, ed., *Britannica Review of Foreign Language Education*, vol. 2 (Chicago: Encyclopaedia Britannica Educational Corp., 1969), pp. 133–55; Harry Reinert, "Practical Guide to Individualization," *Modern Language Journal*, vol. 55, no. 3 (March, 1971), pp. 156–63, and Ronald L. Gougher, "Individualization of Foreign Language Learning: What Is Being Done," in Dale L. Lange, ed., *Britannica Review of Foreign Language Education*, vol. 3 (Chicago: Encyclopaedia Britannica Educational Corp., 1970), pp. 221–45.

result, high-aptitude students were not challenged and low-aptitude students were not passed.

In addition, the teacher-centered organization of the class was unsatisfactory. It did not allow students enough time to practice speaking freely and prevented the teacher from helping individuals with their particular learning problems.

Goals: The teacher decided to try improving her instruction by using techniques of individualization. She set the following goals for herself:

1. To teach for 80 percent mastery of basic material.

2. To promote student use of French in free communication situations.

3. To vary time, materials, and goals in order to give each student a chance to succeed.

She also set this affective goal:

4. To promote enjoyment of French.

Achievement of the goals stated would be measured by test results, student questionnaires, and teacher observations.

Method: The teacher gave her students xeroxed sheets that described in performance terms the tests they would have to pass to demonstrate their mastery of the material in the new unit. This contract also included learning steps that prepared students for each test: vocabulary lists and exercises, self-correcting drills, conversation and discussion questions, and tape and reading assignments. Each step had to be checked and initialed by the teacher before students were allowed to take their test. Also, communication assignments were offered for extra credit.

In cooperation with a colleague who also wanted to adopt this method, three alternate forms of each test were written and stored in a locked file cabinet. Students were to take each test when ready. If they failed to reach a performance level of at least 80 percent, they discussed their errors with the teacher, spent additional time studying, and then took one or two retests as needed in order to achieve the desired mastery.

Full-class explanation of new material was eliminated in favor of teaching new work to small groups of students when they were ready. Four days a week, students worked in small groups with the teacher or student aide, with the tape recorder, with their friends, or on their own. One day a week, the class met as a whole to see films and slides or to discuss culture or current events.

One or two student aides from more advanced classes helped the teacher each period by handing out examinations, correcting short-answer tests, recording grades, filing each student's tests in his folder, and offering supplementary explanations.

Student evaluation: A questionnaire administered to students at the end of the ten-week grading period indicated overwhelming approval of the individualized teaching method by most, although not all, of both the honors and regular students. Reasons cited included less daily pressure, better grades because of the chance to take retests, a more relaxed class atmosphere, and enjoyment of the chance to learn on one's own and with one's friends.

Teacher self-evaluation: For several reasons, the teacher was pleased with the method adopted. Freed from much of the clerical work attached to giving tests, she was able to spend more time teaching, advising students on how to study, and helping them with individual problems. Once the lock-step was broken, she found time for activities that had never before been feasible: individually administered speaking tests, personal conferences to discuss composition errors, and compensatory instruction to students needing extra help.

She also felt that her relationship with students had improved, since it had lost its former adversary-like nature. Students knew she was there to help them with their learning problems and to offer additional tests if they did not pass their first one. As a result, the dropout and failure rate decreased markedly from what it had been the year before.

There were also some unanticipated benefits. With an open, or informal, classroom, the teacher's well-planned lessons could no longer be ruined by fire drills, assemblies, outside trips, extracurricular activities, or heavy absenteeism. Moreover, tests could be returned to students almost immediately after they were submitted; there was no more running after absentees to have them make up their work. The problems of writing extra make-up exams or of not returning tests until all students had taken them were also eliminated.

Difficulties encountered: Not all aspects of the class were positive, however. Several problems were encountered with individualized instruction. Most students had difficulty adjusting to the freedom of taking tests when ready. The highly talented students did the minimum amount of work and then relaxed; the slower students relaxed without doing the work. The teacher faced this problem by instituting some new policies.

All skill tests (Stages 1, 2, and 3 behaviors) would be graded pass/fail with 80 percent needed to pass. Students passing all these tests plus required communication assignments would get a grade of eighty on their report cards. If they wanted higher grades, they would have to complete extra-credit communication assignments, such as speeches, compositions, and book reports, as described in their contract. Failure to pass a required test meant that five points would be deducted from the report card grade. (For a sample of this contract, see Appendix.)

Although initially students considered this unfair, they changed their attitude when the teacher explained that she was encouraging them to use French naturally—for communication—not just for artificial activities like vocabulary learning, reading, and grammar tests. These knowledge and skill tests were not ends in themselves, but would enable them to use French to express their own thoughts orally and in writing. Furthermore, if students wanted, they could emphasize a particular language skill or negotiate a balance of the skills.

Another problem involved excessive use of English as students worked on their contracts. To remedy this situation, the first fifteen minutes of each forty-minute class were devoted to small-group conversations in French. Students could choose to speak freely, to act out skit ideas written on index cards, to discuss topics listed on a hand-out, or to ask and answer lists of questions related to current grammar assignments. This popular activity resulted in increased fluency, comprehension, and accuracy for all students.

The teacher handed out a recommended time schedule and encouraged students to take each test in class before the deadline specified. If they were not ready by this date, they could no longer take the test in class, but were allowed up to a week more during which to take it out of class. All students had to take each test once before the out-of-class deadline, but could retake outside of class any test they wished during the entire ten-week grading period. This policy succeeded in making the students work more diligently both in class and out, but it resulted in heavy time pressure on the slowest students, whose grades at times fell below 80 percent.

Conclusions: On the whole, the teacher felt she had accomplished most of the goals set for herself. She had succeeded in promoting the use of French in free communication situations, particularly in her honors classes, and had achieved her aim of varying to some extent the time, material, and objectives of the course according to individual needs. Since her students looked interested and involved in class—in contrast to their glassy-eyed stares before the experiment—the teacher was led to believe she had indeed accomplished her affective aim of promoting enjoyment of French. This was confirmed by the student responses to her questionnaire.

Her main failure was that not all students reached 80 percent mastery of the material, given the time limits necessarily imposed. Still, she found encouragement in the fact that the dropout and failure rate decreased markedly from what it had been the year before.

Although individualized instruction did not solve all the problems connected with teaching French, the teacher felt its advantages far outweighed its drawbacks. Furthermore, she believed that if she could be freed from having to cover a year's work in a year's time, the problems encountered could be solved. She hoped to win administrative support for a plan whereby credit would be awarded only when students had completed all the course requirements with at least 80 percent mastery. In this way, slower students would no longer fail, while faster students could be rewarded for superior effort with credit for learning, rather than just with high grades.

4.6.2   *Continuous Progress in a High School French II Class*

One student in the honors class of the teacher discussed in the preceding section asked if he might increase his learning pace so that by the end of the year he could take the French III regents exam rather than the French II final and earn credit for two years of study in one.

Although it was March, the teacher agreed, since French was his second foreign language and he was unusually capable. She freed this student from the formal French II requirements and designed assignments tailored to his needs.

When the whole class met for culture and listening comprehension, the continuous-progress student was freed to work with more advanced tapes and culture materials. Within the framework of the open classroom, the teacher had little difficulty finding time to meet twice a week for fifteen minutes with the advanced student, who ultimately earned ninety-three on the Regents.

What may be most significant is that continuous progress operated effectively within the rigid framework of a highly traditional school. Although administrative support for this concept and more free time would have been highly desirable, the program functioned satisfactorily without these luxuries.

4.7 THE TRANSITION FROM FULL-CLASS TO INDIVIDUALIZED INSTRUCTION

The transition from full-class to individualized instruction can be traumatic to all involved unless a certain amount of thought and preparation precedes the changeover.

4.7.1 *New Teacher and Student Roles*

Both the teacher and students must understand fully their new roles. The teacher must no longer consider himself as the stage-center distributor of all new knowledge and information. Rather, he must see himself as the director and manager of student-centered activities, many of which can go on without his direct presence. He must accustom himself to making explanations to small groups of four or five students and to not having the attention of the full class at any one moment.

Students, in turn, must learn that they are no longer passive receivers of the knowledge the teacher dispenses. They must now assume some responsibility for their learning progress. It is up to them to assign themselves homework and to judge when they are ready to take tests. It is their decision how to use their new freedom wisely and to find out how they learn most successfully.

4.7.2 *Stages in the Transition*

In view of the new roles that both teachers and students must assume, it is advisable to make the changeover gradually. At the beginning of the year, the teacher should teach to the full class until he has familiarized himself with each individual and his work habits. This time period, which can vary considerably in different situations, also allows students to become used to the teacher's methods. Then group-work activities can be introduced into the formal class. After teacher presentation and explanation, students can do pattern drills in pairs. Discussion questions on a story read can be given to students who must answer them orally while working in groups of three or four. Students can also write compositions or skits in small groups. Retests can be offered to individuals who wish to improve their work. Once students have become used to learning from one another and to taking responsibility for their foreign-language success and the teacher has gained experience in managing group activities, the class should be ready to move into individualized instruction.

If the teacher feels hesitant about implementing the new approach, he might try it with his best class and then apply the technique to the others once he has gained more confidence. If possible, the teacher should observe a classroom where individualized instruction takes place.

4.7.3 *Preparations for Individualized Instruction*

It is a good idea for the teacher to spend a day explaining to his class what innovations will be made and the advantages of the new method over the old one. Since many students tend to be conservative and to resent sudden changes in the classroom, some promotion is needed to smooth the transition. This orientation session should also include a description of the students' new role and responsibilities. An example of one teacher's explanation is found on pages 216–21 of the Appendix.

The teacher may then distribute a list of performance objectives for the new unit that state clearly the purpose of each test, the student behaviors expected, the conditions under which the behaviors are to occur, and the minimum level of performance desired. In addition, criteria used to evaluate expressive speaking and writing objectives should be specified. Next, the learning steps—reading assignments, tape drills, written exercises, and so on—which the student must follow in preparing himself for each test, are distributed. Supplementary communication assignments may be included in addition to the minimum core of required tests. During the first few days of studying the unit, the teacher may negotiate with each individual the amount and quality of work to be done.

4.7.4 *Evaluation*

At the end of the unit, it is advisable to hand out questionnaires to students so that they may evaluate the instruction and identify problems that may exist. At all times, the teacher should remain sensitive to student needs and be aware of difficulties that may be developing. He should maintain an open, receptive attitude toward responsible student criticisms and should strive to implement reasonable suggestions for improvement.

It is quite possible that in spite of a teacher's best efforts, the attempt to individualize instruction will not work for a particular class. In such cases, it is advisable that the teacher return to his former methods of instruction. In doing so, he should avoid making students feel responsible for the failure. Rather, he should inform his classes that his main concern is helping them learn in whatever way is best for them, not in forcing them to conform to a new and inappropriate teaching technique.

4.8 IMPLEMENTING PERFORMANCE OBJECTIVES IN THE SCHOOL

The decision to implement performance objectives in a school may be made by the individual teacher or by the foreign-language department, or it may be issued as an administrative fiat. The adoption of any new educational approach poses problems. In this section, we shall suggest answers to questions that may arise in connection with the adoption of performance objectives.

4.8.1 *Departmental Attitude*

It is easy to sit back and read professional literature about innovations in education. It is quite another thing to decide to experiment with one's own classes. Not all experiments are successful. A teacher who does not try a new approach knows he avoids the risk of failure. Unfortunately, he also misses the chance to increase his teaching effectiveness.

The attitude of a foreign-language department toward experimentation determines to a large extent whether the implementation of a performance curriculum will result in success or failure.

4.8.1a AN ILLUSTRATION: THE CASE OF NEIGHBORING SCHOOLS

Once there were two neighboring towns, Nowecant and Tryansee. Each town had a high school, and each high school had a foreign-language department, and each department had the same problems to solve. Interest in foreign languages was diminishing. Enrollment was decreasing, and teacher and student morale was declining. Only the dropout and failure rates were skyrocketing.

So, the language departments in each school met to discuss the possibilities of using performance objectives and individualized instruction to increase the effectiveness of their courses. Here are some reactions of the foreign-language teachers in Nowecant:

Noah Waves: But we've *always* taught the way we do now.

Ivan Gudonuv: Right. What was good enough for *us* is good enough now. *We* learned foreign languages, didn't we?

Tim Id: I'm not sure about this new approach. We've never done it before.

Ike Kant: How in the world with all our myriad responsibilities could we *possibly* find the opportunities to effect the item under discussion?

Ivy Moss: I've got to cover the book. That comes before all else.

And here are some of the comments of teachers in Tryansee:

Freddie Reddy: Performance objectives and individualized instruction might help us improve the quality of our instruction, and then again they might not. Perhaps we can try this approach on a limited basis—maybe only one or two classes at the start.

Ima Willing: If we work together on our preparations and swap exercises and tests, we can find the extra time to write performance objectives for each unit.

Ann Able: The administration might not like this idea. They're all from Nowecant. If we don't fail enough students and if our enrollment increases, they will have to spend money on additional language teachers and books. We'll have to think of a way of presenting this idea to them. Maybe if we developed better relations with parents who want their children to pass, we could gain parental support of our idea.

*   *   *

The years passed. Things stayed pretty much the same at Nowecant, but at Tryansee sweeping changes were made in the language curriculum. The attitudes of Reddy, Willing, and Able made all the difference.

4.8.1b   GOAL ORIENTATION VS. PROBLEM ORIENTATION

In the story above, Nowecant High School was *problem oriented*. Once a new idea was proposed, everyone thought of reasons why it should not be initiated. As a result, the idea was never even given a chance. The staff in Tryansee High School was *goal oriented*. The new idea was first considered in the light of its potential contribution to the instructional goals of the department. Once the staff had accepted the value of the new idea, the problems they might encounter were discussed and solutions were offered. Their attitude involved staff cooperation in implementing a new approach and modifying it, if necessary, to their own particular situation.

4.8.2   *Questions on Performance Objectives and Mastery Teaching*

In this section, we shall give answers to some frequently asked questions.

4.8.2a   QUESTIONS FROM TEACHERS

Question: If I understand correctly, the key concept in teaching for mastery is that you proceed from one unit to the next only when the class has mastered the first one. Is that correct?

Answer: Yes. You determine the performance objectives of the lesson and then stay on that lesson until a certain proportion of the students have mastered the objectives. You also determine the level of mastery, for example, 90 percent of the students getting 80 percent of the items correct.

Question: Is this the same as knowing the lesson cold?

Answer: Not at all. You as the teacher look at the lesson. You pick out the essential features the student must master if he is not to have trouble with the following lessons. You may then decide on only one main objective that will determine movement from one lesson to the other—for example, that the student is to understand spoken sentences containing the basic structures and vocabulary of the lesson. This might be tested by having the student hear the sentences and demonstrate his comprehension by selecting the appropriate English equivalent on an answer sheet.

Question: Must every lesson or unit have the same kind of objectives?

Answer: No, you can set different objectives for different lessons. Just make sure the students know what the objectives are. And most important, remember that in beginning classes you should have at least one transfer objective, while in classes that are beyond the very initial language-learning stages you should have at least one communication objective.

Question: Suppose I give the unit tests and half the class scores above 80 percent. My mastery level says 90 percent of the class must make scores above 80 percent. What do I do with those who have done well the first time around?

Answer: You could have the faster students tutor the slower ones. Or you could give the faster ones a special project, like preparing a bulletin board. You could also give them some independent reading or research.

Question: Won't the faster students get bored?

Answer: Not if they are actively contributing to the progress of the class. If you have a few very fast learners, you may want to let them work ahead of the remainder of the class, or some other arrangement can be made.

In one school, for example, a particularly gifted child went to Latin three days a week and to Italian twice a week, since both courses were scheduled at the same time. At the end of the year, the student had accumulated full credit in both Latin and Italian.

Question: How often do you teach the same thing?

Answer: You continue teaching for a specific performance objective until it has been met, but this does not mean that you go over the same point in the same way *ad nauseum*. If your presentation was effective with part of the class and if other students are still having trouble, look for new methods of presentation for the others. Perhaps students can team up, with the stronger ones tutoring the weaker ones. Perhaps your department library has other textbooks available; some students might understand another explanation of a grammatical point better than the one in their own book. Or perhaps you have on hand tapes from a series you no longer use; these might provide the needed variety. Students from more advanced classes might tutor the slower learners during a study hall. Once you begin looking for ways to vary instruction, your students will also provide you with ideas.

Question: But in our school the language classes are rather large. I can't quite visualize the various types of activities you suggest.

Answer: Precisely because the classes are large, one teacher cannot hope to keep the attention of all the students all the time. You might try teaching your usual way for the first half of the class period. Then you might divide the class into small groups of two or three students for oral work. Let one person in each group ask the questions or lead the drill and have the others give the answers; then switch roles. Meanwhile, you can walk around from group to group answering the students' questions—which they feel freer to ask, since they won't appear stupid in front of the entire class. Once your class gets used to this conversation session at the end of each period, you can vary the groups and the activities.

Question: But doesn't this small-group activity create noise and disorder?

Answer: At first noise can be a problem until students become used to showing consideration for others. However, if small-group activities are well structured, there may actually be fewer discipline problems than in a conventional teacher-versus-class situation.

Question: Won't students in small groups make pronunciation mistakes that will go uncorrected?

Answer: Students responding in choral classwork also make mistakes the teacher does not notice. Certainly the silence of students in full-class situations is no guarantee of pronunciation accuracy. Furthermore, constant teacher correction of foreign-language mistakes has the effect of inhibiting students who seek to avoid responding in order to avoid making errors.

Small-group work offers two advantages in the teaching of audio-lingual skills. First, all students are listening and speaking; they do not tune out in small groups. Second, as the teacher supervises each group, he can work with individuals or pairs of students on their particular pronunciation difficulties. This is far more effective than teaching one sound to an entire class of students, many of whom are already capable of producing it correctly.

Question: What about mistakes in vocabulary and grammar? Won't they go uncorrected?

Answer: This depends on the type of oral activity. Students in pairs can practice pattern drills and exercises where the student giving the stimulus or asking the question also can read the correct reply. (If the book does not contain correct answers, these may be mimeographed and distributed for small-group work.) Some of the activities will be of the free-response variety at Stage 4 of the taxonomy. At this point, students are encouraged to try to say what they want to, even if they make mistakes. Gradually they will begin to correct their own errors. It should not be forgotten, either, that the teacher is circulating in the room and acts as a resource person to help students express themselves more easily and accurately. Student aides can also help.

Question: How are grades assigned if you are using performance objectives?

Answer: The attainment of the performance objectives at the minimal acceptable level should be graded B, or 80. For higher levels of performance, grades of B+ (85) or A (95) may be awarded. Quarter or semester grades would be recorded in two parts: number of lessons, units, or levels mastered and grade received.

Question: I am the only teacher in my department who is teaching to performance objectives. My chairman tells me that I have given too many A's and B's. What can I do?

Answer: As a teacher, your first responsibility is toward those you are teaching—your students. Obviously, your position is difficult if you are the only one in your department who is teaching for specific performance objectives. However, if you are confident that you have set appropriate objectives and if all or almost all of your students have mastered the objectives, then in all honesty to yourself and your students, you must assign a preponderance of high grades. If challenged, you can always show the test results of your students.

If this is not enough and if conditions in your school are such that you are not free to teach your students a foreign language in such a manner that they are able to learn it and master it, then you should consider looking elsewhere for another teaching position.

Question: The chairman insists that we cover a certain number of lessons per semester. How can I reconcile this predetermined pace with the teaching toward performance objectives?

Answer: You can't. Teaching toward performance objectives means that you spend the time needed by your students to attain the stated objectives, and this amount of time may vary from class to class. You might try the following. Go over the required lessons and pick out the important vocabulary, patterns, and structures. Set your own minimal objectives for each lesson, selecting those points that are crucial to the successful completion of the subsequent lessons. Teach toward those minimal objectives and do not continue on to another lesson until those goals have been attained. By the end of the semester you may be somewhat behind the other classes, but your students will actually have acquired a stronger language base.

If you have several sections, you may want to try the above with one section and teach your other sections at the preestablished pace. You can then compare performances at the end of the semester.

4.8.2b QUESTIONS FROM CHAIRMEN

Question: As a department chairman, I would like to orient our program toward specific performance objectives, but my teachers are unfamiliar with performance objectives and I have no money to run a workshop. What can I do?

Answer: First do some homework. Analyze the effectiveness of your present program. What percentage of the students in your school are taking foreign languages? How many do you lose between the first and second year? Between the second and third year? Between the third and fourth year? Especially significant are the third- and fourth-year figures, for these reflect the percentage of students who freely elect foreign languages beyond college entrance requirements.

Is your program really teaching the students another language? Do your students demonstrate an interest in continuing language study? Present these questions to your staff members at a department meeting. If they agree that the program has room for improvement and if they feel that the lower third of their students are learning very little, then suggest the adoption of performance objectives.

At this point you may wish to negotiate with the principal for released time for your teachers to prepare performance objectives. Perhaps they can be freed from study-hall assignments in order to work on curriculum. If only some teachers are interested in the experiment, let them work out their own performance objectives and try them out on an experimental basis.

Question: What if none of the teachers seem interested?

Answer: Then take one of your own classes. Select just one or two minimal objectives and teach for mastery of those objectives. If the program is successful, add other objectives and involve more of your classes. If the program is not successful, have the department go over the project and suggest possible modifications. The improvement of your language program will be the result of the combined efforts of you and your staff and not the product of attendance at a workshop.

Question: The principal will not be pleased if all my teachers start turning in mainly A's and B's. What do I tell him?

Answer: First of all, the primary function of your language teachers is to teach language, not to assign grades. Grades in themselves are meaningless, for one teacher's C may equal another teacher's A. A semester grade that indicates the student's level of achievement with respect to specific objectives is a much more meaningful evaluation of his performance than a grade that simply ranks him among his classmates.

Once you have convinced all your teachers that the new grading system is not only more objective but fairer to the students, you may present your principal with the departmental position. If he is recalcitrant, some negotiating may be necessary.

4.8.3 *Questions on Individualized Instruction*

The following are questions that teachers often ask in connection with individualized instruction.

Question: If students learn grammar when they are ready, doesn't this mean that the same explanation must be given several times? Isn't this inconvenient?

Answer: Yes, explanations must be repeated if students work on their own, but this system is preferable. When made to a small group of students, explanations take much less time. Just by looking at the students' faces, the teacher can tell if they understand or not. Also, students in small groups are far more likely to ask questions and pay attention than they are in full-class situations.

Question: How can a teacher maintain control over so many different groups?

Answer: It is helpful to establish separate areas for different activities: test-taking, individual study, group work, and work with tapes. If some students still find the class too noisy, they may be allowed to work outside in the hall. The teacher might also want to keep a bell that he can ring if he needs the attention of the full class for an announcement.

Question: If one student gets a ninety on his first test but another student needs three tests in order to get this score, would both be awarded the same grade?

Answer: Yes, why not? The teacher's job is to motivate students to perform as well as they can. A ninety is a ninety whether it is earned on Monday or on Friday.

Question: But if a seventy student needs three tests to achieve a ninety, won't he just forget the material and thus invalidate his grade?

Answer: There is no such thing as a seventy student. Given sufficient time, most students can raise considerably the standard of their accomplishment. It is wrong to condemn a student to a seventy grade with no chance to improve, since this teacher expectation will actually lead to the mediocre level of performance. Furthermore, even granted that forgetting does occur, isn't it better that it begin from the achievement of a ninety than from a grade of seventy?

Question: If students know they have two or three chances to take a test, will they study for the first one?

Answer: Definitely. In fact, they tend to study harder, since they would prefer to pass the first time and not have to go through the trouble of taking the retests.

Question: But the real world doesn't offer second and third chances. Shouldn't schools prepare students for the way things will be in life?

Answer: Here it is very important that each teacher examine his goals. If he finds that his ultimate purpose is to show students the harshness and brutality of the real world, then he should find more effective ways of weeding out more students. As it is, too many students pass in school but fail in life. However, if the final aim of his instruction is to equip students to deal successfully with the real world, he will make every effort to see that they master the knowledge and skills offered in school. Moreover, the existence of cruelty in the real world is no justification for perpetuating it in the classroom. On the contrary, if present society is to be transformed into a better one, tolerance, kindness, trust, and understanding should be valued in the schools and should characterize the behavior of teachers.

Question: If students take tests when ready, isn't there a lot of cheating once the first few students know what the questions are?

Answer: There is actually less cheating under this system, because students are under less pressure. They know the system is working for them rather than against them. If they do not do well on a test, they know they will receive extra help, extra time to study, and another chance to show that they have mastered the material.

Cheating can also be discouraged by several other procedures. Since students do not know which of three tests they will receive, any answers they might have would be of limited value. Time limits can also make it inadvisable to wait for the test about which one had some information. All tests can be administered in one testing area that the teacher can easily supervise. Students taking the same test may be given different forms so that students cannot copy answers. Multiple-choice answers should be eliminated, since some students enjoy memorizing answer keys. Instead, students can place an X beside their unnumbered, unlettered answer choice, and the exams can be graded by placing over them a grid on which the answers are punched out.

Question: How is listening comprehension taught?

Answer: Some listening-comprehension practice can occur on days when the students meet as a full class. Also, learning steps may specify that students listen to tapes first with their books open and then with them closed. Listening comprehension can be tested indirectly by grading student responses to questions during individual speaking tests, or it can be tested directly through listening comprehension tests administered by the teacher or presented on tape.

Question: Doesn't the preparation for this type of teaching involve an enormous amount of work?

Answer: Yes, but the rewards are also greater. If two or more colleagues can cooperate in preparing the contracts, learning steps, exercises, and alternate forms of each test, the preparation time can be reduced considerably. Summer workshops offer another means of handling the advanced preparation needed to implement individualized instruction.

It should also be noted that classroom aides can free the teacher from much time-consuming grading and recording of objective tests, thereby enabling the teacher to concentrate his energies on the more creative aspects of foreign-language teaching.

Question: What if students are unhappy under individualized instruction?

Answer: The teacher should determine how many students are not satisfied. If they constitute a minority, he should explain to them quite frankly that although they might have done well under the full-class teaching system, he cannot continue to teach this way because of the very wide range of ability in the class. He can also assure them that they can still have all the help they need if they just ask for it. The teacher should attempt to identify which students are dissatisfied and should make every effort to give them extra attention.

If the majority of the class seems to oppose the individualized instruction, it would be wise to find out via questionnaires or open discussions the reasons for this attitude. Do students understand clearly what is expected of them? Are they receiving enough personalized instruction from the teacher? Do they need more guidance in how to study? Are they capable of assuming responsibility for their own success or failure? Are they mature enough to handle freedom? Is the teacher providing too much or too little structure? If the problems identified cannot be solved, it would be wise to abandon individualized instruction in this particular class.

In evaluating the results of an experiment in individualized instruction, it is also important that the teacher examine his own attitudes toward this method. Does he genuinely feel comfortable managing small-group instruction? Can he teach even if the room is noisy? Does he truly believe in a student-centered classroom? Does he enjoy being a manager of learning activities rather than a stage-center distributor of knowledge?

Unless the teacher's attitudes toward individualized instruction are positive, the method is likely to fail when used in the classroom. A teacher should individualize his instruction because he believes it will increase his teaching effectiveness, not because it seems like the thing to do. For example, one teacher who felt compelled to use this method said angrily to his class, "If you don't want to listen to me, then I'll put you on contracts." Since his students perceived this method as punishment for misbehavior, they were very hostile to it and did not cooperate well.

4.8.4   *A Concluding Statement to Teachers and Chairmen*

Once you begin evaluating your instruction in terms of achievement of performance objectives, you find certain other changes taking place in your attitudes. You become acutely aware of your own successes and setbacks. Adopting performance objectives in no way implies automatic success. On the contrary, if you have set a goal for yourself or for your students and if you have set this goal in specific terms of a performance objective, you cannot fool yourself about the effectiveness or ineffectiveness of your teaching.

You find yourself spending a great deal of time thinking about the goals of your instruction and about ways to improve it. Each failure becomes a personal challenge, and you ask yourself, "How can I transform this failure into a success?" You attempt to find better ways of teaching these points.

You become more realistic in setting your objectives. Since you now expect all students to attain your performance objectives, you establish these objectives in terms of what types of behaviors you find the students capable of acquiring. You ask yourself, "Are the students failing to meet this objective because the instruction is inadequate or because the objective itself is inappropriate for these students?" You may begin developing different types of objectives for different types of students.

You find yourself less interested in grading students from A to F and more concerned with bringing all students to the A or B level. In other words, since performance objectives are worded in pass-or-fail terms, you begin establishing a rather high pass-or-fail level—perhaps 85 percent. Since you have carefully defined the outcomes of your instruction, you now want all students to attain those objectives.

You grow more pragmatic in your outlook and less concerned with the theoretical underpinnings of specific approaches and methods. You are interested in what works in the classroom, what works with you and with your students, and not in what ought to work. You still read about what other teachers are thinking and doing, but your concern is whether these things have direct application in your own situation. A dialog method may be very effective in a ghetto school where children are turned off by books, but students in an upper middle-class suburban school might learn faster with a more cognitive approach.

You grow more skeptical about the claims of experts or manufacturers or publishers. You become a Doubting Thomas who has to try out new materials, new methods, new techniques in his own classroom with his own students to see whether they can help him meet his own performance objectives.

In a word, you become more professional. You are willing to experiment with new methods and new techniques, but you judge their effectiveness in terms of preestablished performance objectives. You vary these objectives to meet the needs of the students. You follow the progress of your students with the aim of helping each student learn a second language.

And the students? They will have discovered that the learning activities in the foreign-language classroom have become more meaningful. They will have found that the teacher is now encouraging them to master a new language, rather than sitting back in judgment on their efforts.

CHAPTER FIVE
DEVELOPING AND MEASURING ATTITUDES, FEELINGS, AND VALUES

5.1 GENERAL CONSIDERATIONS

Although teachers obviously cannot directly control the inner workings of their students' minds, they can nevertheless exert considerable indirect influence over the development of positive attitudes, feelings, and values in foreign-language learners. Furthermore, it is vitally important to do so, since negative student attitudes can nullify the most effective presentations of subject matter. The most competent teachers using the soundest methods and best materials will fail to bring all their students to **Stage 4: Communication** unless these students want to acquire the foreign language and value it in terms of their personal goals. For this reason, it is imperative that teachers attach far more importance to the affective results of their instruction than has been the case so far.

One means of motivating students is simply to inform them of the affective goals that it is hoped they will achieve. These goals may be communicated as expressive performance objectives. Another important influence on students is the teacher's own behavior, which reflects his personal attitudes toward the foreign language and culture. Finally, positive feelings may be developed through classroom activities specially designed for this purpose.

The first section of this chapter will deal with specific ways of promoting desired student behaviors at each of the first three stages of the affective taxonomy. The second section will deal with ways of measuring attainment of affective goals.

5.2 DEVELOPING POSITIVE AFFECTIVE BEHAVIORS

5.2.1 Stage 1: Receptivity: *Awareness*

An initial awareness lesson for beginning students might consist of having them listen for a few minutes to a tape of a foreign-language conversation or text. They could then discuss the characteristics that strike them as different, such as sound, rhythm, speed, and melody. The teacher might explain that what seems very strange, foreign, and difficult to them now will become quite easy and familiar in a short while.

A subsequent lesson could deal with instances of foreign-language words used in English, as well as English words that occur in the foreign language. Students might be asked to develop their own lists of examples. These assignments can serve to show students the relevance of foreign-language study.

Students could also keep diaries for a month in which they note all chance encounters with the foreign language and culture under study. These might include finding foreign-language words or phrases in books, magazines, or newspapers. They might record having heard the language used on television, in a movie, or by passersby on the street. An enjoyable class session can result from asking each student to tell about his most interesting or unusual entry. In this situation, peer-group pressure can be employed to good advantage. Since everyone in the class will have had some personal contact with the foreign language or culture, this will seem the "in" thing to do. This session can impress strongly on students the relevance of the foreign language to their daily lives.

Another awareness assignment might consist of weekly or monthly discussions of current events in the foreign country. In advanced classes, these discussions might be conducted in the foreign language. During these sessions, the teacher might point out the importance of being aware of events in foreign countries, since they often have considerable bearing on those in one's native land. A bulletin board featuring current news items as well as other material related to the foreign country is another way of stimulating student awareness. Responsibility for the bulletin board may be rotated among student committees appointed for this purpose.

Positive attitudes might also be developed by having students keep scrapbooks of material relating to a variety of subjects: current events, travel brochures, articles about life in the foreign country, ads for products from the foreign country, entertainment, and so on. Scrapbooks may be exchanged among students during a class period, or they may be made available in the classroom library to students who would like to browse through them after having completed their work ahead of time. A minimum number of entries for the time period allotted could be set, and the scrapbooks subsequently evaluated as pass, fail, or outstanding.

5.2.2   Stage 1: Receptivity: *Attentiveness*

Student attentiveness in fulfilling classroom obligations depends to some extent on the behavior the teacher models. A teacher's consistent attendance and promptness in beginning class demonstrates that he values these characteristics and also tends to produce this behavior in students. The teacher can encourage student attentiveness to homework by checking to see that each assignment has been completed. This may be accomplished by collecting homework or simply by walking around class to look at student papers. In cases where assignments have not been carried out, it is more effective to call for their completion the next day than to assign penalty grades, since this would, in effect, defeat the original purpose of the homework.

Cases where students persist in neglecting assignments call for further action. The teacher might try to find out why the work was not done. Perhaps the problem might be solved by pointing out the relevance of the homework to the goals of the course. Perhaps a choice of homework assignments might be offered that would appeal to the individual interests of the students. Perhaps a conference with the student or with his parents is necessary. Whatever the answer, the teacher's insistence on the importance of completing assignments should, in most cases, result in student attentiveness.

Another important area concerns student attention in class. Here, too, teacher attentiveness is a major influence on student behavior. It is the teacher's responsibility to see that his students are participating in the planned class activities, rather than sleeping, chatting with a friend, or doing homework for another subject. In addition, the teacher must provide for variety in daily class activities to prevent the boredom that often results in student inattention. The use of supervised small group work as well as independent study are effective means of promoting attentiveness.

5.2.3   Stage 2: Responsiveness: *Tolerance*

An important idea to convey to students is that the word "different" is a neutral term; it means neither "good" nor "bad." The reason your own language and culture may seem best is that they have become so familiar to you. For example, the first time you hear a popular song, you may not like it, but after hearing it several times, you like it more and more. Furthermore, it is hard to evaluate a native language and culture unless you can compare them to other linguistic and cultural systems. Certainly, people in foreign countries must also consider their language and culture superior to all others. Ideas such as these can be communicated most effectively through open-ended full-class or small-group discussions, rather than by lecturing. Such discussions might begin with questions such as, Is the American way of life (or the English language) the best in the world? Why?

Other opportunities for developing tolerance may present themselves when students balk at a new spelling or grammatical pattern that seems to them very difficult and illogical. In such cases, the teacher might want to point out inconsistencies in their native language. For example, the pronunciation of the words "though," "through," "tough," and "bought" must surely pose difficulties when foreign students try to learn English. Or the teacher may write the patterns "May I?" "Have I?" "Can I?" and contrast them with "Do I work?" rather than "Work I?" More advanced students might be asked to supply examples of difficulties that their native language can cause foreigners trying to acquire it. Role play can be used profitably in this situation. The teacher or his students could take the role of a foreign student who is frustrated because of the difficulty he is having in English class.

In order to promote cross-cultural tolerance and understanding, it is important that the teacher demonstrate through his behavior an attitude of acceptance toward each member of the class. If appropriate, he might tell his students that even though they look different from each other and perform at different levels of ability, he nevertheless believes in their worth as individuals and tries to help them. A teacher familiar with role play or psychodrama techniques might for one day purposely discriminate in subtle ways (withholding praise or attention, frowning, scolding) against half the members of the class and the next day against the other half. On the third day, the class might discuss against whom the discrimination was directed each day and how it made them feel.

Through daily observations of relationships among members of his classes, a teacher might become aware of students who are disliked by their classmates. He might attempt to modify the behavior of the class by showing tolerance or appreciation of the isolated students and involving them in small-group activities. Or, he might say that he is aware that certain students are ignored by the rest of the class. This makes him feel unhappy, since he would hope that people in a foreign-language class would show tolerance toward others.

5.2.4   Stage 2: Responsiveness: *Interest and Enjoyment*

Here, too, the behavior that a teacher displays exerts considerable influence on that exhibited by his students. If a teacher looks bored, angry, or unhappy, if he gives the impression that he would love to be anywhere else but in the classroom, then his students can hardly be expected to behave otherwise. Whenever relevant, the teacher should communicate to his students the reasons why he is interested in the foreign language and why he enjoys it.

In seeking to promote student interest in foreign-language study, it is important that the teacher recognize the diversity of interests among students in his classes. With this in mind, he should provide for a variety of parallel classroom experiences and homework assignments from which students may choose those they prefer to do. For example, students may elect to write out an exercise on the new grammar, or they may write original sentences or a composition in which they demonstrate ability to use the new patterns. After reading a book they have chosen, students may wish to take a test on the vocabulary lists they have made, or they might want to summarize the book either orally or in writing. Unless the contents, goals, and methods of instruction are individualized to meet student needs, no teacher can expect to capture the interest of each student enrolled in his course.

Enjoyment of a foreign-language class depends considerably on its atmosphere. This atmosphere results mainly from the rapport a teacher establishes with his students. Obviously, a relationship characterized by mistrust, sarcasm, complaints, and generally negative remarks about the entire class is not enjoyable, and students will seek to avoid it.[1] Although students do not always merit praise, criticism of them should be made privately and tactfully. It should be limited to a specific piece of work or to a particular instance of behavior. Generalizations concerning intelligence, language aptitude, or personality serve no constructive purpose and must be avoided.[2] The teacher should seek to establish an accepting, supportive class atmosphere where there is kindness, understanding, and concern for the success of each individual.[3] He should not attempt to pigeonhole his students or to predict their academic success or failure. Too often, negative evaluations of student potential become self-fulfilling prophecies. The teacher should realize that a student's failure to excel in foreign-language study does not detract from his worth as an individual.

In addition to establishing a positive class atmosphere, a teacher wishing to promote enjoyment in his classes should prepare activities he believes his students would like. Language games, songs, dances, skits, films, and slides are but a few of the techniques teachers have traditionally used to promote enjoyment of foreign-language study. Not all classes, however, enjoy the same activities. Therefore, the teacher might prepare a checklist on which students mark the activities they prefer. The most popular ones can then be incorporated into the teacher's lesson plans.

---

[1] For a more complete listing of positive and negative classroom factors, see Robert Mager, *Developing Attitude Toward Learning* (Belmont, Calif.: Fearon Press, 1968).

[2] See Haim G. Ginott, *Between Parent and Child* (New York: Macmillan, 1965) and *Between Parent and Teenager* (New York: Macmillan, 1969).

[3] For a more complete discussion of this topic, see John Holt, *How Children Fail* (New York: Pitman Press, 1964) and *How Children Learn* (New York: Pitman Press, 1967).

More informally, a teacher might express quite frankly to his students his desire that they enjoy the class and might encourage them to tell him at any time how it might be improved. A suggestion box is often highly effective in soliciting sound ideas from students who wish to remain anonymous.

Another means of promoting enjoyment is to provide students with feelings of accomplishment in their work. Student success may be increased by offering them the opportunity to take again the tests on which they did not perform as well as they might. These retests can contribute significantly to reducing the anxiety that results from the pressure to achieve high grades.

In order to develop in students a sense of satisfaction with their language progress, a teacher might present material that is far below their current language ability. Replaying familiar dialogs or oral comprehension tests that have become easy for students is an effective way of showing them how much they have learned. Similarly, students gain a sense of satisfaction from reading unfamiliar material in which all vocabulary and structure are known to them.

Student participation in class activities is also important in the development of enjoyment and can be promoted by the use of group work. Students who normally feel shy about speaking a foreign language in front of the teacher and the whole class lose a considerable part of this inhibition when talking to only three or four classmates. Students who would ordinarily balk at writing a composition at home enjoy greatly writing skits in class with their friends. Similarly, students who are allowed to dramatize in pairs the situations described on note cards perform with much greater enthusiasm than if compelled to answer discussion questions posed by their teacher. The note card situations may relate to the vocabulary and structure of particular lessons, or they may be based on ideas submitted by students. Once a pair has exhausted the conversational possibilities of one card, it may be exchanged for another.

Students can gain an enormous sense of satisfaction from foreign-language study if they see they are able to communicate. To achieve this goal, a teacher could discuss with his classes the importance of using the foreign language at all times in class. He could then distribute a list of commonly used classroom expressions and encourage students to use them when needed. The list might include foreign-language equivalents of asking the teacher for a repetition, an explanation, a page number, and so on. Whenever a student slips into English, the teacher could keep pretending he does not understand until the student uses the appropriate foreign-language expression. Good-natured pretense is far more effective than a sharp reminder to speak the foreign language.

Feelings of progress and achievement can also be promoted by showing students that they can communicate orally with each other to some extent in the foreign language. This may be accomplished by allowing ten minutes or more of class time in which students may discuss anything they want with their friends—as long as they promise to use the foreign language exclusively. The teacher, in turn, promises not to correct anything he hears, unless asked.

He then visits each small group and listens without comment despite overpowering natural urges to correct mistakes. In this way, the teacher plays a supportive rather than judicial role and helps students develop feelings of confidence and fluency that will ultimately encourage them to improve their performance and correct their own mistakes. A school newspaper written in the foreign language is another means of promoting students' pride in their achievements.

In some school systems, student interest and enjoyment is hindered by lack of articulation. For example, several elementary schools whose students differ widely in language background may attend one junior high with the result that learners are forced to begin language study all over again. Or, the goals of a junior high may differ so greatly from those of its senior high school that students are caught helplessly in the ideological crossfire. In such cases, it is imperative that teachers from different schools in one system meet and set common performance objectives. Unless they do so, students are bound to feel frustrated and discouraged when they see how little progress they have made after four, six, or eight years of exposure to a foreign language.

5.2.5   Stage 3: Appreciation: *Valuing*

Leading students to see the value of studying a foreign language or culture is one of the most difficult tasks facing the foreign-language profession. This problem is compounded by the fact that students often assimilate attitudes held by their parents, attitudes that may not always be favorable. For this reason, it is vital that the foreign-language department maintain good public relations with the community. Parents need to be informed of the goals of the foreign-language curriculum as well as the desired results of the program. One way of accomplishing this is by communicating to them the performance objectives of the foreign-language department. Publication of outstanding achievements of students and teachers in the area of foreign language is another means of demonstrating to parents the effectiveness of the school program. Students' feelings of pride in their accomplishments and satisfaction with their progress can also have the beneficial effect of convincing the community of this subject's value.

Community involvement with the foreign-language curriculum is a highly desirable means of developing the support essential to a strong language program. This participation may be enlisted in a number of ways. Parents might be invited to a foreign-language night featuring student performances of songs, dances, skits, and poems. Another possibility involves joint efforts by teachers, parents, and students in a fund-raising drive to bring a foreign-exchange student to the school for a year. In cooperation with local merchants, there might be an international fair featuring food or manufactured products from foreign countries. Residents of the community who are native speakers of a foreign language or who have traveled abroad might be invited to share their background and experiences with foreign-language classes.

Adults who must use a foreign language in the course of their work could talk about the career value of foreign-language learning.

Student valuing of foreign-language study may be enhanced by providing a wealth of experiences beyond those usually offered in a formal class. In addition to the extracurricular programs, foreign-exchange students, and guest speakers already mentioned, language learners could also profit from language club activities as well as from trips to concerts, museums, plays, and foreign-language films. Exchanging pen-pal letters, school newspapers, or tape recordings with a class in the foreign country is also highly effective. Tasting-parties or dinners offering typical food and drink of a foreign country invariably meet with highly positive student responses. In some instances, a teacher might arrange through an accredited organization to take a group of students to the foreign country during a school vacation. This is the best motivation of all.

5.2.6   Stage 3: Appreciation: *Involvement*

Once enrichment activities are made available, the teacher will want to encourage participation in them. This participation must be voluntary if the student behaviors are to be classified at Stage 3. Therefore, while a teacher should not compel his students to engage in extra leisure-time reading or to attend foreign-language club meetings or cultural events, he should nevertheless create a classroom environment conducive to such voluntary involvement. A classroom library rich in attractive foreign-language books and periodicals or even international cookbooks can stimulate the curiosity natural to most students. A classroom bulletin board may include announcements of foreign-language cultural programs in which students might profitably take part. Another might be devoted to posters and brochures advertising foreign pen pals and travel or study abroad. Students may be encouraged to report to the class about voluntary out-of-class activities in which they participated. The attention they receive should have the effect of encouraging other students to follow their example.

The behavior the teacher models is of prime importance in this area. A teacher who shares with his students the results of his reading and research, who willingly looks up the information needed when he cannot answer a question, who gives evidence of participating freely in professional and cultural events, is far more effective in promoting involvement than a teacher who merely exhorts his students to study independently and to seek out knowledge on their own once the course is over.

5.3   MEASURING ATTAINMENT OF AFFECTIVE GOALS

An attitude is not an absolute quantity. That is, a student cannot have 85 percent of an attitude in the same way that he might demonstrate 85 percent mastery on a test of knowledge. For this reason, it is more practical to evaluate student attitudes, feelings, and values in terms of their growth or decline. For example, how do measures of student attitudes taken in June compare with those of the preceding September? Are student attitudes at the end of the year at least as positive as they were at the beginning?

There are three basic approaches to measuring student attitudes, feelings, and values: anonymous questionnaires, teacher observations, and statistical data. Each of these approaches will be discussed in relationship to the taxonomic stage for which it is an appropriate measurement technique. While some illustrative test items will be presented here, a more complete listing of them will be found in Chapter Seven.

Certain ideas should be kept in mind regarding measurement of the affective outcomes of a course. Questionnaires should be completed anonymously in order to ensure the validity of student responses. A teacher should also make clear to his students that their answers will in no way affect their grades. It might also be useful to say that the purpose of a questionnaire is to give the teacher insight into his classroom effectiveness, rather than announce to students that their attitudes are being measured.

Since attitudes, feelings, and values develop slowly over long periods of time, too frequent measurement will not always reveal significant changes. Therefore, it is normally inadvisable to measure them more often than two or three times during the school year. Finally, teachers must not consider as wasted the time and effort spent preparing and administering affective measures. In view of the tremendous influence of affective behavior on foreign-language achievement, teachers can no longer be content with only imprecise knowledge or highly subjective impressions of the affective outcomes of their instruction.

5.3.1   Stage 1: Receptivity: *Awareness*

Questionnaires concerning students' experiences with the foreign language and general knowledge of its culture can be useful measures of their awareness. One questionnaire might involve checking whether or not a student has ever met a native of the foreign country, eaten food typical of the country, seen a film made there, and so on. A somewhat different questionnaire might involve awareness of the contributions of the foreign civilization. A student might be presented with a general category, such as painter, politician, or musician, and be asked to name a well-known French, Spanish, or German figure in each field. An easier format for beginning classes could require students to match the well-known people in the left-hand column with their accomplishments or fields in the right-hand column. Awareness of geography or other areas of civilization could be tested by a series of short-answer questions, such as: What is the capital of the foreign country? What is a major export of the country? A simpler version of this test could present this type of question in a true-false or multiple-choice format.

A word of caution is in order regarding the awareness tests listed above.

It is not at all unusual for student performance on them to be somewhat disappointing. At all costs, however, the teacher should avoid displaying astonishment or frustration because of apparent student ignorance. Since, after all, these are tests of *awareness*, not of knowledge, remarks about student intelligence are out of place. Rather, positive student attitudes can be developed if the teacher accepts the performance of his students and assures them that he will help them become more aware of the foreign culture, and their scores will be higher on similar subsequent tests.

5.3.2   Stage 1: Receptivity: *Attentiveness*

A simple and effective way of measuring student attentiveness is by teacher observation. A teacher can note, mentally or in writing, factors such as daily student attendance and tardiness. He may also keep track of whether or not assignments are completed and handed in on time. Observation of students during class is also important in determining whether they are paying attention or not.

5.3.3   Stage 2: Responsiveness: *Tolerance*

Students can mark on questionnaires whether they agree or disagree with statements expressing tolerance or intolerance toward the foreign language, culture, and people. Although the answer the teacher would like can be quite obvious, such questions are useful. Even student lipservice to attitudes they do not genuinely hold, but know are considered desirable, represents a certain amount of teacher influence on their behavior.

A less transparent way of measuring tolerance could consist of presenting students with a situation and asking them to respond to it freely. For example, they might write what they would say or do if they met a person who spoke no English and needed help in finding his way. Or, they might react to a friend's expression of prejudice against foreigners. In order to facilitate objective scoring, each situation could be followed by multiple-choice answers, rather than a blank.

5.3.4   Stage 2: Responsiveness: *Interest and Enjoyment*

Enrollment statistics provide a reliable objective measure of whether this stage of the affective taxonomy is being reached. If students are interested in foreign-language study, are enjoying it, and are experiencing success in it, they will not drop out in the middle of the year or at the end of the first or second required courses.

At a department or district level, a study of school enrollments over a period of years is revealing. Are foreign-language enrollments rising or falling in proportion to total school enrollments? How does the growth or decline in language courses compare with fluctuations in size of the general school population? What is the dropout rate from required language courses? How does this rate compare to that of other required subjects in the curriculum? At the classroom level, a teacher can determine the interest and enjoyment generated in his course simply by asking each student at the beginning of the year to indicate whether or not he intends to take the next course in the foreign-language sequence. This question can be repeated at the end of the year and the results compared, or he can compare the dropout and failure rate in his course with comparable figures from preceding years.

Teacher observations of behavior at this stage can center on how students appear in class. Do they look happy or unhappy? Are they eager to participate? Do they attempt to use the foreign language to communicate their own thoughts? Is student performance minimal, or do some students exceed the basic requirements of their assignments? (Extra work performed without regard to grades can be classified at both Stages 2 and 3.)

Questionnaires can also serve as measurement techniques at this stage. Students might be asked to write which one of three adjectives (one negative, one neutral, one positive) best describes his feelings toward foreign-language class. Alternatively, they might be asked to supply a suitable completion to an open-ended statement such as, Studying foreign language is _____. Another way of measuring attitudes is to have students indicate whether they agree or disagree with a series of statements describing their foreign-language class. Or, they may choose which of several negative and positive descriptions best fit their experiences in the class. A different technique could involve students' rating various elements of the course, such as textbooks, tests, learning activities, teacher personality, and so on, by circling a number from one to five, with one standing for the most negative evaluation and five for the most positive.

5.3.5   Stage 3: Appreciation: *Valuing*

Statements expressing the reasons commonly offered for taking foreign languages might be presented to students who indicate whether they agree or disagree with them or whether they are uncertain. Another measure is provided by comparing from year to year the percentage or number of students who continue their foreign language once they have met such requirements as college entrance or graduation. If students truly value language study, they will freely elect more advanced courses, and some will choose to begin studying a second foreign language. In some cases, it might be possible to note also the number of students who indicate a strong desire or intent to live or travel abroad.

5.3.6   Stage 3: Appreciation: *Involvement*

Students can list the out-of-class activities relating to foreign-language study in which they have participated voluntarily, or they might check the language or cultural events they have freely attended. This could include seeing a foreign-language movie, participating in a language club, buying a foreign record or magazine, speaking the language with a friend, and so on. This test should not be announced in advance, so that students do not prepare for it. June and September results can be compared.

5.3.7   Stage 4: Internalization: *Conceptualization*

Although Stage 4 behavior goes beyond that which might normally be expected in most foreign-language classes, teachers of advanced or specialized professional courses might want to see if their students express a strong preference for foreign language over other subject areas. This may be accomplished by asking students to list all the subjects they are currently taking and then number them in order of preference. Point values may be assigned in descending order of preference with the highest awarded to the students' favorite subject and no point to their least favorite. The total point value given to foreign language can be compared to that awarded other subjects.

A variation of this technique calls for pairing foreign language with each of the other subjects that students are carrying. The students indicate which subject in each pair they prefer. The number of times foreign language is preferred over another subject is tallied and measured against a "perfect" score, a number equal to that of the subject pairs.

CHAPTER SIX
EVALUATING TEACHER PERFORMANCE

Performance objectives may be developed to measure teacher performance as well as student performance. Institutions that train teachers are now supplementing their evaluation of curriculum (Which courses has the candidate taken? Does he meet the certification requirements of the state? Does he have enough credits for graduation? Is his grade point average acceptable?) with an evaluation of educational outcomes (How well does the candidate control the foreign language? What teaching techniques can he demonstrate? Is he familiar with the professional organizations and their contribution to the improvement of language teaching?). The results of teacher preparation lend themselves to objective evaluation through the use of performance objectives.

Performance objectives may also be used in measuring the effectiveness of the teacher in the classroom, whether he is a student teacher working for a grade or a more experienced teacher up for tenure.

6.1 GENERAL CONSIDERATIONS

Teacher evaluation may be thought of as consisting of two complementary aspects: the evaluation of the teacher's personal qualifications and the evaluation of his effectiveness in the classroom.

6.1.1   *Personal Qualifications*

A teacher's personal qualifications fall into three categories: subject-matter competence, professional competence, and personal attitudes. In foreign-language teaching, subject-matter competence refers to the teacher's command of the foreign language, his acquaintance with the foreign culture, and his knowledge of the literature and civilization of the country or countries where the language is spoken. Professional competence refers to the teacher's behavior in the classroom, his ability to plan lessons, his use of specific teaching techniques, his preparation of appropriate tests, and the like. Teacher attitude is the affective aspect of the teacher's professional activities. It concerns his attitude toward his subject matter, his colleagues, and his students and their problems.

6.1.2   *Classroom Effectiveness*

The teacher's effectiveness in the classroom can be measured in terms of results. In the subject-matter area this refers to the students' attainment of subject-matter performance objectives. In the affective domain, this refers to the students' attitude in class, their motivation, and their extracurricular activities related to foreign-language learning.

6.2   CLASSIFYING TEACHER BEHAVIORS

Teacher qualifications may be stated in performance objective terms. What must the teacher do to demonstrate that he possesses the required qualifications? The list of desirable teacher behaviors might then be classified in the form of a taxonomy, much as student behaviors were in Chapter Two. This taxonomical classification allows the evaluator to rank the behaviors from the simplest and most elementary to the most complex. Such a breakdown shows him whether certain types of behaviors are being omitted and, if so, allows him to decide whether the omission is warranted.

6.2.1   *Subject-Matter Competence: a Taxonomy*

The classification of teacher behaviors in the area of subject-matter competence parallels that of student behaviors in the subject-matter area. Can the teacher pronounce the foreign language in an acceptable manner (Stage 1)? What is the size of the teacher's vocabulary (Stage 2)? Does the teacher know the inflected forms of nouns, verbs, adjectives, and so on (Stage 2)? Does he know grammatical rules and patterns (Stage 2)? Can the teacher form new sentences and write new exercises accurately (Stage 3)? Can the teacher use the language fluently for conversation and oral presentations (Stage 4)? Can the teacher write authentic-sounding dialogs, stories, and descriptions (Stage 4)? Can the teacher analyze a paragraph or a broadcast and comment on the choice of words, structures, intonations, and so on (Stage 5)?

6.2.2 *Professional Competence: a Taxonomy*

The taxonomy of behaviors relating to professional competence follows the same model as the taxonomy of subject-matter behaviors. The stages and categories remain the same and only the content changes to reflect the aims of foreign-language teaching. The stages are described below. Sample teacher behaviors will be found in Chapter Fourteen.

Stage 1: Mechanical Skills

The initial stage of teacher behavior is **Mechanical Skills.** The teacher notices the physical aspects of the classroom and the students. He controls his speech and movements to have the maximum effect on his students. These behaviors are physical and as such they are not specific to foreign-language teaching but are applicable to the process of teaching in general.

The internal aspect of Stage 1 is *Perception.* The teacher is aware of exterior conditions: the lighting, the heat, the chalkboard. The teacher notices which students are absent. He realizes whether students look interested or bored. He can tell who is whispering or passing notes. He realizes whether students are speaking loudly enough for their classmates to hear what they say. At this point the teacher is simply conscious of these things and could enumerate them to an observer. He does not yet act on the basis of these outward signs he has noticed.

The external aspect of this stage is *Reproduction.* In his conduct, the teacher carries out those physical actions that are essential to effective teaching. He speaks clearly and distinctly with a pleasant tone of voice. He writes legibly on the board and the overhead projector. He moves around the classroom rather than sitting behind the desk for the entire period. At this stage only the teacher's general classroom behavior is judged. This category does not include the teacher's ability to vary his manner in response to classroom situations.

Stage 2: Knowledge

Knowledge is the second stage of the taxonomy of professional competence. Although the preparation of teachers includes many areas, such as educational psychology and philosophy and the history of education, this taxonomy is limited to those areas of knowledge that are specific to second-language teaching. At this stage, the teacher is familiar with the professional literature. (This behavior is usually acquired in a foreign-language methods or curriculum course.)

The internal aspect of this stage is *Recognition*. The teacher can demonstrate his knowledge of theories, techniques, research, terminology, and the like, on multiple-choice, matching, true-false, and similar tests.

Recall (external behavior) requires the teacher to define and explain terms, concepts, and practices related to foreign-language methodology. He can repeat the instructions he has learned for using audio-visual equipment. He can also identify texts and classroom materials with which he should be familiar.

Stage 3: Transfer

Stage 3 of the taxonomy is called **Transfer.** Under guidance, the teacher prepares and engages in actual or simulated classroom activities. At this stage he follows instructions and carries out workshop or teaching activities in accordance with preestablished guidelines. He is not responding at this stage to the reactions of the students he is teaching.

The internal aspect of this level is *Reception*. The teacher applies the ideas of others rather than using his own initiative or imagination. He teaches a lesson according to the format prescribed by the teacher's manual or by his supervising teacher. He uses audio-visual equipment according to the manufacturer's instructions. He can write test items to fit a given model. He writes performance objectives under guidance.

The external aspect of this stage is *Application*. Here the teacher acts independently. He writes his own exercises, drills, and tests. He teaches according to his own lesson plans and writes his own performance objectives. Activities in this category are applications to the classroom situation of the material that has been previously taught.

Stage 4: Communication

Stage 4 in the professional taxonomy of teacher qualifications is **Communication.** This is the stage that distinguishes the conscientious but unimaginative teacher from the creative teacher. The unimaginative teacher can function at the application level, planning his classes and performing the activities expected of him. The creative teacher enters into two-way communication with students, colleagues and administrators, and other members of the profession.

The internal aspect of this stage is *Comprehension*. Within the classroom, the teacher is sensitive to the mood of the students and to their performance. He can tell by the way they look and respond whether they have understood or not. He is sensitive to the needs and concerns of the other members of his department and to the wishes of his administrators, even if he does not always agree with them.

The external aspect is *Self-Expression*. The teacher is quick to vary classroom activities in response to the changing needs and moods of his classes.

He modifies his teaching techniques in an effort to attain the performance objectives he has set for his students. He works harmoniously with his colleagues and actively promotes the goals of his profession.

Stage 5: Criticism

Criticism constitutes Stage 5 of the taxonomy. The teacher studies his own performance in an effort to improve his teaching. These self-study activities usually take place after the end of the formal school day.

The first internal aspect of this stage is *Analysis*. The teacher, either alone or in cooperation with a colleague, teacher, or friend, looks at his teaching as objectively as possible. He may simply have discovered that something failed to work in the classroom (the students did not reach a performance objective, the class cheated on a test, and so on) and he wants to discover why by analyzing the situation.

The external aspect of Stage 5 is *Synthesis*. Once the teacher has discovered the possible reasons behind his failure, he may work out another way of approaching the problem. Perhaps the performance objective needs to be modified. Perhaps the situation that led to the cheating can be changed. On a broader scale, the teacher may plan to try to restructure his classes by using small-group work or performance contracts, for example.

The second internal aspect of this stage is *Evaluation*. Behavior in this category is closely linked to the behaviors of analysis and synthesis. As the teacher discovers weaknesses in his teaching and experiments with different ways of promoting student learning, he evaluates his own effectiveness. He may use a specific self-evaluation technique, such as those suggested in section 4.5.

6.2.3 *Teacher Attitudes: an Affective Taxonomy*

The feelings and attitudes of teachers toward their profession fall in the domain of affective behaviors. The stages in the teacher taxonomy are identical to those in the student taxonomy (see section 2.3.1).

Stage 1: Receptivity

At Stage 1 the teacher's professional learning activities are directed by others: a master teacher, a university training program, or an institute. The teacher follows the instructions he is given and is at least neutral in his attitude toward his profession. His attitude might be something like: "After all, it's a job, and we all have to work to earn money." He does not resist learning and is open to the material presented.

Stage 2: Responsiveness

Stage 2 characterizes the teacher who has a generally favorable attitude toward his profession and the activities it involves. He tolerates differences among teachers and teaching methods. He enjoys his work on the whole, both the personal preparation and the classroom teaching. His attitude is reflected in the statement: "As long as I have to work, I'm glad I can teach languages. Basically I do enjoy teaching and working with young people." He participates in department meetings, attends language conferences, and subscribes to professional journals at the suggestion of his superiors.

Stage 3: Appreciation

At Stage 3 the teacher attaches value and worth to his professional work. He voluntarily joins professional organizations, tries to attend local and regional meetings, and participates in activities designed to improve his personal command of the language he teaches. He regularly reads at least one professional journal. His attitude here is: "I want to do what I can to become a better language teacher."

Stage 4: Internalization

The teacher at Stage 4 views language learning as valuable for his students and strives to help all students have a positive learning experience with a second language and culture. He now says: "I am dedicated to language teaching as my profession," and he acquires a professional outlook. In addition to demonstrating concern for all students in his classes, he devotes a major portion of his time and energy to a variety of professional activities. He reads several professional journals. He attends several professional meetings a year at the local, regional, and, if possible, national levels. He signs up for workshops, goes to summer school, takes graduate courses at a nearby university, either in education or in foreign languages. He makes an effort to travel abroad periodically. He engages in self-evaluation in an effort to improve his teaching.

Stage 5: Characterization

At Stage 5 the teacher assumes a leadership role in his profession. His attitude is: "I want to contribute to the improvement of language teaching." He may concentrate all his energies at the district level, building up a program that may eventually inspire others. He may also help organize state, regional, and national meetings; speak at workshops or conventions; write books and articles; and engage in language-learning or literary research.

6.3 USING PERFORMANCE OBJECTIVES IN TEACHER TRAINING

Colleges and universities that train foreign-language teachers may find it profitable to introduce performance objectives into their curriculum. In fact, the freedom offered individual professors at the university level facilitates the restructuring of foreign-language or education courses around specific student behaviors. Performance objectives may also be used to describe what the student should be able to do before he is accepted into a student-teaching program.

6.3.1 *Performance Objectives in College Courses*

It is well known that young teachers, in spite of their education and methodology courses, very frequently end up teaching the way they themselves were taught. A methods teacher lecturing on performance objectives is too often an example of the phrase "Do as I say, not as I do" and usually fails to achieve the desired change of behavior in the students.

6.3.1a AN EXPERIMENT AT BOSTON COLLEGE

One of the objectives of the foreign-language methods course at Boston College is that the students be able to identify certain terms and concepts, such as "minimal pair," "pattern drill," and so on. In the 1967 course, the teacher distributed a list of seventy terms the students were to study for the knowledge section of the final examination. Only two students out of fifteen attained a score of 90 percent. The teacher was not satisfied with these results, since his aim was that all students be able to identify the terms. The following year, the teacher distributed the same list and formulated the following performance objective:

Purpose: To know terms related to language teaching.

Desired behavior: Given a term related to language teaching, the student will identify it in writing and give an example where appropriate.

Conditions: The list of seventy terms will be distributed one week before the test. About fifty to sixty actual terms will appear on the test which will be given on (date). No notes may be used.

Criterion: The passing grade is 90 percent (B+). Students may take the test three times. There will be no penalty for repeating the test. Only the highest score will be recorded.

The students realized that they had three chances to earn a high honor grade. The teacher was pleased to find that fifteen out of eighteen students passed the first test and that the remaining three attained 90 percent on the second test (an alternate form of the first test).

6.3.1b DISCUSSION

In the case above, the teacher, who the previous year had been less than 15 percent effective in bringing the students to master professional terminology, became 100 percent effective with the adoption of a performance objective and the test-retest approach. Students realized that the system was not rigged against them, that the bell-curve did not dominate the classroom, and that the teacher was committed to having them acquire certain professional terminology.

More important than the gain in subject-matter learning was the gain in the affective domain. The students experienced the relaxing effect of a test-retest approach. In this unpressured situation they all studied harder and learned more than they would have otherwise. The 90-percent criterion was a very high standard, but they all reached it. Probably those students not accustomed to achieving at this level gained an extra measure of self-confidence. Furthermore, the students who took this methods course are probably more willing to experiment with performance objectives in teaching their own classes than their classmates of the previous years who were taught by conventional methods.

6.3.2 *Specifying Minimum Requirements for Student Teaching*

The language teachers at high schools and colleges in the greater Boston area, under the sponsorship of the Massachusetts Foreign Language Association, have been working together to establish minimum standards students are to meet before they may be accepted into a student-teaching program. Ultimately, this is an indirect attempt on the part of the foreign-language profession to raise the certification standards in the state.

This group of teachers prepared two documents that were distributed in the spring of 1971. The first is a list, in behavioral terms, of the minimum qualifications expected of students applying for student teaching. The second is a descriptive list of the types of activities student teachers should engage in when in the schools. It is understood that a secondary school can refuse any student teacher who does not meet the minimum requirements. On the other hand, a college may refuse to send student teachers to a school that does not provide for the variety of activities specified on the list. The lists will be distributed to prospective language majors early in their college career. In this way the students themselves will know what types of behaviors are expected of them and what types of things they should be introduced to during their student teaching. (Copies of the first version of both of these documents are found in Appendix B.) The universities, too, will be encouraged to revise their curricula to prepare more adequately their language majors.

6.4 SUPERVISION OF TEACHERS

Department chairmen are frequently required to supervise younger teachers, especially those being considered for tenure. Classroom teachers may be asked to supervise a student teacher assigned to them. Performance objectives can provide an objective criterion with which to judge the teacher's effectiveness in the classroom.

6.4.1 *An Illustration: the Case of the Evan Gard School District*

Excitement, tension, and apprehension greeted the anouncement: The Evan Gard School District had just appointed the new foreign-language coordinator and supervisor. Reactions varied as widely as the personalities of the teachers involved.

Lotta Rapport smiled confidently. She was an unusually attractive and charming woman and people naturally liked her. Students appreciated her kindness, warmth, understanding, and tolerance. Whenever her classes were observed, the students outdid themselves to be cooperative. Dozens of hands shot up to answer questions, and expressions of eager anticipation were on every face. In fact, Lotta Rapport's classes performed so much better when observed than they did from day to day that she hoped the new supervisor would visit her quite often.

Martin Ette read the announcement briskly. A native speaker of the language he taught, he prided himself on classes run strictly and efficiently. Within a forty-five minute period he could present a dazzling array of ten different activities. His lessons were characterized by meticulous preparation, split-second timing, and firm-handed discipline. Woe to the laggard who couldn't keep up in his classes! An observer could never fail to be impressed with him.

I. Mona Stage was already looking forward to a visit from the new supervisor. Thanks to her background in theater, art, and music, her classes offered spectacular performances. They did authentic native folkdances at the drop of a hat. They sang on request in four-part harmony. They staged playlets complete with costumes and props. They welcomed chances to suspend their regular classwork in order to entertain visitors.

As soon as Mac Anick had read the announcement he began to dream up his newest extravaganza. Having a natural talent with audio-visual equipment, he decided to prepare for observation by keeping on hand a culture filmstrip he could use at any point in the course. Since the filmstrip came with a synchronized tape, he could be free to write down new vocabulary words and project them onto a screen with the overhead. He would record individual student responses on a second tape recorder while his actions were being preserved on video tape. Certainly no one could say his teaching was old-fashioned.

Terry Fide didn't know what to think. She was about to begin her first year of teaching and supervisors had always made her nervous. She had been an honors student and felt she could teach well, but not with someone watching her. If only her normal classes could be observed without her knowledge. . . .

Heidi Evidentz merely shrugged. Her knowledge of the language she taught was, at best, "impressionistic," but she had succeeded long ago in perfecting an ideal façade. First she learned to give directions in the foreign language with impeccable grammar and pronunciation. Then whenever she was observed she assigned an in-class composition that relieved her of any further teaching responsibilities. If asked why her lessons did not correspond to the one in her planbook for that day, she discoursed solemnly on the evils of rigid planning and the need to be reponsive to individual situations. Several supervisors had already despaired of ever seeing her teach.

Olaf A. Minit chuckled as he read the news. As a child he had wanted to be a clown, but eventually he decided that teaching was a more practical occupation. Still, his love of fun and games persisted. His classes normally played "hide and go speak," "verbingo," "pin the tail on the noun," and "ring around a pronoun." He always got along well with supervisors.

Philomela Grench looked worried. She wished she could emulate the showmanship of her more flamboyant colleagues, but then she wouldn't be true to herself. Quiet and self-effacing by nature, she easily faded into the walls at faculty parties. In the classroom, however, she displayed admirable control of the foreign language as well as commendable skill in teaching it. Would the new supervisor appreciate her efforts?

Several weeks passed and the supervisor finally arrived. She called a meeting of language teachers in order to get acquainted with them and to present some of her ideas. Before reading the text of what she said, here are some questions to consider:

1. If you are a classroom teacher, on what basis would you want your teaching evaluated?

2. If you are a supervisor, what criteria would you apply in evaluating teachers as different from one another as those in the Evan Gard district?

The Supervisor's Remarks

"First of all, I hope you all relax. I am not here to tell you how to teach. Researchers have failed so far to define exactly what constitutes good teaching. No one personality or method has ever been proven unquestionably superior to all others. Thus, it would be foolish for me to try to impose on you one standard teaching procedure. I recognize that every person here is a different individual and each of you has evolved (or is in the process of evolving) teaching techniques that work for you and your particular classes.

"On the other hand, in spite of the lack of absolute objective criteria for good teaching, it is clear that some techniques prove more effective than others. What works well in one situation, though, may be ineffective in another. How, then, can various styles of teaching be evaluated fairly? Even more important, how can foreign-language instructions at Evan Gard be made more effective?

"Here is what I propose. Since I feel classroom observations are of only limited value, I should like to discuss with each of you the outcomes of your instruction rather than the instructional process itself. In other words, I am not so much interested in what I see you doing in class—although this will be considered too—as I am in what your students can do as a result of your teaching. In this way, I am not judging you; I am judging what you do for your students.

"In order to succeed in this, I need your help. You each have a copy of the district language curriculum established by your elected representatives. Within its broad outlines of general course objectives, I would like all of you to establish specific performance objectives for each of your classes. After completing each unit of work, what will your students be able to do that they could not do before?

"Obviously, I do not expect all of you to produce the same objectives. They will probably vary according to the different emphases you place on each of the language skills. They will differ according to your personal interests and background. There will also be variations due to differences in the abilities of your students. This is fine with me. After observing your classes, two questions will be of foremost concern during our conference. First, are the performance goals you selected appropriate to your particular teaching situation? Second, have your students achieved the goals set? If they have not, we can discuss the reasons for this. Perhaps the goals are unrealistic. Perhaps other teaching techniques could improve the quality of instruction. Perhaps it is something entirely different.

"As you can see, you are free to teach in any way you feel will help you achieve your objectives. The main purpose of my supervision, then, is to help you evaluate your own instruction and to discuss with you ways in which it might be improved. Thus, both you and I share a common goal: improving the foreign-language performance of the students at Evan Gard.

"It is in this spirit of cooperation and mutual respect that I look forward to working with you. Together, perhaps we can find new answers to old questions."

6.4.2   *The Production Criterion*

The case of Evan Gard district suggests that teachers be evaluated in terms of whether or not they have reached Stage 4 behavior on the taxonomy of professional competence. In other words, teachers are not judged on their physical appearance, nor on their personality, nor on the order or disorder prevailing in their classrooms. They are not judged on their professional knowledge, nor on their mastery of specific techniques. Only two questions are asked:

1. Has the teacher set appropriate performance objectives for his students?

2. Is the teacher, by whatever means he employs, enabling his students to attain these performance objectives?

6.4.2a ATTAINING SUBJECT-MATTER PERFORMANCE OBJECTIVES

It is essential that the appropriateness of subject-matter objectives be evaluated. One teacher may bring his students to master his performance objectives, but the objectives might be very low ones, such as memorizing dialogs from an audio-lingual text or memorizing vocabulary items and paradigms from a traditional text. It is also possible that students in another class will fail to meet the teacher's performance objectives because he has set them too high. For example, expecting average first-year students to be speaking fluent French by the end of the second semester is unrealistic. In either of these cases, the supervisor and the classroom teacher can discuss how these objectives might be made more suitable to each teaching situation.

Furthermore, one teacher may set performance objectives for each period of instruction, while another may direct his efforts toward unit performance objectives. In the latter case, it is not advisable to evaluate that teacher on the basis of an isolated classroom visit during the middle of the unit. It would be more appropriate to have the teacher give his class a pretest at the beginning of the unit and an equivalent posttest at the end of the unit and then measure objectively how much progress the students have made.

If performance objectives have been established for all the classes in a school or district—and especially if unit pretests and posttests exist for the teaching materials being used—the teacher's effectiveness in meeting subject-matter objectives can be objectively evaluated.

6.4.2b ATTAINING AFFECTIVE OBJECTIVES

The teacher may also set affective objectives for his classes. His objective may be: "The students will participate willingly and cheerfully in classroom activities" (Stage 2). On visiting this teacher's classes, the supervisor would make note of student reactions (whether or not the students were actively participating, and whether or not they seemed happy about what they were doing).

Another teacher's affective aim might be: "The students will demonstrate their interest in foreign languages by bringing to class related materials they have discovered on their own, such as advertisements, newspaper clippings, labels, and realia" (Stage 3). The fact that students look for samples of the foreign culture and instances of the foreign language outside of class and bring their findings to the teacher is a demonstration of Stage 3 behavior only if no grades or marks are given for this activity. In fact, the teacher must be careful not to let students feel that by bringing material to class they can compensate for deficiencies in subject-matter learning. Once these conditions are met, the supervisor can check whether students are bringing extra material to class. Moreover, if students are attaining this stage of behavior on the affective taxonomy, they are very likely to be alert and active during classroom activities (Stage 2).

On a school-wide level, affective behaviors may take the form of increased enrollments and a corresponding drop in the attrition rate from year to year. The size of third- and fourth-year language classes is a good measure of the effectiveness with which the department is attaining the affective goals.

6.5   TEACHER SELF-EVALUATION

Teacher self-evaluation can be classified at Stage 5 on the professional taxonomy. Although this self-evaluation make take many forms, the results are always private. It is the teacher himself who receives and analyzes the findings. He is the only one to become aware of his professional shortcomings and the only one who can do something about improving his weaknesses and further developing his strong points. The teacher may set himself a goal. His success or failure in reaching that goal will be known to him alone. The term "self-evaluation" indicates that the teacher himself takes the initiative for improving his effectiveness in the classroom. In arriving at his evaluation, however, he may choose to elicit opinions and assistance from others.

6.5.1   *Evaluation Through Student Performance Objectives*

The teacher sets student performance objectives, either subject-matter goals or affective goals or both for his classes. For example, he may decide to modify his program to reduce the attrition rate. An increase in the following year's enrollments will then be his criterion. The teacher may also set subject-matter performance objectives for each unit and a date by which he expects the student to have reached these goals. Finishing on or before the announced date is considered success.

6.5.2   *Evaluation Through Student Reactions*

Some teachers distribute evaluation sheets at the end of the semester or year, which their students fill in. Students need not sign their names to the sheets.

It is most helpful to ask for student suggestions on ways to improve the course.

Student reaction in class is also a valid means of self-evaluation. Do the students participate readily in discussions? Are they eager to answer questions? Do they occasionally go beyond the required work or bring samples of the foreign language or culture to class without being told to do so? Are they alert? If attendance is not compulsory, the percentage of students attending class becomes itself a measure of teacher effectiveness.

6.5.3 *Interaction Analysis*

Interaction analysis[1] objectively shows which kinds of interaction take place in the class period. Who is doing the talking? Who is initiating the discussion? How much time is being wasted in unproductive silence? Does the teacher dominate all activities, or is there considerable interaction between student and teacher and among the students themselves?

Interaction analysis cannot determine whether learning is actually taking place, but it does provide an effective way of studying what types of exchanges occur during the period.

6.5.4 *Evaluation Through a Native Informant*

If the teacher is not a native speaker of the language he teaches, he may often profit from the assistance of a native informant in improving his own subject-matter competence. One American teacher of German paid a local native German lady to visit one of his classes from time to time and to note all his mistakes. Later, he would sit down with her in private and have her correct his grammar and pronunciation.

The teacher who is a native speaker of the language he teaches and for whom English is a second language may likewise profit from the assistance of an American informant. He might regularly meet with this person in an effort to correct the little mistakes he makes in English. Students are more willing to accept corrections from a teacher of foreign background if they know that their teacher is himself working to improve his command of English.

6.5.5 *Evaluation Through Personal Rating Scales and Questions*

The teacher can evaluate his own professional growth by periodically examining his own activities over the past month and asking himself: "How many professional magazines did I read this month? Did I participate actively in

---

[1] Gertrude Moskowitz explains an interaction analysis technique in "The Effects of Training Foreign Language Teachers in Interaction Analysis," *Foreign Language Annals*, vol. 1 (1968), pp. 218–35, and in "Interaction Analysis—A New Modern Language for Supervisors," *Foreign Language Annals*, vol. 5 (1971), pp. 211–21.

department meetings? Have I made provisions in my class for the very slow learner and for the very fast learner? Have I been to a foreign-language film? Have I spoken the foreign language outside the classroom?" The teacher might also make a resolution for the coming month, such as: "This month I will listen to at least one twenty-minute foreign-language broadcast each week," or "I will identify one problem I am having in my class and discuss it with one or two colleagues." [2]

---

[2] Ray H. Simpson provides many suggestions for the teacher who plans to evaluate his own classroom performance in his *Teacher Self-Evaluation* (New York: Macmillan, 1966).

PART TWO
CLASSIFYING STUDENT BEHAVIORS

CHAPTER SEVEN
ATTITUDES, FEELINGS, AND VALUES

Student attitudes, feelings, and values are in the affective domain. Goals in this domain are most appropriately stated as expressive performance objectives, since the conditions under which the behaviors occur are not always predictable and the criteria for measuring them are often subjective.

A simple way of determining how students feel about a course is to have them fill out questionnaires. Since students are often disarmingly frank, much information can be obtained in this manner. However, this one measure may not always be sufficient. Frequently, students will tend to provide answers they think their teacher wants, rather than those that truly reflect their feelings. For this reason, it is advisable to combine anonymous student questionnaires with a variety of other evaluation techniques, such as teacher observation, enrollment figures, and attrition rates.

In this chapter, the first section classifies student behaviors and the second section describes measurement techniques. The third section offers attitude tests for the reader of this book.

7.1 EXAMPLES OF AFFECTIVE BEHAVIORS

This section contains examples of the five stages of behavior in the affective taxonomy.

7.1.1 *Classification*

Stage 1: Receptivity: *Awareness*

Purpose: To develop awareness of foreign language and culture.

Student behaviors:

Demonstrate awareness of differences between the foreign language and culture and one's own language and culture.

Notice instances of the foreign language or culture in one's own language or culture.

Demonstrate awareness of foreign language or culture as reflected in daily life or media (newspapers, magazines, TV).

Receptivity: *Attentiveness*

Purpose: To fulfill all obligations and assignments of the foreign-language class.

Student behaviors:

Listen willingly in class.

Attend class regularly and on time.

Attend class, laboratory session, film, concert, play, lecture, as assigned.

Display care and attention in the completion of all assignments.

Stage 2: Responsiveness: *Tolerance*

Purpose: To demonstrate tolerance of foreign ways in language and culture.

Student behaviors:

Accept that different societies have different ways of expression in words and actions.

Accept that there is no one right or best system of language and culture.

Accept that foreigners consider their language and culture to be as natural, simple, and correct as you do your own.

Accept seemingly strange foreign actions and reactions as appropriate to members of that culture.

Display tolerance in relations with others in class.

Responsiveness: *Interest and Enjoyment*

Purpose: To develop attitudes of interest in and enjoyment of foreign-language learning.

Student behaviors:

Consider learning foreign language and culture interesting and enjoyable.

Evaluate favorably on a questionnaire the material and activities assigned.

Express a desire to learn more about the foreign language and culture in the course.

Express a sense of satisfaction with personal progress and achievements in foreign-language learning.

Participate actively in class.

Stage 3: Appreciation: *Valuing*

Purpose: To consider learning about the foreign language and culture as worthwhile and valuable.

Student behaviors:

Hold the belief that knowledge of the foreign language and culture contributes to the enrichment of one's life.

Hold the belief that it is important for others to learn the foreign language.

Hold the belief that the foreign culture has made valuable contributions to civilization.

Hold the belief that every person should study at least one foreign language.

Consider the foreign language and culture worthwhile and valuable.

Express interest in continuing the study of language and culture even after the end of the course.

Express desire to travel abroad.

Appreciation: *Involvement*

Purpose: To engage voluntarily in out-of-class activities associated with foreign language and culture.

Student behaviors:

Seek on one's own initiative additional information regarding the foreign language and culture from such sources as teacher, library, travel agency, native informant.

Perform additional work above the minimum required by an assignment.

Find opportunities outside of class to use one's foreign-language knowledge and skills (attend language club meetings, talk to exchange students, practice the foreign language with friends or relatives, see a foreign film).

Find ways of promoting international communication and understanding (write to a pen pal, invite an exchange student home).

Travel to the foreign country.

Stage 4: Internalization: *Conceptualization*

Purpose: To develop concepts relating to the foreign language and culture.

Student behaviors:
Hold the belief that the foreign language, culture, or literature offer valuable insights and understandings.
Seek the influence of foreign culture, ideas, and values in the formation of one's personal philosophy.
Hold the belief that the fields of foreign language, literature, and culture are worthy areas of professional study.

Internalization: *Commitment*

Purpose: To commit oneself to advanced study in the field of the foreign language, literature, or culture.

Student behaviors:
Pursue the study of the foreign language, literature, or culture at advanced levels.
Live in the foreign country for an extended period of time.

Stage 5: Characterization: *Integration*

Purpose: To integrate the foreign language, culture and values into one's own personal outlook on life and one's value system.

Student behaviors:
Hold the desire to become bilingual and bicultural.
Make important life decisions (choice of career, home, and so on) with the view of further self-development in the area of foreign language and culture.

Characterization: *Leadership*

Purpose: To exercise professional leadership in promoting the study of foreign language and culture.

Student behaviors:
Work to persuade others to accept the values of foreign-language study.
Conduct original research directed toward the improvement of foreign-language teaching.
Work actively in one's profession to increase international understanding and tolerance.
Write articles and books, give speeches to promote knowledge of and interest in foreign languages and culture.

7.1.2a SELF-TEST

Take this self-test to see how well you have understood this section. Classify the following affective behaviors according to this key: 1 = **Receptivity,** 2 = **Responsiveness,** 3 = **Appreciation.** Write the appropriate number in the blank.

a.＿＿ Demonstrate awareness of the foreign-language culture in popular media (magazines, newspapers, TV, and so on).

b.＿＿ Accept the worth of people and culture different from one's own.

c.＿＿ Engage willingly in the performance of assigned activities.

d.＿＿ Feel a sense of personal satisfaction with one's progress and achievements in foreign-language study.

e.＿＿ Volunteer for out-of-class activities related to language learning.

f.＿＿ Hold the belief that knowing a foreign language is an important part of a well-balanced education.

g.＿＿ Express interest in continuing foreign-language study even after required courses are over.

h.＿＿ Fulfill the minimal obligations of the course.

i.＿＿ Seek out on one's own ways of communicating with natives of the foreign country.

j.＿＿ Consider the study of the foreign language interesting and enjoyable.

Answers: a. 1   b. 2   c. 1   d. 2   e. 3   f. 3   g. 3   h. 1   i. 3   j. 2

7.2 MEASURING AFFECTIVE GOALS

In this section, a variety of techniques appropriate for measuring affective behaviors are suggested. Although several of the examples refer to French language and culture, the items may easily be adapted to any other language.

7.2.1 Stage 1: Receptivity: *Awareness*

7.2.1a AWARENESS IN THE STUDENT'S DAILY LIFE

Instructions: Check "yes," "no," or "uncertain." Have you ever:

1. Heard French spoken for more than a few   yes   no   uncertain minutes?

2. Eaten in a French restaurant or had French   yes   no   uncertain
food at home?

3. Seen a French film (with English subtitles)?

4. Met a native French person?

5. Seen pictures of France in magazines or newspapers?

6. Seen a painting by a French artist?

7. Read a book translated from French into English?

8. Seen or heard an opera or concert by a French
composer?

9. Seen clothes designed or made in France?

10. Seen in someone's home, objects (statues, vases,
ashtrays, dishes, souvenirs) made in France?

11. Sung or heard a French folksong?

12. Had French wine?

13. Seen a French-made car?

Suggested scoring: Count two points for each "yes," one for each "uncertain," zero for each "no." Record the total number of points.

7.2.1b AWARENESS OF CIVILIZATION

Instructions: Name as many Frenchmen or Frenchwomen or items as you
can that would fit into each of the categories below. The people you name
may be living or dead.

1. Painter	7. Magazine, newspaper
2. Politician	8. General (army)
3. Actor or actress	9. Automobile
4. Composer	10. City (not Paris)
5. Designer	11. Book (not a textbook)
6. Author	12. Song, piece of music

Another way of administering the test above would be to write multiple-
choice questions, such as: Which of the following men is a French painter?
a. Gauguin b. Debussy c. Sartre.

Suggested scoring: Count one point for each correct item. In-class correction of this test can be very enjoyable. It might also be profitable to add the

following question at the end of the test: How do you feel about your score on this questionnaire? Students frequently write that their score is not very good and that they wish they knew more.

7.2.1c AWARENESS OF FAMOUS PEOPLE

Instructions: Write the professions of the following Frenchmen and women.

1. Pierre Renoir
2. Claude Debussy
3. Albert Camus
4. Yves St. Laurent
5. Jacques Truffaut
6. J.-J. Servan-Schreiber
7. Yves Montand
8. Jean-Paul Sartre
9. Jeanne Moreau
10. Françoise Sagan

A different way of administering this test would be to present the items as matching questions with the names of the people on the left and their professions on the right.

Suggested scoring: Each correct answer can count as one point.

7.2.1d AWARENESS OF GEOGRAPHY

Instructions: Answer the following questions briefly in one or two words.

1. Which is the largest city in France?
2. What kind of climate does France have?
3. Name a major river in France.
4. Name a major export of France.
5. How large is France compared to the United States? (Approximate percentage of U.S. land area.)
6. How far away is Paris from New York (or local city)?
7. What is the approximate population of France?
8. Name a body of water that is a boundary of France.
9. Name a country that borders on France.
10. Name a mountain range in France.
11. Name a major industry in France.
12. Name a major French agricultural product.

The items above can also be presented as true-false statements or as multiple-choice questions.

Suggested scoring: Each correct answer can count as one point.

7.2.2   Stage 2: Responsiveness: *Tolerance*

7.2.2a   QUESTIONNAIRE: STATEMENTS REFLECTING TOLERANCE

Instructions: Indicate the extent to which these statements represent your feelings by writing +1 if you agree, 0 if you are uncertain, −1 if you disagree.

____1. Different people should have different ways of living and acting.

____2. You should not make fun of people who are different from you.

____3. There is more than one workable system for expressing ideas.

____4. Though differences in system make studying a foreign language hard, these differences must be accepted as part of learning.

____5. Though the foreign language may be hard for me, it probably is not hard for native speakers.

Scoring: Total the +1's and the −1's.

7.2.2b   QUESTIONNAIRE: STATEMENTS REFLECTING LACK OF TOLERANCE

Instructions: Circle whether you agree *(A)*, disagree *(D)*, or are uncertain *(U)* in regard to these statements.

A U D 1. English is better than other languages, and the American way is the best way.

A U D 2. It's silly to learn a foreign language when you already know a language.

A U D 3. Foreign ways and people are strange, different, and unappealing.

A U D 4. The foreign way of saying things just does not make sense.

A U D 5. The foreign language sounds strange and makes me feel uncomfortable and stupid when I try to speak it.

Scoring: Count each *A* as −2, each *U* as −1, and each *D* as +2. Total the scores. To simplify scoring, it is easier not to mix statements expressing tolerance with those expressing lack of tolerance. If mixing the questions is considered desirable, then a special answer key must be prepared.

7.2.2c SITUATION QUESTIONS

Instructions: Answer the following question:

1. Suppose you met a foreign lady on the street who needed directions but didn't speak English. Which of the following things might you do? You may check as many or as few as would apply to you.

_____a. Try to understand what she was saying.

_____b. Explain politely you did not speak her language.

_____c. Try to find someone who could understand her.

_____d. Smile and walk away.

_____e. Try to communicate by gestures, pictures, writing, street names.

(a, c, e are scored at +1; b and d at −1)

2. Pretend a foreign-exchange student has just arrived at your school. What would your attitude and actions be toward him? Check as many items as would apply to you.

_____a. Try actively to meet him.

_____b. Look him over to see if he looks interesting enough to talk to.

_____c. Offer to help him with questions or problems he may have.

_____d. Try to meet him if your friends say he doesn't look funny.

_____e. Try to talk to him before school or at lunch.

Scoring: a, c, e are scored at +1; b and d at −1.

3. You hear a person expressing very strong prejudices against people in the foreign country and against their language and culture. Which of the following things would you probably say or do? Check as many items as would apply to you.

_____a. Defend the people in the foreign country, their language, and their culture.

_____b. Listen quietly.

_____c. Explain to him his prejudice is not rational and is not based on fact.

_____d. Agree with him.

_____e. Try to persuade him that other opinions are possible.

Scoring: a, c, e are scored at +1; b and d at −1.

7.2.3 Stage 2: Responsiveness: *Interest and Enjoyment*

7.2.3a SEMANTIC DIFFERENTIAL TECHNIQUE

Instructions: Circle the letter that best describes your feelings in each of the following statements:

1. Studying foreign language is a. boring, b. not bad, c. interesting.

2. Language class is a place where I a. sleep, b. survive, c. participate.

3. If language class were cancelled for an assembly I'd say, a. "Whoopie!" b. "So what?" c. "Shucks!"

4. When I speak or write the foreign language I feel a. like a clod, b. I'm passing, c. I'm making progress.

5. The foreign culture I am learning about is a. unimportant, b. of average interest, c. very interesting.

Scoring: Count no point if the *a* is circled, five points if *b* is circled and ten points if *c* is circled.

7.2.3b FREE RESPONSE TECHNIQUE

Statements such as those above can be read or presented one at a time on an overhead projector without the accompanying three ending choices. Students are to write as rapidly as they can the first suitable ending that comes to mind. Endings judged unfavorable can be given a negative value; those judged favorable can be given a positive value.

7.2.3c BIPOLAR ADJECTIVE SCALE

Instructions: Evaluate each of the items listed according to how you feel. Use the following scale to express your opinions: 1 = very negative, 2 = negative, 3 = neutral, 4 = positive, 5 = very positive.

The list may include anything a teacher would like to evaluate, such as textbooks, classroom atmosphere, daily lessons, teacher personality, learning progress, and so on.

7.2.3d ATTITUDE SCALE

Instructions: How well do the following statements reflect your attitudes toward the study of foreign language and culture? If you strongly agree, write +2; if you agree write +1; if you are undecided write 0; if you disagree write −1; if you strongly disagree write −2.

_____1. Language learning is enjoyable.

_____2. New ways of saying ideas are interesting.

_____3. It is fun to learn about how other people live.

_____4. I look forward to coming to language class.

_____5. I like trying to speak the foreign language even if I make mistakes.

7.2.3e   ATTITUDE CHECK LIST

Instructions: Check the statements that most accurately reflect your feelings in foreign-language class. You may check as many or as few as apply to you.

_____ 1. I'm generally pleased with my progress in foreign-language learning.

_____ 2. Most of the time foreign-language class is pretty interesting.

_____ 3. I feel very afraid to speak in the foreign language.

_____ 4. The teacher's personality helps me learn more.

_____ 5. I count the minutes until foreign-language class is over.

_____ 6. Learning a foreign language is impossible for me.

_____ 7. I enjoy trying to express my ideas in a foreign language.

_____ 8. Hardly anything good ever happens in foreign-language class.

_____ 9. I can't wait until I finish taking foreign language.

_____10. I look forward to improving my foreign-language skills.

Scoring: Checks by answers 1, 2, 4, 7, and 10 count as +1 each. Checks by answers 3, 5, 6, 8, and 9 count as −1.

7.2.4   Stage 3: Appreciation: *Valuing*

7.2.4a   ATTITUDE QUESTIONNAIRE

Instructions: Read each of the following statements and write *A* if you agree, *D* if you disagree, and *U* if you are undecided.

_____1. To be well-educated, one must know at least one foreign language.

_____2. The foreign culture has made important and worthwhile contributions to civilization and should be studied.

_____3. World tolerance and understanding can be promoted through cultural exchange and by learning languages of other countries.

_____4. Foreign languages and cultures can be very rewarding and worthwhile.

_____5. If people in different countries were able to understand each other better, there would be less war in the world.

Scoring: Count each *A* answer $+2$, *U* $+1$, and *D*-2.

7.2.5   Stage 3: Appreciation: *Involvement*

7.2.5a   INVOLVEMENT CHECK LIST

Instructions: Check which of the following activities you have participated in this past year without being required in any way to do so.

_____ 1. Participated actively in language or human affairs club.

_____ 2. Sought out native speakers of the foreign language in order to talk to them.

_____ 3. Wrote letters to a pen pal in the foreign country.

_____ 4. Read news articles about the foreign country.

_____ 5. Read a book about the foreign country or about famous people from that country.

_____ 6. Tried out a recipe from the foreign country, ate food from the foreign country, or sampled food typical of it.

_____ 7. Bought a foreign-language book, record, or dictionary.

_____ 8. Listened to or watched a program related to the foreign country or culture.

_____ 9. Wrote away for information about study abroad.

_____10. Talked to a guidance counselor or teacher about career opportunities in foreign languages or schools with strong language programs.

_____11. Convinced someone that language study is worthwhile.

7.2.5b   FREE RESPONSE TECHNIQUE

Instructions: Ask students to list what they have done voluntarily in order to increase their knowledge or understanding of the foreign language or culture.

7.2.6 *Self-Tests*

Take the following tests to see how well you have understood this section. Refer back to it as needed.

Test 1: Classify the following statements from questionnaires on language attitudes according to their taxonomic stage. Use the following key: 1 = **Receptivity:** *Awareness,* 2 = **Responsiveness:** *Tolerance,* 3 = **Appreciation:** *Valuing.*

a.＿＿ The foreign country exerts economic and cultural influence in my own country.

b.＿＿ Learning a foreign language promotes international understanding and cooperation.

c.＿＿ Language learning is enjoyable.

d.＿＿ I am pleased with the progress I am making in language class.

e.＿＿ Assignments in language class should be completed conscientiously.

f.＿＿ I look for opportunities to listen to or speak the foreign language outside of class.

g.＿＿ One should not make fun of people just because they speak or dress differently.

h.＿＿ I intend to continue studying the language next year.

i.＿＿ It's fun to try to express ideas in a strange language.

j.＿＿ Everyone should have the chance to study at least one foreign language.

Key: a. 1   b. 3   c. 2   d. 2   e. 1   f. 3   g. 2   h. 2 or 3   i. 2   j. 3

Test 2: Classify the following student behaviors according to their taxonomic stage. Use the following key: 1 = **Receptivity:** *Attentiveness,* 2 = **Responsiveness:** *Tolerance, Interest and Enjoyment,* 3 = **Appreciation:** *Involvement.*

a.＿＿ Corresponds with a pen pal abroad.

b.＿＿ Turns assignments in on time.

c.＿＿ Participates fully in class discussions.

d.＿＿ Corrects his own speaking errors voluntarily.

e.＿＿ Reads foreign magazines of his own accord.

f.＿＿ Performs his homework every day.

g.——— Looks happy when in class.

h.——— Converses in the foreign language even when not required to do so.

i.——— Treats all his classmates with respect.

j.——— Demonstrates self-confidence when speaking in class.

Answers: a. 3   b. 1   c. 2   d. 3   e. 3   f. 1   g. 2   h. 3   i. 2   j. 2

7.3.   THE READER'S ATTITUDES

At this time you may be interested in measuring your own attitude toward the idea of performance objectives in general and this handbook in particular. The first test measures Stage 2 affective behaviors; the second one measures Stage 3 behaviors.

Test 1: Reader's Attitude Scale.

Stage 2: Responsiveness: *Tolerance*

Read each of the following statements. In the blank write *A* if you agree with the statement or *D* if you disagree with it.

——1. There just might be a method to the madness in this book.

——2. All this new-fangled terminology is just a waste of time.

——3. The material has been generally comprehensible and readable.

——4. I haven't yet been lost, turned-off, bored, or confused.

——5. There's little in this book I and my classes don't already know.

Interpretation: How many of your answers correspond to the following? 1. A, 2. D, 3. A, 4. A, 5. D. You must have at least four out of five of these answers for your attitude to be classified as tolerant.

Test 2: Reader's Attitude Scale.

Stage 2: Responsiveness: *Interest and Enjoyment*

In the blank at the left of each number write the letter that best expresses your own reactions.

——1. The information in this book is a. boring, b. typical "educationese", c. interesting.

——2. After finishing this questionnaire, I would most like to a. throw the book away, b. go to sleep, c. read further.

___3. Reading this book is a. a waste of my time, b. unfortunately required, c. enjoyable at times.

___4. If I had it to do over again I would have a. never bought this book, b. bought this book sooner.

___5. So far, as a result of reading this book a. I'd like to quit the teaching profession, b. My teaching hasn't been harmed, c. I'm learning many interesting new ideas.

Count one point for each of the following answers: 1. c, 2. c, 3. c, 4. b, 5. c. A score of four or five indicates that you have an attitude of interest.

Test 3: Reader's Attitude Scale

Stage 3: Appreciation: *Valuing*

Read each of the following statements. In the blank write −2 if you violently disagree, −1 if you disagree somewhat, 0 if you have no opinion, 1 if you agree somewhat, and 2 if you strongly agree.

___1. Reading this book is worthwhile.

___2. The information I have learned so far will be valuable to me in my teaching.

___3. Language teachers would do well to apply the information in this book.

___4. I'm going to recommend this book to my colleagues.

___5. What I have learned so far should prove useful in my classroom.

Interpretation: Add up the five numbers. A score of five or more shows that you value the information in this book.

Test 4: Reader's Attitude Scale.

Stage 3: Appreciation: *Valuing*

React to the statements using the key given for the preceding test.

___1. I intend to write formal and expressive objectives for the subject-matter and affective goals of the courses I teach.

___2. I will classify my objectives according to the subject-matter or affective taxonomy in this handbook.

___3. I will measure student attitudes, feelings, and values related to my courses.

_____4. I intend to include **Stage 4: Communication** goals in the objectives I write.

_____5. I am planning ways to individualize my foreign-language instruction according to suggestions in this book.

Interpretation: Total your points. A score of five or more shows that you value the material presented in this handbook.

Test 5: Reader's Check List.

Stage 3: Appreciation: _Involvement_

Check each of the following activities in which you have already engaged.

_____1. Wrote performance objectives for the subject-matter goals of at least one unit.

_____2. Established affective goals for a course of study.

_____3. Communicated subject-matter and affective goals to students, parents, or administrators.

_____4. Developed performance objectives for **Stage 4: Communication.**

_____5. Individualized classroom instruction.

Interpretation: The number of items checked out of the five activities indicates the extent of your involvement with the material provided in this handbook.

CHAPTER EIGHT
LISTENING

In the area of listening, the teacher is primarily concerned with the student's understanding of the spoken language, presented either live or on tape. The behaviors involved are internal.

8.1 STAGES OF BEHAVIOR

Stage 1: Mechanical Skills: *Perception* (*Internal*)

The student perceives differences between his native language and the foreign language. He can discriminate among two or more foreign-language utterances based on the sounds he hears. However, he does not necessarily understand the meaning of the elements among which he makes auditory distinctions.

Stage 2: Knowledge: *Recognition* (*Internal*)

The student understands the meanings of words and sentences he has been taught. He can carry out familiar commands, match utterances with appropriate pictures, and select an English equivalent of a sentence he hears. All test material appears as it has been taught, and normally only one sentence at a time is presented.

Stage 3: Transfer: *Reception* (*Internal*)

The student understands recombinations of the structure and vocabulary he has been taught.

He can answer true-false questions, select appropriate completions to statements or answers to questions, and comprehend passages consisting of several sentences.

Stage 4: Communication: *Comprehension (Internal)*

The student understands instructions and explanations given in the foreign language. The student can understand the general meaning of passages containing unfamiliar vocabulary items or new cognates. He guesses intelligently at what he does not understand and has sufficient skill to fill in elements he may not have heard distinctly. At the highest development of this behavior, the student can understand with ease rapid native speech heard in plays or films and on radio or TV programs.

Stage 5: Criticism: *Analysis (Internal)*

The student can analyze the manner in which a message has been expressed. He can distinguish between various standards of language and perceive geographical regions or social classes represented in speech. In addition, he can comprehend implicit as well as explicit meanings of what he hears. He is conscious of nuances of meaning conveyed by intonation and stress and can describe the mood or tone of the speaker according to his manner of delivery.

Criticism: *Evaluation (Internal)*

The student can judge the effectiveness of the speech he has heard, its internal consistency, and the appropriateness of the language to the ideas conveyed.

8.2   EXAMPLES

This section contains examples of partial performance objectives in the area of listening skills. They include student behaviors and test items that can be used to measure them. Since conditions and criteria will vary considerably according to class size, type of student, language level, and facilities, these aspects of the performance objectives have not been specified here. It is left to the individual teacher to formulate them for his own situation. The purpose of all the partial performance objectives presented here is to develop listening skills.

Stage 1: Mechanical Skills: *Perception (Internal)*

Student behavior (1-a): Distinguish between English and foreign-language words.

Test item (1-1): If the word you hear is in English, circle "English"; if in French, circle "French."

Tape: 1. bell   Answer sheet: 1. (English)   French

2. parc   2.   English   (French)

Student behavior (1-b): Distinguish among foreign-language sounds.

Test item (1-2): Check the appropriate box to indicate whether the paired words you hear are the same or different.

			same	different
Tape: 1. tout	tu	Answer sheet: 1.		✓
2. vu	vu	2.	✓	

Test item (1-3): Circle the letter of the word that is different from the other two.

Tape: 1. a. pas, b. bas, c. bas

Answer sheet: (a.) b. c.

Test item (1-4): You will hear a word and then three words after it. Mark an X c   the letter of the word that rhymes with the first one heard.

Tape: 1. í   a. Tür, b. nur, c. teuer

Answer sheet: X̷ b. c.

Student behavior (1-c): Distinguish between grammatical signals in the foreign language according to the instructions.

Test item (1-5): If you hear "elle," check "feminine"; if you hear "il," check "masculine."

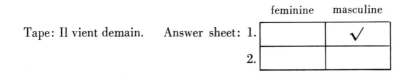

		feminine	masculine
Tape: Il vient demain.	Answer sheet: 1.		✓
	2.		

Student behavior (1-d): Discriminate between foreign-language sentences.

Test item (1-6): You will hear two sentences. If they are the same, circle "same"; if different, circle "different."

Tape: 1. Je le prends.   Je la prends.

Answer sheet: 1. same (different)

Student behavior (1-e): Distinguish between foreign-language intonation patterns.

Test item (1-7): Circle the letter of the intonation pattern that matches the one in the sentence you hear.

Tape: 1. Paul me cherche?

Answer sheet: 1. a. ⋀   b. ╱   c. ╲

Student behavior (1-f): Demonstrate perception of differences in stress.

Test item (1-8): Circle the syllable that is stressed. (Each dash stands for a syllable.)

Tape: 1. Está

Answer sheet: 1. — ⊖

Stage 2: Knowledge: *Recognition (Internal)*

Student behavior (2-a): Demonstrate understanding of familiar utterances.

Test item (2-1): Carry out the command the teacher gives you.

Teacher: Levez la main droite. (Raise your right hand.)

Test item (2-2): When shown a picture or flashcard, indicate whether the statement about it is true or false by circling "true" or "false" on your answer sheet.

Picture of sunny weather.
Teacher says: Il neige. (It is snowing.)

Answer sheet: 1. true (false)

Test item (2-3): When shown a picture or flashcard, circle the letter of the sentence that correctly describes it.

Picture of sunny weather.

Tape: 1. a. It is sunny. b. It is raining.

Answer sheet: 1.(a.) b.

Test item (2-4): After hearing a dialog line, mark an *X* by the written English translation that corresponds to it.

Tape: Quién eres?

Answer sheet. 1. __X__a. Who are you?

_____b. Who is he?

_____c. Who is she?

Stage 3: Transfer: *Reception (Internal)*

Student behavior (3-a) Demonstrate understanding of grammatical signals.

Test item (3-1): Listen to the following sentences and check the appropriate box to indicate if the verb you hear is in the present or future tense.

	present	future
Tape: 1. Les filles danseront. Answer sheet: 1.		✓
2.		

Student behavior (3-b): Select appropriate grammatical forms.

Test item (3-2): Circle the response that is most appropriate to the initial statement.

Tape: 1. Où est le livre?

a. Il est là-bas.

b. Elle est là-bas.

Answer sheet: 1. (a.) b.

Student behavior (3-c): Demonstrate understanding of vocabulary words in recombined contexts.

Test item (3-3): Circle the letter of the vocabulary word that best completes the statement.

Tape: Ich lese   a. ein Buch, b. einen Bleistift, c. eine Schule.

Answer sheet: (a.) b. c.

Test item (3-4): In the space below draw a picture according to the directions you hear.

Tape: Dessinez une fille qui porte un chemisier rouge et une jupe bleue.

Student behavior (3-d): Demonstrate understanding of recombined sentences.

Test item (3-5): Show, by underlining the appropriate word, if the sentences you hear are true or false.

Tape: Il neige souvent en été.

Answer sheet: true   false

Test item (3-6): Circle the letter of the response that is an appropriate completion or continuation of the first statement.

Tape: Il neige souvent   a. en hiver.   b. en été.

Answer sheet: (a.) b.

Student behavior (3-e): Demonstrate understanding of recombined passages.

Test item (3-7): Listen to the paragraph and write the word "true" or "false" to indicate whether each of the following statements about it agrees with the information given. (On the tape is a recorded passage followed by several statements.)

Test item (3-8): Listen to the paragraph and write the letter of the response that best completes each statement. (On the tape is a recorded passage followed by completion questions.)

Stage 4: Communication: *Comprehension (Internal)*

Student behavior (4-a): Show the ability to grasp the general meaning of material containing unfamiliar cognates or vocabulary words.

Test item (4-1): Listen to the following passage and answer orally or in writing the following general questions. (Short-answer, multiple-choice questions on weather reports, newscasts, speeches, jokes, stories, and so on.)

Test item (4-2): Summarize orally or in writing the taped material you have heard. (Recording of a speech, scene from a play, a film sound track.)

Student behavior (4-b): Show the ability to comprehend rapid discourse with ease.

Test item (4-3): Indicate if the following rapidly spoken sentences are true or false. (Description of a picture, factual statements.)

Stage 5: Criticism: *Analysis (Internal)*

Student behavior (5-a): Show the ability to understand implied meanings.

Test item (5-1): Listen to the following passage (or dialog) and indicate by writing "yes" or "no" whether each of the statements after it may be logically implied from the information given. (Questions on number of speakers, topic of discussion, point of view of speaker(s), location, attitudes, feelings, intentions, extrapolated actions.)

Student behavior (5-b): Show the ability to perceive standards of language.

Test item (5-2): Listen to the following passages and mark with an *X* the standard of language being used. (Is the speech sample formal, familiar, colloquial, vulgar?)

Student behavior (5-c): Show the ability to distinguish regional speech or social class differences.

Test item (5-3): Circle the region, country, or class the speaker apparently represents. (Castilian or Mexican Spanish, northern or southern French, upper- or lower-class speech, and so on.)

Student behavior (5-d) : Show the ability to understand significant intonation and stress patterns.

Test item (5-4) : Listen to the following passages and circle the adjective that best describes the mood of the speaker. (Happy, angry, satirical, and so on.)

Test item (5-5) : Write the letter of the foreign-language word that best describes the feelings of the speaker in each of the following passages. (Embarrassed, annoyed, and so on.)

Criticism: *Evaluation (Internal)*

Student behavior (5-e) : Show the ability to evaluate a passage heard.

Test item (5-6) : While listening to the following passage, prepare yourself to answer these questions and to cite evidence to support your conclusions. (Consistency in standard of language, appropriateness of language to idea, persuasiveness, success in terms of purpose, organization, clarity, pronunciation.)

8.3   SELF-TESTS

Take these self-tests to see how well you have understood this section. Refer back to it as needed.

Test 1: Classify the following student behaviors according to their taxonomic stage. Use this key: 1 = **Mechanical Skills:** *Perception*, 2 = **Knowledge:** *Recognition*, 3 = **Transfer:** *Reception*, 4 = **Communication:** *Comprehension*, 5 = **Criticism:** *Analysis, Evaluation*. Write the appropriate number in the blank.

a.___ Demonstrate understanding of recombined familiar dialog material.

b.___ Distinguish between English and foreign-language sounds.

c.___ State the standard of language used in a taped passage.

d.___ Judge the appropriateness of language to the idea expressed.

e.___ Demonstrate understanding of a foreign-language news report.

f.___ Mark whether two sentences are the same or different.

g.___ Demonstrate understanding of a lecture in the foreign language.

h.___ Write whether sentences are singular or plural according to grammatical signals.

i.___ Match familiar expressions with appropriate pictures.

j.___ Select appropriate completions to unfamiliar foreign-language sentences.

Answers: a. 3   b. 1   c. 5   d. 5   e. 4   f. 1   g. 4   h. 1   i. 2   j. 3

Test 2: Classify the following test items according to this key: 1 = **Mechanical Skills:** *Perception,* 2 = **Knowledge:** *Recognition,* 3 = **Transfer:** *Reception,* 4 = **Communciation:** *Comprehension,* 5 = **Criticism:** *Analysis, Evaluation.* Write the appropriate number in the blank.

a.___ Underline the one vocabulary word that best completes each sentence you hear.

b.___ Write the letter of the picture that corresponds to the familiar weather expression you hear.

c.___ Describe the mood of the speaker.

d.___ Write the letter of the diagram that best describes the intonation pattern you hear in each sentence.

e.___ Answer in writing these factual questions on the unfamiliar short story you have heard.

f.___ According to the pronunciation you hear, write from which region each speaker apparently comes.

g.___ Circle the letter of the one word that does not rhyme with the two others.

h.___ According to the sound signals you hear, indicate by a check mark whether the subject of each of the following sentences is masculine or feminine.

i.___ Summarize in writing the main points of the lecture you will hear.

j.___ Make a check mark to show whether the sentences you hear are appropriate or not to the pictures you see. (Recombined material.)

Answers: a. 2 or 3   b. 2   c. 5   d. 1   e. 4   f. 5   g. 1   h. 1
          i. 4   j. 3

Test 3: Check the test items that might be appropriate measures of the desired behavior listed above them. In each case, the number of items to be checked is indicated in parentheses after the desired behavior.

1. Demonstrate comprehension of familiar sentences. (2)

    ____a. Write the familiar expressions you hear.

    ____b. Write the letter of the familiar expression you hear that corresponds to each picture you see.

    ____c. Repeat the sentences you hear.

    ____d. Write the number of the picture you see that corresponds to each expression you hear.

2. Demonstrate understanding of the recombined material heard. (2)

    ____a. Indicate which one of the vocabulary words you hear best completes each sentence.

    ____b. Circle whether each statement you hear is true or false.

    ____c. Write the answers you have memorized in response to these familiar questions.

    ____d. Write whether the paired sentences you hear are the same or different.

3. Show understanding of utterances containing unfamiliar material. (1)

    ____a. Write any new or unfamiliar words you hear.

    ____b. Write the standard of language used in each passage.

    ____c. Answer briefly the short-answer general questions covering material heard.

    ____d. Write the tense of each of the sentences you hear.

4. Demonstrate the ability to perceive differences in material heard. (2)

    ____a. Write whether each word you hear is pronounced in English or in the foreign language.

    ____b. Write the number of the English translation that best suits each of the familiar expressions you hear.

    ____c. Mark with an X whether the word pairs you hear rhyme or not.

    ____d. Indicate with a check mark the standard of language being used in each passage.

5. Demonstrate ability to analyze speech samples. (3)

_____a. Write the letter of the choice that best represents the implied meaning of each passage.

_____b. Underline from which of these geographical regions the speaker apparently comes.

_____c. Write "yes" if the standard of language is appropriate to the content and "no" if it is not.

_____d. Write a check mark by one of the three choices to show if each speech sample you hear is characteristic of upper-, middle-, or lower-class speech.

Answers: 1. b, d   2. a, b   3. c   4. a, c   5. a, b, d

CHAPTER NINE

SPEAKING

Speaking skill involves active participation on the part of the student. Speaking behaviors are usually developed in conjunction with the listening behaviors described in Chapter Five. It must be remembered that students are likely to understand many more words and structures than they use in speaking. In this sense, the student's speaking performance at a given point may appear weaker than his listening performance.

9.1 STAGES OF BEHAVIOR

Stage 1: Mechanical Skills: *Reproduction (External)*

The student can imitate native models of the foreign language. He reproduces native pronunciation, rhythm, stress, juncture, elision, and liaison. He can recite dialogs, poems, sayings, or series of items from memory. He is capable of correctly reading aloud material he has memorized. Although he may comprehend what he is saying, the student can also function at this stage without understanding precisely what each word or phrase means.

Stage 2: Knowledge: *Recall (External)*

The student can answer familiar questions according to what he has been taught. He can produce appropriate grammatical forms in familiar contexts. He can read aloud familiar material with accuracy. At this stage, understanding of the material is needed to produce the information requested.

Stage 3: Transfer: *Application* (*External*)

The student can vary his responses according to instructions. He applies his knowledge of grammar to the creation of new utterances. The situation in which he does this is highly controlled; he is given precise directions as to what structures he is to use and what changes or transformations he is to make. All types of pattern practice, sentence combination, and guided responses fall into this stage of behavior.

Stage 4: Communication: *Self-Expression* (*External*)

The student can express himself intelligibly and can make his ideas and desires known to others. The most guidance he receives is the assignment of a general topic, a particular structure, or several vocabulary words. At the lower end of this stage, the student's speech may be quite halting but is nevertheless comprehensible. At the upper end of this stage, the student may be bilingual. Fluency, comprehensibility, ease of expression, and effectiveness of communication are more important evaluation criteria than strict grammatical accuracy.

Stage 5: Criticism: *Synthesis* (*External*)

The main concern is no longer whether the student can express his ideas, but rather the manner in which he expresses them. He is capable of using style, tone, and choice of language appropriate to the subject of his discourse and to the people he is addressing.

9.2 EXAMPLES

This section contains examples of partial performance objectives in the area of speaking skills. They include student behaviors and test items that can be used to measure them. Since conditions and criteria will vary considerably according to classes, language level, facilities, and so on, these parts of the performance objective have not been specified here. It is left to the individual teacher to formulate them for his own situation. The purpose of all the partial performance objectives presented here is to develop speaking skills.

Stage 1: Mechanical Skills: *Reproduction (External)*

Student behavior (1-a): Imitate foreign-language sounds, intonation, rhythm, stress, juncture, elision, or liaison.

Test item (1-1): Repeat after the tape or teacher the words you hear. (Scored on pronunciation accuracy.)

Test item (1-2): Repeat after the tape or teacher the sentences you hear. (Scored on pronunciation accuracy.)

Student behavior (1-b): Recite memorized material with accurate pronunciation (accuracy of sounds, intonation, rhythm, stress, juncture, elision, liaison).

Test item (1-3): Recite the sentences or dialog you have memorized. (Scored on pronunciation accuracy.)

Test item (1-4): Recite from memory the dialog line that comes after the one you hear. (Scored on pronunciation accuracy.)

Test item (1-5): Recite the conjugation of the irregular verb you have memorized. (Scored on pronunciation accuracy.)

Test item (1-6): Recite from memory the days of the week, months of year, seasons, and alphabet. (Scored on overall accuracy.)

Test item (1-7): Count from one to one hundred (by two's, five's, ten's, and so on). (Scored on overall accuracy.)

Student behavior (1-c): Read aloud familiar material. (Scored on accuracy of sounds, intonation, rhythm, stress, juncture, elision, liaison.)

Test item (1-8): Repeat after the teacher or tape the words or sentences you hear. (Scored on pronunciation accuracy.)

Test item (1-9): Read aloud the sentences you see. (Scored on pronunciation accuracy.)

Stage 2: Knowledge: *Recall (External)*

Student behavior (2-a): Respond with familiar vocabulary and expressions in familiar contexts.

Test item (2-1): Respond with the appropriate word or expression associated with a picture, flashcard, or question (letters, numbers out of sequence, arithmetic problems, weather, seasons, colors, greetings, and so on).

Test item (2-2): Respond with the appropriate foreign-language expression associated with an English cue (same topics as above).

Student behavior (2-b): Respond with familiar grammatical forms in familiar contexts.

Test item (2-3): Respond with the appropriate form according to the cue given (pattern drills and exercises from the textbook or tape program).

Test item (2-4): Respond with a memorized sentence when presented with an English cue (translation). (These may be dialog sentences out of sequence.)

Student behavior (2-c): Read aloud familiar material (not memorized) with accuracy (accuracy of sounds, intonation, rhythm, stress, juncture, elision, liaison).

Test item (2-5): Read aloud the sentences you see. (Scored on accuracy.)

Stage 3: Transfer: *Application (External)*

Student behavior (3-a): Manipulate simple substitution patterns according to directions.

Test item (3-1): When presented with a structure and a cue word (recombined material), respond by incorporating the cue word into the pattern (pattern drills and exercises not practiced in class, such as substitution of articles, nouns, adjectives, and so on, with no other pattern changes).

Test item (3-2): Respond by incorporating the cue word into the pattern presented (recombined material) and make all necessary changes (substitution of nouns, pronouns, verbs, articles that require changes in other words in the sentence).

Test item (3-3): Respond by changing one part of speech to another according to transformation rules learned (recombined material) (adjectives to nouns, adjectives to adverbs, infinitives to nouns).

Test item (3-4): Respond by changing the following sentences according to directions and making all necessary changes (recombined material) (declarative to interrogative, affirmative to interrogative, affirmative to negative, singular to plural, nouns to pronouns, masculine to feminine, present to past, and so on).

Test item (3-5): Answer the following questions (personal questions, questions based on a picture or story).

Test item (3-6): Engage in the dialog according to directions (directed dialog: ask questions, give answers specified, and so on).

Student behavior (3-b): Combine sentences using appropriate conjunctions and making all necessary changes.

Test item (3-7): Combine each of the following sentence pairs into one sentence (indicative to subjunctive, word order in subordinate clauses, use of coordinating and subordinating conjunctions, relative pronouns).

Student behavior (3-c): Produce a sentence by recombining known elements.

Test item (3-8): Respond to the English sentence you hear with its foreign-language equivalent (oral translation).

Student behavior (3-d): Apply sound or letter correspondence rules in unfamiliar contexts.

Test item (3-9): Circle "yes" if the printed word pairs would rhyme when read aloud and "no" if they would not.

Printed text: 1. though   through

Answer sheet: 1. yes   (no)

Test item (3-10): Underline the one word in each group that does not rhyme with the other.

Answer sheet: 1. tough   rough   dough

Student behavior (3-e): Read aloud unfamiliar material and apply correct sound or letter correspondence rules (rules for sounds, intonation, rhythm, liaison, elision, juncture, stress, and so on).

Test item (3-11): Read aloud the following passage (unfamiliar material).

Stage 4: Communication: *Self-Expression* (*External*)

Student behavior (4-a): Communicate original thoughts orally.

Test item (4-1): Speak for _____ minutes on a topic of your or your teacher's choice.

Test item (4-2): Describe a magazine picture.

Test item (4-3): Narrate the action in a sequence of pictures.

Test item (4-4): Interview a friend.

Test item (4-5): Present a skit in which you give hotel, train, or plane directions to a foreign visitor.

Test item (4-6): Present a skit in which you and a friend talk on the phone, make a date, discuss a party, and so on.

Test item (4-7): Tell how you spent your weekend or vacation.

Test item (4-8): Present a debate on the pros and cons of an issue (foreign-language study, politics, morality).

Test item (4-9): Explain how to do something (cook, sew, assemble, construct, repair, play a musical instrument).

Test item (4-10): Persuade your parents to allow you to do something (borrow the car, travel abroad, get a job, stay out later).

Test item (4-11): Present a summary of a book you have read or a current-events topic.

Test item (4-12): Persuade your teacher to do something (delay a test, cancel homework, raise a grade).

Stage 5: Criticism: *Synthesis* (*External*)

Student behavior (5-a): Speak using appropriate style, tone, choice of language.

Test item (5-1): Act out a situation in which you display a particular emotion (anger, impatience, frustration).

Test item (5-2): Watch a film clip of an incident and describe it from the points of view of those involved.

Test item (5-3): Another motorist ran into your car. Show how you would talk to the other driver, explain the accident to a policeman, describe the incident to your friends.

Test item (5-4): Act out various situations in which apologies must be given to different people (a younger brother, an uncle, the school principal, and so on).

9.3   SELF-TESTS

Take these self-tests to see how well you have understood this section. Refer back to it as needed.

Test 1: Classify the following student behaviors according to their taxonomic stage. Use this key: 1 = **Mechanical Skills:** *Reproduction,* 2 = **Knowledge:** *Recall,* 3 = **Transfer:** *Application,* 4 = **Communication:** *Self-Expression,* 5 = **Criticism:** *Synthesis.* Write the appropriate number in the blank.

a.＿＿ Perform appropriate introductions as learned.

b.＿＿ Form a new sentence according to a given cue.

c.＿＿ Mimic a taped utterance.

d.＿＿ Carry on a conversation with people of different ages.

e.＿＿ Ask for needed information on classwork. (Original sentences.)

f.＿＿ Read aloud a memorized dialog.

g.＿＿ Engage in directed dialog situations. (Recombined material.)

h.＿＿ Present a speech using the structures and vocabulary learned.

i.＿＿ Describe the action in a picture you see. (Unfamiliar.)

j.＿＿ Speak so as to illustrate different emotions.

Answers: a. 2   b. 3   c. 1   d. 5   e. 4   f. 1   g. 3   h. 2   i. 4   j. 5

Test 2. Classify the following test items according to this key: 1 = **Mechanical Skills:** *Reproduction,* 2 = **Knowledge:** *Recall,* 3 = **Transfer:** *Application,* 4 = **Communication:** *Self-Expression,* 5 = **Criticism:** *Synthesis.* Write the appropriate number in the blank.

a.＿＿ Prepare a skit in which you and a friend make social plans.

b.＿＿ Imitate the sentences you hear, paying special attention to pronunciation, intonation, rhythm, and stress.

c.___ Combine the two sentences you hear, using either the indicative or subjunctive.

d.___ Do the following math problems orally.

e.___ Read aloud the following unfamiliar sentences.

f.___ Imitate a ten-year-old boy begging his older brother to take him along to the movies.

g.___ Recite with a friend the dialog you have memorized.

h.___ Give directions to a foreign visitor.

i.___ Show how you would greet and converse with a friend and then a teacher, both of whom you meet by chance.

j.___ Recite the twelve months of the year in order.

Answers: a. 4   b. 1   c. 3   d. 2   e. 3   f. 5   g. 1   h. 4   i. 5   j. 1

Test 3: Check the test items that might be appropriate measures of the desired behavior listed above them. In each case, the number of items to be checked is indicated in parentheses after the desired behavior.

1. Respond appropriately with material taught in class. (1)

   ___a. Look at the positions of the clock hands and tell the time (as learned).

   ___b. Change these sentences (recombined) from present to imperfect.

   ___c. Repeat each sentence (recombined) with the new cue word given and make necessary changes.

   ___d. Repeat the dialog sentences you hear.

2. Use vocabulary and grammar learned in new situations. (3)

   ___a. Answer the following (unfamiliar) personal questions in past tense.

   ___b. Tell the class how you spent your vacation.

   ___c. Change the following sentences from present to future.

   ___d. Read aloud the following unfamiliar material, observing sound-letter correspondences learned.

3. Pronounce the foreign language accurately. (2)

   ___a. Write whether the words you hear are pronounced in English or in the foreign language.

_____b. Present the dialog you have learned.

_____c. Write whether the paired words you see written rhyme or do not.

_____d. Imitate as accurately as you can the sentences you hear.

4. Carry on a conversation in which differences in tone are evident. (3)

_____a. Describe the items in the classroom.

_____b. Play the role of someone arguing with his parents.

_____c. Pretend you are speaking to a young child.

_____d. Call up your best friend and make plans to go out.

5. Speak extemporaneously in the foreign language. (3)

_____a. Debate the pros and cons of studying a foreign language.

_____b. Tell how you plan to spend your vacation.

_____c. Describe what the people in the picture (unfamiliar) are doing.

_____d. Write out a skit with a friend and present it to the class.

Answers: 1. a   2. a, b, c   3. b, d   4. b, c, d   5. a, b, c

CHAPTER TEN
READING

In this section "reading" refers only to the ability of the student to perceive and understand what is written or printed. This skill, then, involves internal behavior. Although reading aloud has occasionally been considered as part of the reading skill, it will not be included here, since it really aims to develop speaking, rather than reading, skill. Nor does reading here include the student's ability to choose a grammatically correct sentence completion (My sister *brang, bringed, brought* the book), since such exercises constitute an indirect measure of the student's ability to write correctly.

10.1 STAGES OF BEHAVIOR

Stage 1: Mechanical Skills: *Perception (Internal)*

The student can differentiate between spellings in the foreign language and can tell if they are the same or different. He does not necessarily understand what he sees, however.

Stage 2: Knowledge: *Recognition (Internal)*

The student understands the meaning of the familiar statements he reads. He can tell which statement corresponds to a picture he sees or which of several translations is appropriate to a particular statement. He can also tell which of several sentences he sees before him is being read. Reading at this stage is usually of the sentence-at-a-time variety. The material presented in the test situation is virtually the same as that of the learning situation.

Stage 3: Transfer: *Reception (Internal)*

The student understands recombinations of the vocabulary and structure he has learned. He can read several paragraphs and answer true-false, completion, or multiple-choice questions about them. He can indicate which of several vocabulary words is appropriate to a new context. All the elements presented to the student are familiar to him, but their combination or order of presentation is not.

Stage 4: Communication: *Comprehension (Internal)*

The student reads with comprehension materials containing unfamiliar cognates and new vocabulary or structural items. Although he may not understand every word read, he nevertheless comprehends the main points of the passage. The highest development of this stage of behavior includes reading speed and fluency comparable to the student's ability in his native language.

Stage 5: Criticism: *Analysis (Internal)*

Understanding the denotational, or surface, meaning of an unfamiliar passage no longer constitutes a problem for the student. At this stage, he is capable of discerning connotational or implicit meanings, point of view, and standard of language. He is sensitive to nuances of style and to the suggestive meanings of the words used. The student reads between the lines.

Criticism: *Evaluation (Internal)*

The student makes judgments in regard to the expression and style of an author. He determines if the style of a text is internally consistent and if it is effective in accomplishing its purposes.

10.2 EXAMPLES

This section contains examples of partial performance objectives in the area of reading skills. They include student behaviors and test items that can be used to measure them. Since conditions and criteria will vary considerably according to classes, language level, facilities, and so on, these parts of the performance objectives have not been specified here. It is left to the individual teacher to formulate them for his own situation. The purpose of all the partial performance objectives presented here is to develop reading skills.

Stage 1: Mechanical Skills: *Perception (Internal)*

Student behavior (1-a): Distinguish between letters and combinations of letters.

Test item (1-1): Circle whether the letters you see are the same or different. (Russian, Arabic, Hebrew letters, accent marks, Japanese, Chinese characters.)

Test item (1-2): Underline the word whose vowels are different from those of the other two words.

1. tout   <u>taux</u>   nous

Student behavior (1-b): Distinguish between sentences read.

Test item (1-3): Write *s* if the sentence pairs you see are the same or *d* if they are different from each other.

<u>d</u> 1. Il la prend.   Il l'apprend.

Stage 2: Knowledge: *Recognition (Internal)*

Student behavior (2-a): Demonstrate recognition of the written form of familiar sounds or words heard.

Test item (2-1): After hearing three items, circle the letter of the item that is the same as the one written on your paper.

Tape: a. ils sont, b. ils ont, c. elles ont.

Answer sheet: ils ont   a.   ⓑ   c.

Test item (2-2): Underline the word or words that are the same as the one(s) heard.

Tape: cent

Answer sheet: sein   <u>cent</u>   sente

Student behavior (2-b): Demonstrate recognition of different spellings of the same sound.

Test item (2-3): Circle the word that does not rhyme with the others.

Answer sheet: 1. cent   rang   temps   (lente)

Student behavior (2-c): Demonstrate understanding of familiar words.

Test item (2-4): Write an X by the statement whose meaning corresponds to the picture you see.

Picture: A house

Answer sheet: X a. C'est une maison.

b. C'est un magasin.

Test item (2-5): Check the appropriate column to show whether a statement is true or false according to the picture you see.

Picture: Sun shining   Answer sheet:

	T	F
1. Il fait beau.	√	

Test item (2-6): Write the number of the picture that illustrates the meaning of each statement you read (pictures of clocks with times, each numbered.)

Answer sheet: _____Il est midi et demi. (Student writes number of clock showing 12:30 in the blank.)

Test item (2-7): Match the words or sentences at the left with an appropriate picture at the right (as with clocks, using objects, adjectives, comparisons, numbers, and so on).

Student behavior (2-d): Select an appropriate translation for familiar words or sentences.

Test item (2-8): Circle the English word that corresponds to the underlined foreign-language word.

C'est un chien. a. cat b. (dog) c. chair

Test item (2-9): Write the letter of the English sentence that translates the foreign-language sentence.

<u>a</u> 1. Je vais bien.   a. I feel well.

     b. I go far.

     c. He's fine.

Student behavior (2-e): Match idioms or vocabulary words with definitions.

Test item (2-10): In the right hand column write the letter of the definition or translation that corresponds to the underlined idiom or vocabulary word in the sentence to the left.

<u>b</u> 1. C'est le coup de foudre.   a. dead end

     b. love at first sight

Stage 3: Transfer: *Reception* (*Internal*)

Student behavior (3-a): Demonstrate comprehension of vocabulary words in recombined contexts.

Test item (3-1): Write the letter of the choice that most appropriately completes the sentence.

<u>a</u> 1. Ich fahre mit   a. einem Bus.

     b. einer Strasse.

     c. einer Stadt.

Test item (3-2): Write the letter of the choice that is the most appropriate synonym (antonym, definition, translation) of the word or words underlined in the sentence.

1. <u>b</u> Je viens tout de suite   a. tard.

     b. immédiatement.

     c. après.

Student behavior (3-b): Demonstrate comprehension of recombined sentences.

Test item (3-3): Check the appropriate column according to whether the sentences you read are true or false.

	True	False
1. La neige est blanche.	√	

Test item (3-4): Circle whether the sentences you read are true or false or appropriate or inappropriate to the picture or paragraph above.

Picture: Summer scene at sea shore

Text: 1. On fait du patin.

Answer sheet: 1. appropriate   (inappropriate)

Test item (3-5): Check which of the responses best completes the initial statement.

1. Maman prépare un grand déjeuner parce que

   √a. c'est mon anniversaire.

   b. je viens de manger.

   c. nous sortons ce matin.

Test item (3-6): Write the letter of the response that best continues the thought of the initial question or statement.

c 1. Es geht mir nicht gut.

   a. Du gehst zur Schule?

   b. Es geht immer schlechter.

   c. Bist du krank?

Test item (3-7): Translate the following sentences into natural, idiomatic English.

1. Bei mir bist du schön.

2. Er sieht sie böse an.

Test item (3-8): Write the letter of the English translation that is most appropriate to the foreign-language sentence(s).

<u>b</u> 1. Es geht ganz gut.

    a. He feels all well.

    b. Things are really swell.

    c. It's going fairly well.

Stage 4: Communication: *Comprehension (Internal)*

Student behavior (4-a): Read unfamiliar material with understanding.

Test item (4-1): Answer the following short-answer or multiple-choice questions on the story, novel, play, essay, article, or poem you have read.

Test item (4-2): Summarize orally or in writing the content of what you have read.

Test item (4-3): List three important ideas, facts, or events from the material read.

Test item (4-4): Define or translate the following underlined words or expressions taken from the reading selection.

Student behavior (4-b): Demonstrate ability to read fluently in the foreign language.

Test item (4-5): Read as rapidly as you can for _____ minutes without losing the sense of the text. Mark the last word read at the end of the time period.

Test item (4-6): Read as rapidly as you can with understanding during the allotted time. Cross out the nonsense words that have been inserted in the passage.

Test item (4-7): Read as rapidly as you with understanding for _____ minutes. Answer the multiple-choice questions on the text read.

Stage 5: Criticism: *Analysis (Internal)*

Student behavior (5-a): Analyze an unfamiliar, unedited reading selection.

Test item (5-1): Write "yes" or "no" to indicate if the following statements may logically be implied from the selection read (number of speakers, location of speakers, time of day or night, mood of speakers, extrapolated actions).

> Example: Two speakers discuss what they will order for lunch.
> Statements:
>
> <u>yes</u> 1. The speakers are in a restaurant.
>
> <u>no</u> 2. It's early evening.

Test item (5-2): Answer the following questions in writing. Support your conclusions with evidence from the text. (Notes may be taken.) (Questions on author's attitude to subject [involved or detached, objective or subjective, pro or con], point of view, style of language, purpose.)

> **Criticism:** *Evaluation (Internal)*

Student behavior (5-b): Evaluate an unfamiliar, unedited reading selection.

Test item (5-3): Answer the following questions in writing. Evaluate the selection read in terms of organization, success in accomplishing purpose, appropriateness or effectiveness of language, ability to hold reader interest, appropriateness of ending, suggestions for improvement, and so on.

10.3   SELF-TESTS

Take these self-tests to see how well you have understood this section. Refer back to it as needed.

Test 1: Classify the following student behaviors according to their taxonomic stages. Use this key: 1 = **Mechanical Skills:** *Perception,* 2 = **Knowledge:** *Recognition,* 3 = **Transfer:** *Reception,* 4 = **Communication:** *Comprehension,* 5 = **Criticism:** *Analysis, Evaluation.* Write the appropriate number in the blank.

a.____ Match familiar vocabulary words in sentences with their correct definitions.

b.____ Circle whether two words are the same or different.

c.____ Demonstrate understanding of implications in material read.

d.____ Demonstrate understanding of recombined reading material.

e.____ Read with understanding material containing unfamiliar words.

f.____ Select which of several sentences is the most appropriate completion of the initial sentence read (recombined material).

g.____ Judge the effectiveness of material read.

h.___ Mark which one of several written words corresponds to the one spoken.

i.___ Give evidence on a timed test of the ability to read with fluency.

Answers: a. 2   b. 1   c. 5   d. 3   e. 4   f. 3   g. 5   h. 2   i. 4

Test 2: Classify the following test items according to this key: 1 = **Mechanical Skills**: *Perception,* 2 = **Knowledge**: *Recognition,* 3 = **Transfer**: *Reception,* 4 = **Communication**: *Comprehension,* 5 = **Criticism**: *Analysis, Evaluation.* Write the appropriate number in the blank.

a.___ Write the letter of the English translation that is most appropriate to the (familiar) foreign-language idiom you see.

b.___ Write the letter of the choice that best fits in the blank.

c.___ Write whether each of the sentences you see is the same as or different from the sentence you hear.

d.___ Read the following unfamiliar material within the allotted time period and answer the multiple-choice questions afterward.

e.___ Mark an *X* by the choice that is the most appropriate answer to each of the questions you see (recombined material).

f.___ Read the following recombined paragraphs and indicate if the statements afterward are true or false.

g.___ Give your opinion on the appropriateness of the ending of the story read.

h.___ Write a paper discussing these points based on the text read: author's purpose, point of view, choice of language.

i.___ Match each familiar statement on seasons of the year with its appropriate picture.

j.___ Circle whether the paired sentences you see are the same or different.

Answers: a. 2   b. 3   c. 2   d. 4   e. 3   f. 3   g. 5   h. 4   i. 2   j. 1

Test 3: Check the test items that might be appropriate measures of the desired behavior listed above them. In each case the number of items to be checked is indicated in parentheses after the desired behavior.

1. Read with understanding unedited material. (2)

___a. Summarize the magazine article you have read.

___b. Outline the newspaper article you have read.

____c. Read the following short story as rapidly as you can.

____d. Underline the words you do not understand in the reading passage.

2. Demonstrate understanding of recombined reading material. (1)

____a. Read aloud the following material.

____b. Write a synonym or antonym for each of the following words taken from the passage read.

____c. Translate the following idioms found in the recombined passage read.

____d. Answer the following multiple-choice questions on the recombined passage read.

3. Differentiate between foreign-language spellings. (2)

____a. Circle which one of the following four words is different from the other three.

____b. Copy the following sentences.

____c. Underline the two words of the following three that rhyme with each other.

____d. Write whether the following sentence pairs are the same or different.

4. Show understanding of familiar vocabulary words and idioms (familiar contexts). (3)

____a. Write original sentences in which the following idioms are used correctly.

____b. Draw a picture that represents the meaning of the words underlined in these familiar sentences.

____c. Indicate by writing an X which of the four familiar sentences after each picture best corresponds to it in meaning.

____d. Translate each of these familiar idioms.

5. Analyze a reading selection (unfamiliar). (1)

____a. Summarize the plot of the unfamiliar story read.

____b. Evaluate the appropriateness of the ending of the story.

____c. Discuss in writing the sources of conflict in the story.

____d. Using notes taken in class and personal ideas, analyze the development of the main character in the story read.

Answers: 1. a, b   2. d   3. a, d   4. b, c, d   5. c

CHAPTER ELEVEN
WRITING

Writing skill usually involves external behavior on the part of students. All activities that require writing in the foreign language fall into this skill area. Indirect measures of writing ability, however, may also be used in foreign-language testing because of their convenience in scoring. On an item such as "I'll take this/these two boxes," students are being tested on whether they know which of two forms to write in order to complete the sentence correctly. Such an item is quite similar to one in which the student would actually write the missing word. (Example: Fill in the blanks of the following sentences with *this* or *these*; or, Fill in the blanks of the following sentences with the appropriate form of the demonstrative *this*.) This treatment of multiple-choice grammar items as indirect writing measures is substantiated by statistical studies made by the Education Testing Service. Items of this type on College Board language tests usually prove to be the most difficult for the candidates. Production of accurate written language is a highly complex and difficult skill.

11.1 STAGES OF BEHAVIOR

Stage 1: Mechanical Skills: *Reproduction* (*External*)

The student can copy accurately material presented to him and can spell correctly from memory or from dictation of memorized material. He does not necessarily understand the material he writes.

Stage 2: Knowledge: *Recall (External)*

The student knows the sound and symbol correspondences of the foreign language. He can spell correctly familiar material dictated to him and can write familiar sentences appropriate to pictures presented to him. He can write correctly the grammatical forms he has learned and can write answers to familiar questions. Understanding is necessary for satisfactory performance at this stage.

Stage 3: Transfer: *Application (External)*

The student can write variations of new patterns according to the rules he has learned. His performance is guided; he is told what changes, recombinations, or transformations he is to make in the patterns presented. Multiple-choice grammar items are indirect measures of behavior at this stage.

Stage 4: Communication: *Self-Expression (External)*

The student communicates his own thoughts in writing. He expresses certain ideas, not because he has been instructed to do so, but because he wants to. At this stage, comprehensibility is considered more important than strict grammatical accuracy. Student written work is not structured by the teacher beyond the assignment of a general topic, a grammatical structure, or certain lexical items.

Stage 5: Criticism: *Synthesis (External)*

The student is already capable of expressing his ideas with facility when writing in the foreign language. At this stage, he demonstrates ability to vary his style, tone, and choice of language in accordance with his subject matter, his purpose, or his intended audience. He approaches native proficiency in his mastery of the nuances of the language and in his selection of appropriate words.

11.2   EXAMPLES

This section contains examples of partial performance objectives in the area of writing skills. They include student behaviors and test items that can be used to measure them. Since conditions and criteria will vary considerably according to classes, language level, facilities, and so on, these parts of the performance objectives have not been specified here. It is left to the individual teacher to formulate them for his own situation. The purpose of all the partial performance objectives presented here is to develop writing skills.

Stage 1: Mechanical Skills: *Reproduction (External)*

Student behavior (1-a) : Copy foreign-language material.

Test item (1-1) : Look at the following sentences and copy them.

Student behavior (1-b) : Spell correctly from memory.

Test item (1-2) : Write the dialog, sentences, or poem you have memorized.

Student behavior (1-c) : Write a sentence substitution involving no other changes.

Test item (1-3) : Recopy the sentence, substituting the words in parentheses for those underlined in the sentence.

Example: Je vais en ville. (à l'école)

Answer: Je vais à l'école.

Stage 2: Knowledge: *Recall (External)*

Student behavior (2-a) : Spell familiar sentences from dictation.

Test item (2-1) : Write the sentences you hear dictated.

Student behavior (2-b) : Write the appropriate grammatical forms as learned. (Articles: definite, indefinite; adjectives: descriptive, demonstrative; plurals, case endings.)

Test item (2-2) : In the blank, write the appropriate form of the definite article required in the sentence.

1. Das Mädchen heisst Lieselotte.

Student behavior (2-c) : Spell a familiar word or grammatical form from dictation.

Test item (2-3): Listen to the following sentences. Look at the incomplete sentences on your answer sheet and write the missing words in the blanks according to what you hear.

Tape: Mes amis parlent beaucoup.

Answer sheet: Mes amis _____ beaucoup.

Student behavior (2-d): Write punctuation marks from dictation.

Test item (2-4): Write the appropriate punctuation marks according to instructions during the dictation.

Student behavior (2-e): Write correct answers to familiar questions.

Test item (2-5): Answer the following questions in writing.

1. What time is it?

2. How old are you?

Stage 3: Transfer: *Application (External)*

Student behavior (3-a): Select the appropriate grammatical form in a recombined pattern.

Test item (3-1): Circle the letter of the appropriate completion.

1. If faut que a. je pars, b. je parte.

Test item (3-2): Write the letter of the appropriate form in the blank.

<u>b</u> 1. Ich _____ durstig.

    a. sind

    b. bin

    c. bist.

(This type of item is also for testing adjective and case endings.)

Test item (3-3): Write the sentences you hear dictated (recombined material).

Test item (3-4) : Write the letter of the pronoun that may be substituted for the underlined words.

<u>c</u> 1. Ich sehe das <u>Buch</u>.

　　a. sie

　　b. ihn

　　c. es

Student behavior (3-b) : Rewrite patterns according to directions and make necessary grammatical changes.

Test item (3-5) : Rewrite the following sentences using the cue word.

1. Je suis ici. Nous

2. Voici une fleur blanche. Livre

Test item (3-6) : Write the appropriate form of the infinitive in the blank.

1. (avoir) Ils _____ faim.

Test item (3-7) : Change the following sentences from present to past, future, conditional, and so on.

Test item (3-8) : Change the following dialog to a narrative (or narrative to a dialog).

Test item (3-9) : Expand each of the following sentences by inserting the word in parentheses (adjectives, adverbs).

Test item (3-10) : Rewrite the following sentences in the negative, interrogative, imperative.

Test item (3-11) : Rewrite the following paragraph, changing all nouns and pronouns from singular to plural and making all other necessary agreements. (Or, change from a masculine to a feminine subject.)

Test item (3-12) : Construct grammatically correct sentences from the following elements.

| Il | achètent | un | disque. |
| Elles | achète | des | cartes. |

(Or, Il/acheter/disque.)

Test item (3-13) : Rewrite the following sentences, replacing the under-lined nouns with pronouns.

Nous regardons <u>les fleurs</u>.

Test item (3-14) : By using the word in parentheses, combine each of the following pairs of sentences into one and make all necessary changes.

Je suis désolé. Paul n'est pas ici. (que)

Ich weiss es. Er ist hier. (dass)

Student behavior: Write guided compositions.

Test item (3-15) : Answer the following questions so that your written responses will form a composition. (How many people are there in your family? What are their names? How old are they? What do they like to do?)

Test item (3-16) : Write a composition using the grammatical structure just learned (past, future, conditional, subjunctive).

Stage 4: Communication: *Self-Expression* (*External*)

Student behavior (4-a) : Demonstrate the ability to communicate one's thoughts in writing.

Test item (4-1) : Write a paragraph, composition, dialog on a topic of your or your instructor's choice (friends, family, hobbies, special interests, unusual activities).

Test item (4-2) : Describe in writing a magazine picture.

Test item (4-3) : Write a narrative of the action in the cartoon series you see.

Test item (4-4) : Write a letter to a friend, a foreign pen pal.

Test item (4-5) : Explain in writing how to do something (cook, sew, play an instrument).

Test item (4-6) : Write an essay that expresses the presumed thoughts of an inanimate object (chair, pencil, blackboard, tree, refrigerator).

Stage 5: Criticism: *Synthesis (External)*

Student behavior (5-a): Demonstrate the ability to communicate one's thoughts in writing, using appropriate style, tone, and choice of language.

Test item (5-1): Write a formal business letter (order merchandise, job application, general inquiry).

Test item (5-2): Write a short story containing narrative, dialog, description, regional dialects.

Test item (5-3): Write an essay from a particular point of view (old man, child, lover).

Test item (5-4): Write an essay that argues for a particular point of view (politics, morality, education, philosophy).

Test item (5-5): Write a personal letter to your five-year-old cousin. Rewrite the same letter to your aunt and uncle.

Test item (5-6): Change the tone of a given paragraph (formal to informal, humorous to serious, ironic to factual).

11.3   SELF-TESTS

Take these self-tests to see how well you have understood this section. Refer back to it as needed.

Test 1: Classify the following student behaviors according to their taxonomic stage. Use this key: 1 = **Mechanical Skills:** *Reproduction,* 2 = **Knowledge:** *Recall,* 3 = **Transfer:** *Application,* 4 = **Communication:** *Self-Expression,* 5 = **Criticism:** *Synthesis.* Write the appropriate number in the blank.

a.＿＿   Circle the one grammatical form that can correctly be used in the blank.

b.＿＿   Copy dialog sentences.

c.＿＿   Write answers to familiar questions.

d.＿＿   Write a letter to a foreign pen pal.

e.＿＿   Rewrite a sentence according to a cue and make necessary grammatical changes.

f.____ Write a formal business letter using appropriate salutations and closings.

g.____ Write a guided composition.

h.____ Write out the entire conjugation of a verb in a given tense.

i.____ Write sentences from memory.

j.____ Write a narrative according to a series of unfamiliar pictures.

Answers: a. 3   b. 1   c. 2   d. 4   e. 3   f. 5   g. 3   h. 2   i. 1   j. 4

Test 2: Classify the following test items according to this key: 1 = **Mechanical Skills**: *Reproduction*, 2 = **Knowledge**: *Recall*, 3 = **Transfer**: *Application*, 4 = **Communication**: *Self-Expression*, 5 = **Criticism**: *Synthesis*. Write the appropriate number in the blank.

a.____ State your beliefs on what makes a good foreign-language course. Style and organization will be counted in your statement.

b.____ Substitute the cue word in parentheses for the underlined word in the sentence and make necessary grammatical changes.

c.____ Change the following sentences from present to past.

d.____ Write the familiar sentences you hear dictated.

e.____ Substitute the cue word for the underlined word in the sentence (no other changes necessary).

f.____ Write the appropriate form of the definite article in front of the familiar nouns presented in the following sentences.

g.____ Write to a hotel abroad and make vacation reservations.

h.____ Write a composition on the career you would like to prepare for.

i.____ Describe your closest friend.

j.____ Change the following dialog to a narrative.

Answers: a. 5   b. 3   c. 3   d. 2   e. 1   f. 2   g. 5   h. 4   i. 4   j. 3

Test 3: Check the test items that might be appropriate measures of the desired behavior listed above them. In each case, the number of items to be checked is indicated in parentheses after the desired behavior.

1. Spell the familiar sentences heard. (1)

    ___a. Copy the sentences you see.

    ___b. Write the dialog you have memorized.

    ___c. Write these familiar sentences from dictation.

    ___d. Indicate by underlining which words in the following sentences are incorrectly spelled.

2. Make grammatical changes in recombined sentences according to direction given. (3)

    ___a. Change the following narrative to a dialog.

    ___b. Combine each pair of sentences using the indicative or subjunctive as appropriate.

    ___c. Rewrite the following paragraph making all the subject pronouns plural and changing other elements as needed.

    ___d. Write the conjugation of the verb "to be" in the future tense.

3. Demonstrate ability to use different standards of language. (3)

    ___a. Write a letter containing personal news to a friend. Write a letter with similar information to a grandparent.

    ___b. Change the tone of a given narrative from formal to informal.

    ___c. Indicate the relationships between the correspondents as indicated by the terminations of their letters.

    ___d. Indicate which of the following endings is most appropriate in letters between people who are related as described.

4. Communicate original thoughts in writing. (1)

    ___a. Answer these questions so that your responses form a coherent composition.

    ___b. Apply for a job, using an appropriate salutation and closing in your letter.

    ___c. Describe your hobbies and leisure time activities.

    ___d. Write an essay from the point of view of a king.

5. Write appropriate grammatical forms according to cues. (3)

___a. Write the letter of the adjective that best fits the blank in the sentence.

___b. Write the appropriate definite article in front of each of the following nouns.

___c. Judging from the verb forms you see, write an appropriate subject pronoun for each.

___d. Expand the following paragraph by modifying the underlined nouns with the adjectives given in parentheses.

Answers: 1. c   2. a, b, c   3. a, b, d   4. c   5. a, c, d

CHAPTER TWELVE
GESTURES

The area of gestures, or body language, is given scant attention in the typical foreign-language course. Teachers, however, may wish to include some of the simpler stages of such behavior among the performance objectives they set for their students.

The taxonomy of behaviors in this area includes internal and external behaviors. Internal behaviors stress the understanding of gestures used by the members of the foreign culture under study. Frequently, this behavior is the only type teachers seek to develop. The external behaviors require the student to act and react physically in a manner typical of the culture being studied. When these aims are taught, the teacher is seeking to train an individual to be bicultural. For example, when the student describes a large fish he caught, he would use one gesture when speaking English and another when speaking French.

12.1 STAGES OF BEHAVIOR

Stage 1: Mechanical Skills: *Perception* (*Internal*)

The student can indicate if gestures he sees are typical of the foreign culture, his native culture or of both.

Mechanical Skills: *Reproduction (External)*

The student imitates a gesture modeled for him.

Stage 2: Knowledge: *Recognition (Internal)*

The student recognizes the meaning of a gesture that has been presented and explained in class. The test situation reproduces the teaching situation.

Knowledge: *Recall (External)*

The student explains the meaning of a familiar gesture in a situation he remembers having been presented in class. He is able to indicate what gestures a native would most probably use in a situation he has already seen.

Stage 3: Transfer: *Reception (Internal)*

The student understands the meaning of a familiar gesture in an unfamiliar situation.

Transfer: *Application (External)*

The student uses a familiar gesture appropriately in a simulated, role-playing situation.

Stage 4: Communication: *Comprehension (Internal)*

The student understands the meaning of gestures he sees in the foreign culture or in a film made in the foreign country.

Communication: *Self-Expression (External)*

The student uses appropriate gestures to convey his ideas in the foreign culture.

Stage 5: Criticism: *Analysis (Internal)*

The student can analyze the speaker's mood and message by observing his gestures.

Criticism: *Synthesis (External)*

The student produces a catalog of common and uncommon foreign-culture gestures or a method of studying or categorizing them.

Criticism: *Evaluation (Internal)*

The student evaluates the appropriateness of certain foreign-culture gestures for the situation in which they are used. He might do this as a director of a play, a teacher in a classroom, and so on.

12.2 EXAMPLES

This section contains examples of partial performance objectives in the area of gestures. They include student behaviors and test items that can be used to measure them. Since conditions and criteria will vary considerably according to classes, language level, facilities, and so on, these parts of the performance objective have not been specified here. It is left to the individual teacher to formulate them for his own situation. The purpose of all the partial performance objectives presented here is to develop skill in the area of foreign-culture gestures.

Stage 1: Mechanical Skills: *Perception (Internal)*

Student behavior (1-a): Distinguish between foreign- and native-culture gestures.

Test item (1-1): Check the appropriate column according to whether the gestures you see are characteristic of your own culture, the foreign culture, or both (model or film clip of handshake, arm movements, facial expression, posture).

Mechanical Skills: *Reproduction (External)*

Student behavior (1-b): Imitate gestures of natives of the foreign culture under study.

Test item (1-2): Imitate the gesture you see (as above).

Stage 2: Knowledge: *Recognition (Internal)*

Student behavior (2-a): Give evidence of understanding the meaning of a familiar gesture in a familiar situation.

Test item (2-1): Mark with an X the one statement of three that best explains each gesture you see (boredom, disagreement, agreement, disappointment).

Test item (2-2) : Write the letter of the gesture shown that is most appropriate to the situation described or portrayed (lack of information, surprise, shock).

Knowledge: *Recall (External)*

Student behavior (2-b) : Show understanding of the meaning of a familiar gesture in a familiar situation.

Test item (2-3) : Explain what the gestures in the following situations mean (descriptions/film clips as above).

Test item (2-4) : Match the picture of the gesture on the left with its correct meaning selected from the list at the right.

Student behavior (2-c) : Produce a gesture appropriate to a familiar situation.

Test item (2-5) : Use a gesture that is appropriate in the following situations (annoyance; relief; greetings between friends, family members, politicians, army buddies).

Stage 3: Transfer: *Reception (Internal)*

Student behavior (3-a) : Give evidence of understanding the meaning of a familiar gesture in an unfamiliar situation.

Test item (3-1) : Write the letter of the statement that best explains each gesture you see.

Test item (3-2) : Write the letter of the gesture that is most appropriate to the situation described or portrayed (new situations, such as a long wait in line, a crowded terminal, an accident).

Transfer: *Application (External)*

Student behavior (3-b) : Give evidence of understanding the meaning of a familiar gesture in an unfamiliar situation.

Test item (3-3) : Explain the meaning of a specific gesture shown in a film clip (speaker tells of accident, listener shakes hand up and down from wrist).

Student behavior (3-c): Show what gesture or gestures might be appropriate to an unfamiliar situation.

Test item (3-4): Act out the gestures natives of the foreign culture would make in each of these situations (two school chums greet each other after summer vacation—two boys, two girls, a boy and a girl).

Test item (3-5): Play one of the roles described. Use gestures to enhance what you say or to replace verbal remarks (two motorists talk to each other after a rear-end collision).

Stage 4: Communication: *Comprehension (Internal)*

Student behavior (4-a): Demonstrate understanding of gestures used by natives in the foreign country.

Test item (4-1): Within the context of the conversation, respond verbally to the gestures made so as to demonstrate your understanding of them.

Communication: *Self-Expression (External)*

Student behavior (4-b): Use appropriate gestures in the course of a conversation.

Test item (4-2): Converse with a native in the foreign language using gestures when and where appropriate.

Stage 5: Criticism: *Analysis (Internal)*

Student behavior (5-a): Identify and explain significant gestures observed in the foreign country or in a foreign film.

Test item (5-1): Observe the people in a given situation. Identify and explain the gestures that seem significant.

Test item (5-2): Write what nonverbal messages the people in the foreign film are communicating.

Test item (5-3): Identify the speaker's social class or background by his posture and gestures.

Criticism: *Synthesis (External)*

Student behavior (5-b): Catalog gestural patterns used by speakers of different social backgrounds, geographical regions, and so on.

Test item (5-4): Establish a "kinesic atlas" defining where characteristic gestures are used.

Criticism: *Evaluation (Internal)*

Student behavior (5-c): Judge whether specific gestures are appropriate to a given situation or speaker.

Test item (5-5): Identify the person in each film clip whose gestures are inappropriate and explain why this is so.

12.3   SELF-TESTS

Take these self-tests to see how well you have understood this section. Refer back to it as needed.

Test 1: Classify the following internal student behaviors according to their taxonomic stage. Use this key: 1 = **Mechanical Skills:** *Perception*, 2 = **Knowledge:** *Recognition*, 3 = **Transfer:** *Reception*, 4 = **Communication:** *Comprehension*, 5 = **Criticism:** *Analysis, Evaluation.* Write the appropriate number in the blank.

a.____ Identify which of several familiar gestures shown is appropriate to the familiar situation described.

b.____ Demonstrate understanding of the meaning of a familiar gesture in an unfamiliar situation.

c.____ Mark whether a gesture is typical of one's own culture, a foreign culture, or both.

d.____ Demonstrate understanding of the meaning of a gesture in the foreign-culture setting.

e.____ Evaluate the appropriateness of a gesture used in a given situation.

Classify the following external student behaviors according to their taxonomic stage. Use this key: 1 = **Mechanical Skills:** *Reproduction*, 2 = **Knowledge:** *Recall*, 3 = **Transfer:** *Application*, 4 = **Communication:**

Self-Expression, 5 = **Criticism:** *Synthesis.* Write the appropriate number in the blank.

f.____ Perform a familiar gesture appropriate to a given familiar situation.

g.____ Mimic a foreign-culture gesture.

h.____ Produce a known gesture appropriate to an unfamiliar situation.

i.____ Communicate in the foreign language using appropriate gestures.

j.____ Produce a list with explanations of gestures observed in the foreign culture.

Answers: a. 2   b. 3   c. 1   d. 4   e. 5   f. 2   g. 1   h. 3   i. 4   j. 5

Test 2: Classify the following test items according to this key: 1 = **Mechanical Skills:** *Perception,* 2 = **Knowledge:** *Recognition,* 3 = **Transfer:** *Reception,* 4 = **Communication:** *Comprehension,* 5 = **Criticism:** *Analysis, Evaluation.*

Internal behaviors:

a.____ Explain the meaning of gestures you observe in the foreign culture.

b.____ Explain the meaning of familiar gestures you see in unfamiliar simulated situations.

c.____ Write an *F* if the gestures you see are typical of the foreign culture, an *N* if typical of your native culture, or *FN* if typical of both.

d.____ Indicate the possible social class or background of the speaker according to his appearance and gestures by writing "upper," "middle," or "lower."

e.____ Match the familiar gestures you see listed with familiar phrases you hear.

Classify the following test items according to this key: 1 = **Mechanical Skills:** *Reproduction,* 2 = **Knowledge:** *Recall,* 3 = **Transfer:** *Application,* 4 = **Communication:** *Self-Expression,* 5 = **Criticism:** *Synthesis.*

External behaviors:

f.____ Perform the gesture appropriate to the familiar expressions you hear.

g.____ Imitate the gestures you see.

h.____ Keep a notebook in which you list significant gestures you observe and the foreign-culture situations that provoked them.

i.____ During a visit abroad, demonstrate that you can use gestures appropriate to what you say.

j.____ Play the role assigned to you in this unfamiliar simulation of a foreign-culture situation, using any gestures that might reinforce what you say.

Answers: a. 4   b. 3   c. 1   d. 4   e. 2   f. 2   g. 1   h. 5   i. 4   j. 3

Test 3: Check the test items that might be appropriate measures of the desired behavior listed above them. In each case, the number of items to be checked is indicated in parentheses after the desired behavior.

1. Use appropriate gestures while speaking the foreign language. (2)

____a. Play a role in this simulated situation.

____b. Indicate which of the following gestures might accompany each of the following sentences.

____c. During a visit abroad, show that you can command the gestures commonly used by natives.

____d. Describe a situation in which each of the following gestures might be used.

2. Differentiate gestures of the foreign culture from those of one's own culture. (1)

____a. Act out the following situation in the foreign language.

____b. Write whether the gestures you see in the following silent film clips are typical of the foreign culture, your own culture, or both.

____c. List five commonly used foreign-culture gestures.

____d. Explain the meaning of the gestures used in the following situations.

3. Analyze a speaker's gestures. (1)

____a. Judging from the gestures observed, write whether each speaker apparently belongs to the upper-, middle-, or lower-class.

____b. Imitate the gestures you see.

____c. Evaluate the effectiveness of the gestures each speaker uses.

____d. Judge the appropriateness of the gestures you see.

4. Demonstrate understanding of foreign-culture gestures. (2)

_____a. Write whether each gesture you see is typical or not of the foreign culture.

_____b. Write an *X* by the one picture in a group of three that shows a gesture appropriate to each situation described.

_____c. Circle the letter of the explanation in each group that most accurately describes the purposes of the gestures shown.

_____d. Explain briefly the significance of the gestures in these film clips.

5. Carry out original research in foreign-culture gestures. (3)

_____a. Present a plan for observing the gestures of natives of the foreign culture.

_____b. Evaluate the effectiveness of the simulations you see.

_____c. Summarize the reading you have done in the field of body language.

_____d. Report the results of your observations of gestures in the foreign culture.

Answers: 1. a, c   2. b   3. a   4. c, d   5. a, b, d

CHAPTER THIRTEEN
WAY-OF-LIFE
CULTURE

Learning about the way of life of the people who speak the foreign language is becoming increasingly important in second-language courses. Primary emphasis seems to be placed on the internal behaviors—that is, in developing an awareness of unique features in the new culture and in understanding values, themes, and concepts of that culture. As in the case of gestures, the development of the external behaviors relating to way-of-life culture leads to the formation of a bicultural individual. The following sections present both internal and external behaviors. It is left to the individual teacher to determine which ones should be emphasized.

13.1 STAGES OF BEHAVIOR

Stage 1: Mechanical Skills: *Perception* (*Internal*)

The student can indicate if the objects, people, or scenes he sees are typical of the foreign culture, his own culture, or both.

Mechanical Skills: *Reproduction* (*External*)

The student sings a foreign-language song or recites from memory a poem, fable, or saying.

190

Stage 2: Knowledge: *Recognition* (*Internal*)

The student recognizes familiar information he has learned. He indicates if facts about the culture are true or false, matches specialized terms with their definitions, and answers factual multiple-choice questions.

Knowledge: *Recall* (*External*)

The student recalls information he has acquired about the way of life in the foreign culture. He answers questions, supplies terminology and definitions, or fills in blanks with the information requested.

Stage 3: Transfer: *Reception* (*Internal*)

The student comprehends familiar elements in unfamiliar situations in the light of his background knowledge of the way of life in the foreign culture.

Transfer: *Application* (*External*)

The student uses his knowledge of the foreign culture to play the role of a member of that culture in simulated situations.

Stage 4: Communication: *Comprehension* (*Internal*)

The student understands what behavior is expected of him in the foreign culture. He notices cultural references within a message and understands what these references mean to natives of the culture.

Communication: *Self-Expression* (*External*)

In the foreign country, the student reacts as a native. At the highest development of this stage he has become bicultural.

Stage 5: Criticism: *Analysis* (*Internal*)

The student compares and contrasts significant aspects of the foreign culture with their counterparts in other cultures or in his own culture.

Criticism: *Synthesis* (*External*)

The student recreates aspects of the culture and can produce a plan for further study of its way of life.

Criticism: *Evaluation* (*Internal*)

The student judges the validity or worth of generalizations regarding the foreign culture. He evaluates the way of life in this culture either in terms of how well it accomplishes social purposes or in terms of his own personal criteria, ethics, or aesthetics.

13.2 EXAMPLES

This section contains many examples of partial performance objectives in the area of way-of-life culture behaviors. They include student behaviors and test items that can be used to measure them. Since conditions and criteria will vary considerably according to classes, language level, facilities, and so on, these parts of the performance objective have not been specified here. It is left to the individual teacher to formulate them for his own situation. The purpose of all the partial performance objectives presented here is to develop knowledge and understanding of the way of life in the foreign culture under study.

Stage 1: Mechanical Skills: *Perception (Internal)*

Student behavior (1-a): Write whether the action, scene, or picture you see is typical of the foreign country, your own, or both.

Test item (1-1): Check the appropriate column to show if the picture you see characterizes the foreign country, your own, or both (street scenes, houses, classrooms, dinner table, café).

Student behavior (1-b): Distinguish objects or behaviors that are typical of the foreign culture but not of one's own culture.

Test item (1-2): Write out what in the picture or scene strikes you as foreign (clothing, animals, types of stores).

Mechanical Skills: *Reproduction (External)*

Student behavior (1-c): Produce orally or in writing a foreign-language song, poem, fable, or saying that has been memorized.

Test item (1-3): Recite or write the material you have memorized.

Stage 2: Knowledge: *Recognition (Internal)*

Student behavior (2-a): Demonstrate knowledge of familiar factual material.

Test item (2-1): Write whether the following statements are true or false (meal times, customs, school system, holidays).

Test item (2-2): Match each definition at the left with the word at the right it defines (cooking terms, ceremonies, sports, feast days).

Test item (2-3): Mark the choice that best completes each of the following statements (generalization on attitudes, cultural values, themes, trends).

Knowledge: *Recall* (*External*)

Student behavior (2-b): Supply factual information that has been learned.

Test item (2-4): Define the following words in terms of the foreign culture: *machismo, la raza, Menschligkeit, Gemütlichkeit.*

Test item (2-5): Respond to the following short-answer or essay questions (current events, trends, problems, or issues in the foreign culture).

Stage 3: Transfer: *Reception* (*Internal*)

Student behavior (3-a): Using one's background knowledge of the foreign culture, demonstrate the ability to make inferences or to draw conclusions in unfamiliar situations.

Test item (3-1): Mark the statement that is the most likely explanation of each news item (man vindicated in a trial of a crime of passion, parents held responsible for crimes of son).

Test item (3-2): Write the letter of the most likely reaction of a native culture in each of these situations (verbal insult, stranger at the door).

Transfer: *Application* (*External*)

Student behavior (3-b): Simulate actions and reactions of members of the foreign culture in role-playing situations.

Test item (3-3): Play the role of a highly critical Frenchman visiting the United States for the first time.

Stage 4: Communication: *Comprehension* (*Internal*)

Student behavior (4-a): Demonstrate understanding of the way of life within the foreign-culture setting.

Test item (4-1): Explain why the native is reacting as he is to conditions or to life in the foreign country (film clips, experience living abroad).

Communication: *Self-Expression* (*External*)

Student behavior (4-b): Demonstrate ability to function as a native in the foreign culture.

Test item (4-2): React as a native probably would in these situations (shopping in stores, ordering food in a restaurant).

Stage 5: Criticism: *Analysis* (*Internal*)

Student behavior (5-a): Observe and describe elements, structures, or institutions of the foreign culture.

Test item (5-1): State what attitudes and values are operating in each of these unfamiliar situations (teacher-student relations, citizen paying or not paying taxes, parent scolding child).

Student behavior (5-b): Compare and contrast one's own culture with the foreign culture.

Test item (5-2): Write about differences and similiarities between the foreign culture and your own (family relations, food, school).

Test item (5-3): Describe what difficulties an American might encounter if his work forced him to move to the foreign country.

Criticism: *Synthesis* (*External*)

Student behavior (5-c): Re-create aspects of the foreign culture.

Test item (5-4): Write a short story or produce a film that conveys information about a significant aspect of the way of life in the foreign country.

Student behavior (5-d): Produce a plan for studying the foreign culture.

Test item (5-5): Describe how you would carry out research in the foreign country.

Criticism: *Evaluation (Internal)*

Student behavior (5-e): Evaluate strengths and weaknesses of the foreign culture in terms of its own purposes.

Test item (5-6): Discuss the advantages and disadvantages of the French desire to increase the influence of the French language and culture.

Student behavior (5-f): Evaluate the foreign culture in terms of one's own native culture.

Test item (5-7): Describe what you like and dislike most about life in the foreign culture.

Student behavior (5-g): Evaluate the worth, reliability, or importance of information or sources of information on the foreign culture.

Test item (5-8): Mark whether the information from each of these sources should be considered highly reliable, of limited reliability, or in need of further investigation (statistics, tourist impressions, travel brochures, book by eminent authority).

13.3   SELF-TESTS

Take these self-tests to see how well you have understood this section. Refer back to it as needed.

Test 1: Classify the following internal student behaviors according to their taxonomic stage. Use this key: 1 = **Mechanical Skills:** *Perception,* 2 = **Knowledge:** *Recognition,* 3 = **Transfer:** *Reception,* 4 = **Communication:** *Comprehension,* 5 = **Criticism:** *Analysis, Evaluation.*

Internal behaviors:

a.____ Recognize familiar facts.

b.____ Demonstrate understanding of the way of life in the foreign country.

c.____ Mark whether a picture or scene is typical of one's own culture, the foreign culture, or both.

d.____ Use background knowledge of the foreign culture to understand an unfamiliar anecdote.

e.____ Contrast patterns of living in one's culture with their counterparts in the foreign culture.

Classify the following behaviors according to this key: 1 = **Mechanical Skills:** *Reproduction,* 2 = **Knowledge:** *Recall,* 3 = **Transfer:** *Application,* 4 = **Communication:** *Self-Expression,* 5 = **Criticism:** *Synthesis.*

External behaviors:

f.____ Sing a foreign-culture song from memory.

g.____ Act as a native in the foreign country.

h.____ Define these familiar terms.

i.____ Play the role of a native of the foreign country.

j.____ Re-create typical aspects of the foreign culture.

Answers: a. 2   b. 4   c. 1   d. 3   e. 5   f. 1   g. 4   h. 2   i. 3   j. 5

Test 2: Classify the following test items according to this key: 1 = **Mechanical Skills:** *Perception,* 2 = **Knowledge:** *Recognition,* 3 = **Transfer:** *Reception,* 4 = **Communication:** *Comprehension,* 5 = **Criticism:** *Analysis, Evaluation.*

Internal behaviors:

a.____ Mark whether the pictures you see are typical of your own culture, the foreign culture, or both.

b.____ Prepare a scrapbook of snapshots (with captions) portraying typical aspects of the way of life in the foreign culture.

c.____ Check the appropriate column to indicate whether the following unfamiliar statements about the foreign culture are true or false.

d.____ Show by appropriate behavior that you understand the way of life in the foreign-culture setting in which you live.

e.____ Using background knowledge of culture, indicate which choice best explains the reactions of the people in each unfamiliar situation.

Classify the following test items according to this key: 1 = **Mechanical Skills:** *Reproduction,* 2 = **Knowledge:** *Recall,* 3 = **Transfer:** *Application,* 4 = **Communication:** *Self-Expression,* 5 = **Criticism:** *Synthesis.*

External behaviors:

f.____ Recite the poem you have memorized.

g.____ Present your plan for studying the patterns of living in the foreign culture.

h.____ State briefly five rules concerning the serving of wine (familiar material).

i.____ Demonstrate in your behavior abroad that you can emulate the actions and attitudes of native members of the culture.

j.____ Play a given role in a simulated foreign-culture situation.

Answers: a. 1   b. 5   c. 2   d. 4   e. 3   f. 1   g. 5   h. 2   i. 4   j. 3

Test 3: Check the test items that might be appropriate measures of the desired behavior listed above them. In each case, the number of items to be checked is indicated in parentheses after the desired behavior.

1. Demonstrate cultural understanding in unfamiliar contexts. (2)

____a. Predict which would be the most likely reaction of a native member of the foreign culture in these situations.

____b. Match the following terms with an appropriate definition.

____c. Write whether the facts in the following statements are true or false.

____d. Explain what the statements of each of the following people mean.

2. Analyze the patterns of living in the foreign culture. (1)

____a. Pattern your daily routine according to that of the surrounding foreign culture.

____b. Compare living in the foreign culture with life in your own culture.

____c. Take the role of a native in the following simulation.

____d. Write whether the following customs are or are not typical of the foreign culture.

3. Display knowledge of the foreign culture. (3)

____a. Recite the poem or fable you have memorized.

____b. Write the term whose definition you see.

_____c. Select the choice that best completes the statement.

_____d. Fill in the blank with an appropriate completion for each of these statements.

4. Apply cultural knowledge to new situations. (2)

    _____a. Explain in writing any three of the cultural conflicts taught in class.

    _____b. List significant cultural themes found in newspaper or magazine articles from the foreign country.

    _____c. Prepare a list of sources that would be helpful for research in a particular area of interest.

    _____d. Describe how a native of the foreign culture would most probably react to the following situations if he encountered them in your native culture.

5. Re-create an aspect of life in the foreign culture. (3)

    _____a. Describe a typical day in the life of a worker (material gained from experience living abroad).

    _____b. Write whether the following customs are typical or not of the foreign culture.

    _____c. Prepare a meal typical of the foreign culture.

    _____d. Describe the routine of a housewife according to your observations while living abroad.

Answers: 1. a, d   2. b   3. b, c, d   4. b, d   5. a, c, d

CHAPTER FOURTEEN
CIVILIZATION

Civilization, as the term is used in this handbook, refers to the physical aspects of the foreign country (or countries), its history, political system, and contributions to the advancement of man in areas such as science and technology, medicine, philosophy, architecture, and the arts. (Literature will be treated separately, since it is an art form that cuts across the areas of language, civilization, and culture.) Behaviors in the area of civilization are primarily of the internal type. The foreign-language student is expected to increase in his knowledge and understanding of the foreign civilization. Of course, it is not the intention of the foreign-language teacher to develop in his students the skills of a scientist, doctor, historian, political scientist, or geographer. However, the teacher might want his students to be able to create plans of study for further independent research into a particular area of interest in the foreign civilization. Consequently, the only external behaviors appearing in the taxonomy below are those of recall and synthesis; all others are internal behaviors.

14.1 STAGES OF BEHAVIOR

Stage 1: Mechanical Skills: *Perception* (*Internal*)

The student notices similarities and differences between styles of music, painting, sculpture, and architecture of both his native and the foreign culture.

Stage 2: Knowledge: *Recognition (Internal)*

The student recognizes familiar facts he has learned. He can identify familiar works of art, buildings, monuments, sculpture, musical works, and so on. He demonstrates his knowledge on matching and multiple-choice tests.

Knowledge: *Recall (External)*

The student produces the information learned. He answers questions, supplies explanations, definitions, and descriptions and lists causes, themes, events, people, dates, and so on.

Stage 3: Transfer: *Reception (Internal)*

The student identifies the artist or style of works he has never seen before. He relates unfamiliar quotations to their author or historical period.

Stage 4: Communication: *Comprehension (Internal)*

The student interprets quotations, cartoons, and statistical or graphic data.

Stage 5: Criticism: *Analysis (Internal)*

The student analyzes a musical or artistic work or a historical document or text. He compares or contrasts two or more works or documents. He relates an artistic work or historical document to its period.

Criticism: *Synthesis (External)*

The student organizes and carries out a research project in one of the social sciences or humanities related to the language and culture under study.

Criticism: *Evaluation (Internal)*

The student judges the merits of works of art or music or evaluates the careers and contributions of famous people (scientists, artists, politicians, philosophers, rulers).

14.2 EXAMPLES

This section contains examples of partial performance objectives in the area of civilization. They include student behaviors and test items that can be used to measure them. Since conditions and criteria will vary considerably according to classes, language level, facilities, and so on, these parts of the performance objective have not been specified here. It is left to the individual teacher to formulate them for his own situation. The purpose of all the partial performance objectives presented here is to develop knowledge and understanding of the civilization of the foreign country or countries under study.

Stage 1: Mechanical Skills: *Perception (Internal)*

Student behavior (1-a): Demonstrate ability to differentiate between architectural and artistic styles.

Test item (1-1): Look at each group of three slides or pictures and mark which two monuments or paintings represent the same style.

Student behavior (1-b): Recognize similarities in musical styles.

Test item (1-2): Listen to portions of these two symphonies or operas and write whether they sound alike or different.

Stage 2: Knowledge: *Recognition (Internal)*

Student behavior (2-a): Recognize familiar information.

Test item (2-1): Match the following monuments or styles, paintings or artists, inventors or inventions, scientists or discoveries, regions or products, countries or capitals, architecture or centuries.

Test item: (2-2): Answer the following multiple-choice questions (on history, art, government, geography, music, famous men).

Knowledge: *Recall (External)*

Student behavior (2-b): Recall familiar information.

Test item (2-3): Name the artist, architect, or composer who created each of the following works.

Test item (2-4): List the major causes of the _____ revolution.

Test item (2-5): Describe the structure of the _____ government.

Test item (2-6): List the major industrial and agricultural products of the foreign country.

Test item (2-7): Answer each of the following questions in one or two words (on history, geography, art, government, music, famous men).

Test item (2-8): Draw a map of _____, indicating the following features: rivers, cities, mountains, boundaries.

Stage 3: Transfer: *Reception (Internal)*

Student behavior (3-a): Apply knowledge to new situations.

Test item (3-1): Identify the style of the following unfamiliar buildings, monuments, paintings, or musical works.

Test item (3-2): Identify the artist or composer of each of these unfamiliar works.

Student behavior (3-b): Demonstrate understanding of brief, unfamiliar quotes of remarks by philosophers, composers, and artists.

Test item (3-3): State in your own words the basic position or idea of the author of each of these short quotations.

Stage 4: Communication: *Comprehension (Internal)*

Student behavior (4-a): Interpret political cartoons.

Test item (4-1): Explain the cartoon below in terms of your knowledge of the historical period or the current events.

Student behavior (4-b): Demonstrate understanding of statistical information.

Test item (4-2): Interpret the data presented in the following chart, graph, or table (population figures, gross national product, industrial or agricultural production).

Student behavior (4-c): Demonstrate understanding of historic, philosophic, and aesthetic ideas.

Test item (4-3): Express in your own words the views presented in this unfamiliar essay or text.

Test item (4-4): Write a letter or diary entry from the point of view of _____ on the day before or after a momentous event in his life (politician, general, king, philosopher, scientist, inventor).

Stage 5: Criticism: *Analysis (Internal)*

Student behavior (5-a): Analyze a work of art.

Test item (5-1): Analyze the unfamiliar painting, sculpture, or musical work (structure, composition, methods of achieving its effects).

Criticism: *Synthesis (External)*

Student behavior (5-b): Formulate a plan of study in the field of civilization.

Test item (5-2): Write out an original hypothesis in a field of interest to you and list the steps you would take to pursue your research.

Student behavior: (5-c): Carry out original research in the field of civilization.

Test item (5-3): Produce a thesis, monograph, or book that contributes significant new information and understanding to the field of _____ (philosophy, art, music, history).

Criticism: *Evaluation (Internal)*

Student behavior (5-d): Evaluate the contributions of the civilization to the world.

Test item (5-4): Evaluate the contributions of _____ to art, music, political science, or philosophy.

14.3   SELF-TESTS

Take these self-tests to see how well you have understood this section. Refer back to it as needed.

Test 1: Classify the following student behaviors according to their taxonomic stage. Use this key: 1 = **Mechanical Skills,** *Perception,* 2 = **Knowl-**

edge: *Recognition, Recall,* 3 = **Transfer:** *Reception,* 4 = **Communication:** *Comprehension,* 5 = **Criticism:** *Analysis, Synthesis, Evaluation.*

a.____ List in chronological order the following familiar historical events.

b.____ Interpret political cartoons in the light of your background knowledge.

c.____ Assess the effect of an important historical event on the nation based on personal research and original thought.

d.____ Identify the style of monuments never seen before.

e.____ State whether two works of art or music belong to the same or different periods.

f.____ Paraphrase the ideas presented in an unfamiliar text by a philosopher studied in class.

g.____ Discuss the subject, technique, and ideas in an unfamiliar painting by an artist previously studied.

h.____ State the philosophical position represented in unfamiliar quotations.

i.____ Present a proposal for individual research into an area of personal interest.

j.____ Fill in the important geographical features of the foreign country on an outline map.

Answers: a. 2   b. 4   c. 5   d. 3   e. 1   f. 4   g. 3   h. 3   i. 5   j. 2

Test 2: Classify the following test items according to this key: 1 = **Mechanical Skills:** *Perception,* 2 = **Knowledge:** *Recognition, Recall,* 3 = **Transfer:** *Reception,* 4 = **Communication:** *Comprehension,* 5 = **Criticism:** *Analysis, Synthesis, Evaluation.*

a.____ Write what trends may reasonably be predicted based on extrapolations from the statistical tables presented.

b.____ Look at the pictures of these unfamiliar buildings and list them in chronological order according to when they were most probably erected.

c.____ List the major agricultural and industrial products of each of the following regions based on information acquired in class.

d.____ Compare and contrast the work of two artists of your choice.

e.____ Paint in the style of an artist of your choice.

f.___ Write an essay discussing the causes of ___ (major historical event that has been treated in the course).

g.___ Develop a research hypothesis in a field of interest to you and outline how you intend to carry it out.

h.___ Discuss the strengths and weaknesses of a work of unfamiliar music by a composer from the foreign country.

i.___ Indicate what architectural period the style of these unfamiliar monuments or buildings represent.

j.___ Indicate which response choice expresses the same meaning of the following unfamiliar quotations from well-known historical figures.

Answers: a. 4   b. 3   c. 3   d. 4   e. 3   f. 2   g. 5   h. 5   i. 3   j. 4

Test 3: Check the test items that might be appropriate measures of the desired behavior listed above them. In each case the number of items to be checked is indicated in parentheses after the desired behavior.

1. Recognize styles of unfamiliar works of art. (1)

   ___a. Number each picture in the following groups of five to indicate their chronological order.

   ___b. Discuss the style of this painting.

   ___c. Match the painting styles on the left with their appropriate definitions on the right.

   ___d. Write which of the following styles is exemplified by each painting shown.

2. Demonstrate understanding of unfamiliar material read. (2)

   ___a. Summarize the philosophic position set forth in this text.

   ___b. Rewrite this historical declaration in your own words.

   ___c. Underline examples of inflammatory prose in the following passage.

   ___d. Write the letter of the political position represented by each of the quotations below.

3. Analyze a work of art. (3)

   ___a. Compare and contrast two paintings of your choice that have not previously been presented in class.

   ___b. Discuss the structure of an unfamiliar musical composition.

____c. Describe the relationship of this monument, not previously shown in class, to its historic period.

____d. List criteria one should use in judging a work of art.

4. Display knowledge of the foreign civilization. (3)

____a. Present in outline form the background causes of the ____ Revolution (familiar).

____b. Match each of the kings on the left with the event on the right that occurred during his reign.

____c. Pretend you are a famous historical figure. Write a letter that he might have written.

____d. List five principal mountains, rivers, and cities of the foreign country being studied.

5. Evaluate the cultural output of a civilization. (3)

____a. Select a favorite painter and explain why you enjoy his work.

____b. Discuss the influence a given philosopher has had on your thinking.

____c. React to the following statements regarding the civilization of the foreign country. You may agree or disagree.

____d. List an important contribution of each of these famous men.

Answers: 1. d   2. a, b   3. a, b, c   4. a, b, d   5. a, b, c

CHAPTER FIFTEEN
LITERATURE

The study of literature in its original language formerly constituted the main goal of foreign-language study. Currently, however, this aim is only one of several. Since students of literature are not expected to produce literary works themselves, behaviors in this area of instruction are generally of the internal type, with the exception of the external behaviors of reproduction and recall.

An important consideration in classifying behaviors in the area of literature is that of familiarity. A student may determine accurately the meter or rhyme scheme of a poem, ostensibly a Stage 3 behavior, but if the poem has previously been analyzed in class, such behavior falls into Stage 2. Similarly, a student may explain figures of speech and symbols (Stage 4) or produce a fine *explication de texte* or an evaluation of a work (Stage 5), but if his work is based on class discussions or lectures, his behavior should be classified no higher than Stage 2.

15.1 STAGES OF BEHAVIOR

Stage 1: Mechanical Skills: *Reproduction (External)*

The student recites a poem or fable that has been memorized.

Stage 2: Knowledge: *Recognition* (*Internal*)

The student recognizes information he has learned regarding authors, dates, places, characters, quotations, literary works, and so on. He answers matching, multiple-choice, or true-false questions on these.

Knowledge: *Recall* (*External*)

The student can recall the authors, dates, places, characters, quotations, literary works, analyses, ideas, and so on, he has learned. He identifies the author of certain familiar works or the person responsible for a familiar quotation. He defines specialized terminology and lists events, ideas, themes, or purposes he has been taught. He summarizes familiar works and writes out the analyses presented in class. All the information he supplies has been gained either from his textbook or from class lectures and discussions.

Stage 3: Transfer: *Reception* (*Internal*)

The student can identify or point out figures of speech in passages he has never seen before. He can determine the meter or rhyme scheme of an unfamiliar poem.

Stage 4: Communication: *Comprehension* (*Internal*)

The student understands unfamiliar figures of speech, irony, symbolism, or parables in literary works presented to him for explanation. He uses his knowledge of an author, character, literary period, genre, or work to explain a given quotation or brief text. He can state the general themes or main ideas of stories or poems not previously encountered.

Stage 5: Criticism: *Analysis* (*Internal*)

The student analyzes unfamiliar literary texts in terms of their structure, style, character, conflicts, themes, ideas, and so on. He compares and contrasts different authors, works, and periods. He is able to explicate in detail an unfamiliar text. Here, as opposed to the behavior in the preceding stage, the student, not the teacher, selects examples to be explained.

Criticism: *Evaluation* (*Internal*)

The student judges the merit or worth of a literary work in terms of its own purposes or criteria or in terms of his personal criteria or aesthetics.

15.2   EXAMPLES

This section contains examples of partial performance objectives in the area of literature. They include student behaviors and test items that can be used to measure them. Since conditions and criteria will vary considerably according to classes, language level, facilities, and so on, these parts of the performance objective have not been specified here. It is left to the individual teacher to formulate them for his own situation. The purpose of all the partial performance objectives presented here is to develop knowledge and understanding of the literature of the foreign language under study.

Stage 1: Mechanical Skills: *Reproduction (External)*

Student behavior (1-a): Memorize a poem or fable.

Test item (1-1): Recite the poem or fable you have learned.

Stage 2: Knowledge: *Recognition (Internal)*

Student behavior (2-a): Recognize familiar facts presented in books or class lectures.

Test item (2-1): Match the following book titles with their authors.

Test item (2-2): Match the following characters or quotations with the works to which they belong.

Test item (2-3): Answer the following multiple-choice or true-false questions (literary history).

Knowledge: *Recall (External)*

Student behavior (2-b): Identify an author, work, character, quotation, or term.

Test item (2-4): Name the author of each of the following works.

Test item (2-5): Name the work in which each of the following characters or quotations appears.

Student behavior (2-c): Demonstrate knowledge of factual material.

Test item (2-6): Answer briefly the following questions based on your text and class notes.

Test item (2-7): State the main ideas of the following works that have been discussed.

Test item (2-8): Define each of the following terms (genres, types of rhymes, figures of speech).

Test item (2-9): Discuss the major characters, themes, or ideas of these literary periods or authors.

Student behavior (2-d): Demonstrate knowledge of literary criticism.

Test item (2-10): Write which school of criticism each of these critics represents.

Test item (2-11): State briefly the opinion of _____ in regard to the work of _____.

Stage 3: Transfer: *Reception (Internal)*

Student behavior (3-a): Identify figures of speech, symbols, meter, or rhyme scheme.

Test item (3-1): Underline the similes, metaphors, or symbols in this unfamiliar poem or passage.

Test item (3-2): Write out the meter and rhyme scheme of this sonnet.

Student behavior (3-b): Identify literary genres.

Test item (3-3): Write whether each of the following texts is a ballad, ode, rondeau, or sonnet.

Stage 4: Communication: *Comprehension (Internal)*

Student behavior (4-a): Demonstrate understanding of unfamiliar figures of speech, irony, symbolism, or parables.

Test item (4-1): Mark an X by the choice that best explains the underlined figure of speech.

Test item (4-2) : Explain the meaning of the underlined figures of speech or of the following fable or parable.

Student behavior (4-b) : Demonstrate understanding of the purpose of an essay, play, novel, or poem.

Test item (4-3) : Explain what the author tries to say or to accomplish in the work you have read that has not been studied in class.

Stage 5: Criticism: *Analysis* (*Internal*)

Student behavior (5-a) : Analyze an unfamiliar work.

Test item (5-1) : Describe the structure, style, conflicts, or themes in the work read.

Test item (5-2) : Discuss the role of women, love, humor, or fate in _____.

Test item (5-3) : Describe how the author's use of figures of speech helps him achieve his effect.

Test item (5-4) : Discuss how the work you have read does or does not reflect its literary period.

Test item (5-5) : Trace the development of the plot in the work read.

Test item (5-6) : Describe the development of the main character throughout the novel read.

Student behavior (5-b) : Explain an unfamiliar text.

Test item (5-7) : Explain the following text. Consider connotations and denotations of words used, style, tone, effects, figures of speech, rhythm, rhyme (if applicable), situation of the text in relation to the life, and work of the author.

Criticism: *Evaluation* (*Internal*)

Student behavior (5-c) : Evaluate a literary work according to intrinsic or extrinsic criteria.

Test item (5-8) : Evaluate the work read according to the aesthetics or criteria proposed by the author.

Test item (5-9): Evaluate the work read according to your personal aesthetics.

15.3 SELF-TESTS

Take these self-tests to see how well you have understood this section. Refer back to it as needed.

Test 1: Classify the following student behaviors according to this key: 1 = **Mechanical Skills:** *Reproduction,* 2 = **Knowledge:** *Recognition, Recall,* 3 = **Transfer:** *Reception,* 4 = **Communication:** *Comprehension,* 5 = **Criticism:** *Analysis, Evaluation.*

a.____ Identify the character who utters a quotation selected from one of the books read.

b.____ Write out the rhyme scheme of an unfamiliar poem.

c.____ Memorize a poem.

d.____ Demonstrate understanding of figures of speech in unfamiliar texts.

e.____ Supply definitions of literary terms presented in class.

f.____ Discuss the role of fate in two plays read outside of class.

g.____ Judge the merit of a book read outside of class.

h.____ Identify the genre of an unfamiliar poem.

i.____ Explain a particular symbol within the context of an unfamiliar work.

j.____ Explain an unfamiliar text.

Answers: a. 2   b. 3   c. 1   d. 4   e. 2   f. 4   g. 5   h. 3   i. 4   j. 4

Test 2: Classify the following test items according to this key: 1 = **Mechanical Skills:** *Perception,* 2 = **Knowledge:** *Recognition, Recall,* 3 = **Transfer:** *Reception,* 4 = **Communication:** *Comprehension,* 5 = **Criticism:** *Analysis, Evaluation.*

a.____ Discuss in writing the literary significance of ____ (work studied in class).

b.____ Study the relationship between form and content in an unfamiliar text of your choice.

c.＿＿ Mark which of the following meanings is appropriate to the figures of speech underlined in the unfamiliar text.

d.＿＿ Circle the figures of speech in the following unfamiliar text.

e.＿＿ Write an essay on whether the following unfamiliar text fulfills the aesthetic criteria proposed by the author. Justify your response with examples from the text.

f.＿＿ Trace the psychological development of the main character throughout a book not previously discussed in class.

g.＿＿ Explain in your own words the meaning of the following unfamiliar parable or fable.

h.＿＿ For each of the following unfamiliar quatrains, write what kind of rhyme the poet employs (riche, plate, embracée, and so on).

i.＿＿ Analyze the characteristics of romanticism and realism based on information presented in class and in the text.

j.＿＿ Attack or defend the idea of the three dramatic unities. Provide illustrations from personal outside reading.

Answers: a. 2   b. 4   c. 4   d. 3   e. 5   f. 5   g. 4   h. 3   i. 2   j. 5

Test 3: Check the test items that might be appropriate measures of the desired behavior listed above them. In each case the number of items to be checked is indicated in parentheses after the desired behavior.

1. Analyze a poem. (2)

＿＿a. Explain the following text.

＿＿b. Discuss the form of a poem read outside of class.

＿＿c. Analyze a poem discussed in class.

＿＿d. Indicate which of the listed genres is exemplified in each of the following poems.

2. Demonstrate understanding of material read. (2)

＿＿a. Characterize the style of each of these passages.

＿＿b. Express in your own words the idea in each paragraph.

＿＿c. Explain the meaning of the underlined figures of speech.

＿＿d. Circle the similes and metaphors in the following paragraphs.

3. Demonstrate recognition of factual material. (2)

_____a. Identify briefly the following authors.

_____b. Define the following literary terms.

_____c. Mark which of the following choices most accurately completes each statement.

_____d. Match authors and their works.

4. Evaluate literary works. (2)

_____a. Explain why you did or did not react favorably to the work read outside of class.

_____b. Summarize several critical opinions of the novel read.

_____c. Discuss in writing whether the book does or does not represent its era.

_____d. Appraise the book in terms of the purposes the author has set forth.

5. Apply one's knowledge to new situations. (3)

_____a. Write out the rhyme scheme of the following unfamiliar poems.

_____b. Judge the play you have seen in terms of your dramatic background.

_____c. Underline examples of alliteration in these unfamiliar passages.

_____d. Mark the meter of this unfamiliar poem.

Answers: 1. a, b   2. b, c   3. c, d   4. a, d   5. a, c, d

APPENDIX

The Appendix includes the following three sections:

A. Sample introductory material and a sample performance contract for a second-year French class in a high school using a pass or fail grading system. Completion dates have been inserted since all students must cover a prescribed amount of work during the school year. Within this limitation, however, students are allowed to retake their tests outside of class until the end of the grading period if they have not yet mastered the material. Grades above seventy are achieved by contracting for additional extra-credit communication tests.

B. A sample introduction, lesson contract, and evaluation forms for a first-year German class in which student progress is evaluated in units of credit completed with a grade of A or B. There are no suggested completion dates, and students receive credit only for the amount of work they have performed. The units of credit that can be earned in one year may range from one to thirty. Each student is theoretically free to "goof off" completely; he would, then, receive no credit for the course, but he would not fail.

C. A sample set of performance criteria that prospective French teachers (college seniors) must meet before acceptance as student teachers in secondary schools.

APPENDIX A

I. INTRODUCTORY MATERIALS

Distribute the following information at the beginning of the school year to orient the students to the contract method of teaching.

A. Advantages of Learning French with the Contract Method

1. Less boredom from:

Listening to explanations you already understand.
Listening to explanations which don't interest you.
Listening to slow-moving homework corrections.
Listening to other students' responses.
Waiting for the rest of the class to finish a test.
Waiting for the teacher to begin class or to hand out papers.
Listening to the teacher for the whole period.

2. More personal attention from:

Classmates who can explain materials to you.
Student aides who can explain your errors on homework and tests.
Your teacher who can present new grammar, offer additional explanations when needed, talk to you informally in French, administer individual oral tests, help you individually with your compositions, and adjust your contract requirements to suit your individual needs.

3. More freedom to:

Regulate the amount of homework you do each night.
Choose the day you want to take certain tests.
Move around in class and learn from your friends.
Follow your own particular interests after consulting your teacher.
Learn at your own rate (within certain limits).

4. More personal responsibility for:

Deciding for yourself how you will use your daily class time.
Assigning yourself homework.
Deciding which extra-credit assignments to do.

The introductory material and performance contract were prepared by Renée Disick for use in Valley Stream Central High School, Long Island, New York, to accompany *A-LM French Level Two*, 2d ed. (New York: Harcourt Brace Jovanovich, Inc., 1970).

Determining which language skills you want to emphasize.

Directing your own learning.

5. Less anxiety from:

Having to participate orally in full-class discussions.

Too much homework on one day.

Too many tests on one day.

Low grades. (You may retake your tests to score higher grades.)

Missing new work because of absence.

Not knowing what tests will be like or how they will be graded.

Not knowing how well you are doing in a course.

6. Better grades because:

You may take most tests three times (or sometimes more) in order to pass.

Only lack of effort on your part can result in failure.

You will be given whatever individual help you need in order to pass.

You will have many opportunities to earn extra credit.

B. How to Learn with the Contract Method

1. At the beginning of each new unit, you will receive a contract describing exactly tests that you are required to take to demonstrate your mastery of the material.

2. There will be a list of activities (learning steps) with each test description that will help you to prepare for the test.

3. The contract will also describe additional communication assignments that you may elect to complete for extra credit.

4. You may take both required and optional tests when you are ready for them, but within the limits of the deadlines stipulated in the contract.

5. All tests will be graded on the "pass/fail" system. On vocabulary and grammar tests, 80 percent is "pass." On optional communication tests, comprehensibility in oral or written work determines a "pass" grade.

6. If you have earned a "pass" on all required tests, your report card grade will be seventy. The points you have earned from extra-credit assignments will be added to the report card grade.

7. At the beginning of each contract, you will sign a statement indicating how many extra points a week you intend to earn

during the ten-week marking period and what report card grade you wish to achieve.

8. You may retake a grammar test as many as three times if you do not pass on the first try. There are no limits (except time) to the number of times you may take vocabulary or oral tests. Each listening comprehension and unit test may be taken only once.

9. There will be no full-class lectures from Tuesday through Friday. You will work instead in small groups, but the teacher will be available for help and explanations when needed.

10. On Mondays, the class will meet as a whole to participate in one or more of the following activities: listening comprehension practice, lectures or discussions on culture, games in French, films, slides, guest speakers, and so on.

11. Contracts will be negotiable. You will have the freedom to discuss your contract with the teacher and to substitute assignments you would enjoy more for some of the ones listed.

12. There will be no homework assigned by the teacher, but you will assign your own homework. You will find that you must work outside of class to meet the deadlines.

13. All exercises and tests will be corrected and checked by the teacher. Tests will be marked immediately after they are taken.

14. Each learning step and required test must be marked with the date it is completed, checked by the teacher, and then initialed.

15. It is advisable to mark or circle the optional communication tests that you have passed on your copy of the contract. In this way, you will know your report card grade in French by adding these extra points to the average of seventy.

16. You will receive up to five extra-credit points on your report card if the teacher observes you speaking French constantly in class.

C.   Student Responsibilities under the Contract System

Students' cooperation is necessary under the contract system. They can help their teacher in the following ways:

1. Work seriously both in class and at home.

2. Avoid any conversation not directly related to French in class.

3. If speaking in a group, speak softly and avoid those who might be studying or taking tests.

4. Keep to the time schedule. The deadlines are rigid and will not be changed; try to work ahead of them as much as possible.

5. Ask for help from friends, the student aide, and the teacher whenever needed.

6. <u>Never</u> discuss a test until all in the class have taken it. (Since there will normally be five forms of most written tests, the information would be of only limited value to others.)

7. Report to the teacher any problems related to the French class.

8. Share with the teacher any complaints or suggestions for improving classroom management. The teacher will provide a suggestion box.

9. The student aide will file all tests and written work. No papers should be kept by the student and no one may use the file cabinet.

10. Work in a normal, diligent manner, especially if a substitute teacher is supervising the class.

11. Take good care of library books, tape recorders, and tapes. Put all books and equipment away neatly.

12. Speak French at all times in class.

D. French Class Rules

1. To obtain a grade of seventy on your report card, each minimum required test must be graded "pass" (80 percent accuracy).

2. For every required test that is not passed with a grade of eighty, five points will be subtracted from the report card grade of seventy.

3. To obtain a report card grade above seventy, extra-credit assignments may be elected. Their point value will be added to the seventy received for passing required tests.

4. To obtain a grade above eighty-five on your report card, you may read an outside book per unit, approved by the teacher in advance, and summarize it orally or in writing. You may also compile a vocabulary list from the book and take an oral test on it.

5. You are encouraged to devise your own communication assign-ments which you would enjoy. You may emphasize listening, speaking, reading, or writing.

6. You are not required to perform the learning steps for a test if you pass the grammar pretest with 90 percent accuracy on or before the pretest deadline.

7. All test deadlines are <u>rigidly</u> observed, and the tests will <u>not</u> be offered afterwards. Exceptions to this rule, for one-day ab-sences or other reasons, will be rare.

8. Deadlines for required tests are for the period in which you have French class, not for the end of a particular school day.

9. Before the student aide gives you a test paper, he will check to see that all of the learning steps have been signed by the teacher. If they are not, you will not be able to take the test until they are completed.

10. While reviewing a test which has been graded and returned, you may not leave the testing area and may not show it to a friend who has not yet taken the test.

11. All tests and written work <u>must</u> be returned to the teacher for filing in your folder after you have reviewed them.

12. Only the teacher or student aide may use the files so that they may remain in good order.

13. The last date on which a required test is offered is <u>also</u> the deadline for submitting the communication assignments of that test to the teacher, but these assignments may be handed in through the last hour of the school day on the day they are due.

14. Tests may be taken <u>only</u> in the designated testing area; if any-one takes a test outside of the test area, his test paper will be destroyed.

15. Write on every other line of the paper for all written work that the teacher must correct.

16. All written work should be original. Any evidence of copying will result in the similar papers' invalidation.

17. If a written exercise requires the use of a minimum number of grammatical examples or vocabulary words, underline and number each item. If the use of a minimum number of words

is specified, write the number of words that you have used at the end of your paper.

18. Label each written communication assignment that you turn in to the teacher (IIA, IIIB, and so on).

19. Tests that are worth two or three points will be given two points for fluency and comprehensibility and three points if they are substantially above the required and are unusually accurate.

20. All point totals which fall between the grade points allowed on report cards (for example, eighty-seven points) will be recorded as the lower figure (eighty-five) and the additional points (two) will be credited to you for the next grading period. The last marking period's extra points will be added to the final test.

21. All exercises that have been corrected by the student must show evidence of self-correction by the use of a red pen.

22. Any student who speaks understandable French in class, whether it is accurate or not, will receive up to five extra points on his report card grade.

23. Although much of the assigned written work may be completed in class, it is advisable to assign yourself homework so that you may complete required tests and communication assignments before the deadlines.

E. French Class Rules for Two-Years-in-One Accelerated Contract

1. Students under the accelerated contract will finish second-year French at the end of the first semester and third-year French at the end of the second semester.

2. Perform only the learning steps that are absolutely needed for each grammar test in order to meet the deadline.

3. Eighty percent accuracy on tests will result in a minimum report card grade of eighty.

4. In order to adhere to the accelerated time schedule, it is advisable to contract for only eighty-five or ninety on your report card grade. If it is easy for you to learn French, you are certainly free to contract for higher grades, but remember that credit is more important than report card grades.[1]

---

[1] A third contract was subsequently added. It provided deadlines for completing the year's work in three grading periods, while the student had freedom for independent study during the fourth grading period.

II. SAMPLE PERFORMANCE CONTRACT

Text: *A-LM French, Level Two*, 2d ed., Unit 16

A. Agreements

1. Regular Contract

I, _____, intend to pass all my required tests on time with at least _____ percent accuracy. In addition, I plan to earn an average of at least _____ points a week during the coming ten-week grading period. This should entitle me to a report card grade of at least _____. I will/will not read one library book in French.

_____
(student's signature)

I have read the agreement.

_____
(parent's signature)

2. Accelerated Contract

I, _____, intend to finish all the required tests of this unit by _____ with at least 80 percent accuracy. In addition, I plan to earn an average of at least _____ points a week during the coming ten-week grading period. This should entitle me to a report card grade of at least _____ percent. I will/will not read one library book in French.

_____
(student's signature)

I have read the agreement.

_____
(parent's signature)

B. Level One Review Tests

In order to be eligible to begin work on Unit 16, you must pass the following two tests of twenty items each and make no more than two errors on each test.

1. Present tense of irregular verbs. Due within four days in class.[2]

   Write the correct present tense forms of the verbs on the attached list.

   Sample item: (avoir)   Tu _____ faim.

[2] On actual contracts, calendar dates are indicated.

2. Past tense (*passé composé*). Due within four days in class.

Write the correct past tense forms of the verbs on the attached list when you are given their present tense forms.

Sample item: Nous sommes ici.   Answer: Nous avons été ici.

C. Extra-Credit Communication Assignments

1. Speaking (two points)

Either tell a story about yourself using at least ten of the present or *passé composé* forms on your list (minimum time of one minute) or present a skit with a friend using these forms (minimum time of two minutes).

Conditions: No notes are allowed.

Grading: You will receive "pass" if your story or skit is understandable.

2. Writing (two points)

Write a story, skit, poem about yourself using at least ten of the verbs on the list in the present or *passé composé* (minimum length of fifty words per person). Up to three people may complete this assignment together.

Conditions: Skip lines and underline and number each verb form used.

Grading: Pass/Fail

D. Contract for Unit 16

1. Vocabulary

Deadline: three days

Demonstrate your knowledge of the Basic Material I vocabulary by supplying the English translation of French words read by the teacher during an oral in-class test of ten words selected from the attached list.

Conditions: No more than three seconds' hesitation is allowed. You may not look at the vacabulary list during the test.

Grading: Only two errors are allowed in order to pass.

You may retake the test as many times as you need until the deadline.

a. Learning Steps

The order in which you perform the learning steps may be varied.

1. Read the dialog and supplement (pp. 67–68). Consult an English translation only if needed. The teacher is available for help if you need it.

2. Listen and repeat the dialog and supplement (pp. 67–68) and Drills 10 and 11 (p. 73) on Tape Reel 1. Report to the teacher for checking.

3. Memorize the words on the attached vocabulary list. Have a friend test you by reading the English words so that you can supply the French translations. Report to the teacher for checking.

4. Report to the teacher for the oral test. Retake the test as many times as necessary until the deadline.

b. Optional Communication Assignments for Extra Credit

1. Speaking (1 point)

Demonstrate your ability to use the new vocabulary words by answering five oral questions given by the teacher. The questions will be based on Vocabulary Exercises 14 and 15 (p. 76) and on Exercises 22 and 23 (p. 81).

a. Learning Steps

(1) Write the answers to the above drills and have the teacher or aide check them for accuracy (optional step).

(2) Practice orally with a friend or the teacher.

(3) Report to the teacher for the test.

2. Pronunciation (one point)

Read aloud the text (p. 67) to demonstrate your ability to pronounce French correctly. You may practice orally with a friend or the student aide.

3. Writing (one point)

Demonstrate your ability to use twenty new vocabulary words in original sentences of at least five words each.

Conditions: Underline each new word used.

Grading: At least fifteen of the sentences should be easily understandable, if not entirely accurate, in order to pass.

4. Writing (two or three points)

Write a dialog, composition, or poem using the new vocabulary (minimum length of fifty words per person). Up to three people may work on this assignment together.

Conditions: Underline and number each of the new vocabulary words.

Grading: You will receive "pass" if the written work is understandable.

5. Speaking (two or three points)

Present an original skit, such as the argument between the parent and child (p. 67). Up to four people may work on this assignment together with a minimum time of one minute per person.

Conditions: No notes are allowed.

Grading: You will receive "pass" if your part of the presentation is understandable.

6. Listening (two points)

Demonstrate your ability to comprehend the vocabulary by listening to short paragraphs or dialogs on the tape and answering in written French four out of five questions.

Grading: You will pass if your answers show that you have understood what you have heard. Only the idea that you express will be graded, not the grammar.

2. Vocabulary (required)

Deadline: three days

Demonstrate your knowledge of the Basic Material II vocabulary by supplying the French translation of English words read by the teacher as in the Vocabulary Test I.

a. Learning Steps

1. Read the paragraph and supplement (pp. 75–76), referring to an English dictionary if necessary.

2. Listen to the paragraph and supplement of Tape Reel 2 and repeat during the pauses. Report to the teacher for oral checking.

3. Memorize the vocabulary list. Have a friend test you by reading the French words so that you can supply the English translations. Report to the teacher for checking.

4. Report to the teacher for the oral test. Remember that only two errors are allowed in order to pass. You may retake the test as many times as needed until the deadline.

b. Optional Extra-Credit Communication Assignments

1. Speaking (one point)

Demonstrate your ability to use the new vocabulary words by answering five oral questions given by the teacher. The questions will be based on Vocabulary Exericses 14 and 15 (p. 76) and on Exercises 22 and 23 (p. 81).

a. Learning Steps

(1) Write the answers to the above drills and have the teacher or aide check them for accuracy (optional step).

(2) Practice orally with a friend, the student aide, or the teacher.

(3) Report to the teacher for the test.

2. Writing (one point)

Demonstrate your ability to use twenty new vocabulary words in original sentences of at least five words each.

Conditions: Underline each new word used.

Grading: At least fifteen of the sentences should be easily understandable, if not entirely accurate, in order to pass.

3. Writing (two or three points)

Write a news story, an interview about current events or school life, or anything that you wish, either humorous or serious (see p. 75 of the text), using new vocabulary words (with a minimum of ten examples). Up to three people may work on this assignment together (minimum length of fifty words per person).

Conditions: Underline and number each of the new vocabulary words.

Grading: You will receive "pass" if your part of the written work is understandable.

4. Pronunciation (one point)

Read aloud the text (p. 75) to demonstrate your ability to pronounce French accurately.

a. Listen to and repeat the text on Tape Reel 2 or practice with the student aide.

b. Report to the teacher for the test.

3. Grammar (required)

Use of *à, de,* or nothing.

Deadline: three days

Demonstrate your ability to write *à, de,* or nothing correctly after ten written expressions based on the lists (pp. 79 and 82). You are to write an appropriate completion to the sentences.

Example: J'ai l'intention _____.

Grading: You are allowed no more than two errors of grammar or appropriateness in order to pass.

a. Learning Steps

1. Read explanations (pp. 78–83). Consult a friend, the student aide, or teacher for help if necessary.

2. Memorize the blue charts (pp. 79 and 82).

3. Ask a friend or student aide to test you by giving several expressions <u>out of order</u> to determine if you know how to use *à, de,* and nothing.

4. Listen to and repeat Drills 20, 21, 25, and 26 (pp. 80–83) on Tape Reel 2. Report to the teacher for checking.

5. Write Exercises 6 through 8 in the Workbook (pp. 39–41) on notebook paper. Number each exercise and correct your paper with the answer sheet that the teacher will give to you. Show your work to the teacher.

a. Complete Drill 24 (p. 82) by writing at least five original words for each sentence. You should make no more than one error with the prepositions.

b. Write Drill 27 (p. 83) and add at least five words of your own. You should make no more than one error.

c. Complete each sentence of the writing exercise (p. 92) by adding five words of your own to each sentence. You should make no more than one error.

6. Report to the teacher for the grammar test. You must make no more than two errors in order to pass, and you are allowed to retake the test only two more times.

b. Optional Extra-Credit Communication Assignments

1. Writing (one point)

Write each sentence in the Sentence Construction (p. 84).

Conditions: Only original work will be accepted.

Grading: In order to pass, you may make no more than two errors in the *passé composé*, articles (*un, le, la,* etc.), or possessive forms (*mon, ton, son, leur,* etc.)

2. Writing (two or three points)

Write a composition using at least ten of the expressions presented in the unit with *à, de,* or nothing before the infinitive (minimum length of fifty words per person). Up to three people may work on this assignment together.

Conditions: Underline and number the expressions used.

Grading: Your part of the composition should be understandable in order to pass.

4. Reading (required)

Deadline: three days

Demonstrate that you have read the story (pp. 85–87) in <u>one</u> of the following ways. Consult the teacher for approval of your choice.

a. Pronunciation

Read aloud any passage indicated by the teacher so that it is easily understood.

1. Learning Steps

(a) Read the passage (pp. 85–87) either silently or aloud, alone or with a friend.

(b) If necessary, ask a friend, the student aide, or the teacher for help.

(c) Report to the teacher for the test.

b. Speaking

Answer five of the ten questions in Exercise 23 (p. 87) so that the teacher can understand what you are saying.

Conditions: No notes or open textbooks are allowed.

Grading: In order to pass, you must make no more than one error.

1. Write the answers to the ten questions (optional).

2. Practice with a friend or the student aide.

3. Report to the teacher for the test. You may retake it as many times as necessary.

c. Speaking

Give a one-minute oral summary of the story in the *passé composé*.

d. Listening

The teacher or a tape will present five brief variations of the text. Before each passage, a question will be asked. The question will be repeated at the end of the passage, and time will be allowed for an oral or written (to be announced) response.

Grading: In order to pass, no more than one error or omission will be allowed. Only the content of your answer will be considered, not the grammatical accuracy.

5. Extra-Credit Assignments

If you finish the unit early, you may do any of the following:

a. Speaking (three or four points)

Hold a five minute conversation with the teacher on a topic of your choice. You will lead the conversation.

Grading: Pass/Fail

b. Writing (one point)

Write Exercise 11 in the Workbook (p. 44).

> Grading: No more than five major errors in grammar (verb
> forms, gender, and so on) are allowed in order to
> pass.

c. Reading (five points)

> Read an outside book from the classroom library after secur-
> ing the teacher's approval for your choice. Keep a vocabu-
> lary list. Present the list to the teacher for an oral test.
> Present a written or oral summary of the story which
> demonstrates that you have indeed read and understood the
> book.

d. Writing (two points)

> Write an article, interview, poem, review (with a minimum
> length of one hundred words) for the French Club news-
> paper.

APPENDIX B

I.   INTRODUCTION: USING *DEUTSCH-KERNSTUFE* IN INDIVIDUALIZED INSTRUCTION

We assume that teachers who intend to use *Deutsch-Kernstufe* in a course of individualized instruction are aware of the rationale for this approach. If not, they might consult Dale L. Lange, ed., *Britannica Review of Foreign-Language Education,* vol. 2 (Chicago: Encyclopaedia Britannica Educational Corp., 1969). The entire volume discusses the individualization of foreign-language instruction.

What follows, then, are specific behavioral objectives and steps for reaching these objectives for each unit of *Deutsch-Kernstufe.* These objectives and learning steps guide the student through the text while they learn at their own rate of speed. Some of the contracts or forms that are used for students at Live Oak High School to measure their learning rate have been included. Teachers who have not developed their own contracts may use these as models.

At Live Oak High School, no evaluation is considered that does not show at least 90 percent of the material learned. If a student scores below 90 percent, he is referred back to the text for more drill or study.

The introduction, sample lesson contract, and evaluation forms were developed by Gerald Logan for use in Live Oak High School, Morgan Hill, California.

Then, he may report for another evaluation. The process is repeated until the minimum performance criteria have been reached.

A sample report card is also included. Each course, such as the one using *Deutsch-Kernstufe,* is divided into ten units of school credit. A student earns credit toward graduation only in proportion to the amount of work completed—with the minimum performance criteria. Thus, a student could end the year with an A or B and only two or three units of credit, rather than the normal ten. He could also end the year with more than ten credits, having finished one course and started, or even finished, another course during the year.

Each student is required to spend fifty minutes per week in a small conversation group of five or six students. If he performs adequately and prepares himself properly for the session, he receives one unit of credit per semester for this work. He may earn ten units of credit by completing *Deutsch-Kernstufe* (there are eight units of text, not counting the two review units) and by participating fully in the conversation groups.

II. SAMPLE LESSON CONTRACT: INSTRUCTIONS FOR INDIVIDUALIZED OR INDEPENDENT LEARNING

Text: *Deutsch-Kernstufe,* Unit Four

A. Objectives

1. To demonstrate your knowledge of the three basic texts in the following ways:

   a. To read any of the texts aloud in an acceptable manner to the teacher.

   b. To answer all the questions concerning the texts (pp. 4–5) orally and in writing with no errors. (You may answer the questions with the short responses that are provided on these pages of the text).

   c. To write all three of the texts as dictations with no errors.

2. To demonstrate your command of German rules of pronunciation by pronouncing any or all of the words on page 6 acceptably for your teacher when the words are pointed out to you in a random fashion or by pointing to the words when you hear them pronounced.

3. To demonstrate your knowledge of the grammatical structures in Units 1 through 4, either orally or in writing, when these

structures must occur in subordinate clauses. Your ability to do the drills on pages 8, 11, 12, 14, and 16 fluently will constitute sufficient evidence of this required skill.

4. To demonstrate orally and in writing your knowledge of all the forms of *sein* as they appear on page 9 and to demonstrate orally and in writing your knowledge of the infinitive and past participle forms of the seven verbs—using *sein* as an auxiliary in the perfect tense—when you are given the English infinitive as a cue.

5. To demonstrate your comprehension of any German words, phrases, or sentences in the unit when you hear or see them by giving the English translation.

6. To demonstrate your comprehension of the story (pp. 27–28) by reading it aloud, answering the questions (p. 33) orally or in writing, and providing an explanation in English of any part of it.

B. Learning Steps

1. Learn Text A of Unit 4 in the usual manner. (See Step 1 of Units 1, 2, and 3 if necessary.) Refer to the tops of pages 136 and 137. First, however, practice with the taped model. When you are sure of your knowledge of Text A, report to the teacher for evaluation.

2. Practice the pronunciation of the "ach" and "ich" sounds and use the appropriate tapes. The text of the tape is on page 141.

3. Study Part 3 at the bottom of page 141 and then practice the first set of drills at the top of page 142. Refer to the taped version first.

4. Practice and learn to write Text A.

.   .   .   .   .

III. EVALUATION FORMS

A. Evaluation sheet for earning credits in German
(Units 1 through 4 of the text)

Name _____

Activities for earning one unit of credit and a grade of B:

	Evaluation (90 percent minimum)	Date of evaluation	Teacher (or aide)
1. Oral test on Text A	_____	_____	_____
2. Oral test on Text B	_____	_____	_____
3. Oral test on Text C	_____	_____	_____
4. Written test on Texts A, B, and C	_____	_____	_____
5. Oral test on ability to form sentences	_____	_____	_____
6. Comprehension test on any sentences in the unit	_____	_____	_____
7. Test on story in the unit	_____	_____	_____
8. Final test in unit (written)	_____	_____	_____
9. Pronunciation test (Unit 4)	_____	_____	_____

Activities for earning one unit of credit and a grade of A:

1. All of the activities above with evaluation of 95 percent or more	_____	_____	_____
2. Supplementary reading as posted on assignment board	_____	_____	_____
3. Sections E and F in text	_____	_____	_____
4. Short oral report on "research" into one additional aspect of German life (choose from posted list)	_____	_____	_____

The student named above has been awarded one unit of credit toward graduation from Live Oak High School.

This credit was earned in German _____.

_____   _____   _____
       date   grade   teacher

B. Evaluation sheet for earning credits in German
(Units 6 through 9)

Name _____

Record of work done to earn one unit of credit in German toward graduation.

The minimum requirements for earning one unit of credit and a grade of B:

Assignment	Date	Grade (90 percent minimum)	Teacher
1. Basic text (Oral)	_____	_____	_____
(Written)	_____	_____	_____
2. Vocabulary (Oral)	_____	_____	_____
(Spelling)	_____	_____	_____
3. New Forms (Oral)	_____	_____	_____
(grammar) (Written)	_____	_____	_____
(Oral)	_____	_____	_____
(Written)	_____	_____	_____
4. Unit test	_____	_____	_____
5. Nacherzählung	_____	_____	_____

The minimum requirements for earning one unit of credit and a grade of A:

1. The activities above at
achievement level of 95
percent or better _____ _____ _____

2. Section B in text _____ _____ _____

3. Section E in text _____ _____ _____

4. Reading assignment
(chosen from list) _____ _____ _____

The student named above has been awarded one unit of credit toward graduation from Live Oak High School.

This credit was earned in German course _____.

_____ _____ _____
date   grade   teacher

C.   Evaluation sheet for earning credits in German conversation groups where a minimum of fifteen participations is necessary for one unit of credit.

Name _____

	Date of activity	Participa- tion (+ or −)	Knowledge of vocab. (+ or −)	Teacher in charge
1.	_____	_____	_____	_____
2.	_____	_____	_____	_____
3.	_____	_____	_____	_____
4.	_____	_____	_____	_____
5.	_____	_____	_____	_____
6.	_____	_____	_____	_____
7.	_____	_____	_____	_____
8.	_____	_____	_____	_____
9.	_____	_____	_____	_____
10.	_____	_____	_____	_____
11.	_____	_____	_____	_____
12.	_____	_____	_____	_____
13.	_____	_____	_____	_____
14.	_____	_____	_____	_____
15.	_____	_____	_____	_____

The student named above has been awarded one unit of credit toward graduation from Live Oak High School.

This credit was earned through weekly participation in a German conversation group.

_____   _____   _____
date   grade   teacher

   D.   Grade and Credit Report Card

Student _____   Freshman   Sophomore   Junior   Senior

Course Title   Teacher _____

   1. _____

   2. _____   (If the student has completed one course and
                               begun another)

Time covered by report: Semester (Fall/Spring)—Quarter (1st/2nd)

Is this a college preparatory type course?   Yes   No

If so, does the student's work at this time show a quality and a quantity that
would indicate success in this subject if he were to continue it in college?

     yes   no   perhaps Jr. College   uncertain now

To what extent is the student applying himself to the work in this course?

     works hard   average effort   little effort

How many units of credit does this course yield when completed?

          1. 0   1   2   3   4   5   6   7   8   9   10

          2. 0   1   2   3   4   5   6   7   8   9   10

How many units has the student completed up to this point?

          1. 0   1   2   3   4   5   6   7   8   9   10

          2. 0   1   2   3   4   5   6   7   8   9   10

How many units were completed during this grading period?

          1. 0   1   2   3   4   5   6   7   8   9   10

          2. 0   1   2   3   4   5   6   7   8   9   10

How long has the student taken to reach this point? _____

What is the "normal" length of time for a student to take in reaching this
point if he is enrolled in German daily? _____

What grade has the student achieved on the work done?

          1. A   B   C   D   E   F   NM   PASSING   INC.

          2. A   B   C   D   E   F   NM   PASSING   INC.

Additional Comments:

_____   _____   _____
        date   parent's signature   teacher

E.   Letter to Parents

Dear _____ :

Your student, _____, has progressed as follows in German up to this point this year:

(   ) 1. Has been doing good work and has completed the normal amount of work, or more, expected of a "full-time" student. If the student continues at this rate, he can expect to receive A or B at report card time with full unit credit, or more.

(   ) 2. Has been doing good work, but has completed less than the normal amount. If the student continues at this rate, he can expect to receive A or B at report card time, but would not receive the full number of units of credit.

(   ) 3. Has been doing very little work. Although he may complete enough to get a grade on his report card, he is likely to receive very few units of credit.

(   ) 4. Is having serious difficulty. The student should either consider changing to a different German course, or dropping German altogether at this time and making a new start later.

EXPLANATIONS

Units of Credit. A full-time student usually earns five units of credit per semester in any course. If a student progresses at a slower rate, he might require more than one year in German to earn credit for completing "a year's course." For example, if the student's overall goal is to complete two years of German to satisfy a college entrance requirement, he may find himself needing two and one half or three years to meet this requirement. Some students can afford this time. Others might not be able to.

Slow Progress. If your student is progressing slower than normal at this time (students often pick up speed later), what do the teachers feel is the reason? We feel at this time that the reason(s) for our checking 2, 3, or 4 above is:

a)   the student does not make full use of the time he has in class.

b)   the student wastes a great deal of time in class in spite of frequent reminders of the consequences.

c)   the student works hard, but finds the subject difficult and finds it necessary to progress slowly.

d)   that we are not certain at this point and will make every effort to find out—and hope you might be able to help us find out.

e)   other:

SOLUTION

In most cases of slow progress, the student should spend more time on German than he has been doing. Can you encourage him to do so? We try. <u>Is he doing homework? Is he taking advantage of the fact that the German room is open and two teachers are available to him personally</u> from 7:15 to 8.00 A.M. daily, during both fifty-minute lunch periods, and after school from 2:30 to 3:30 P.M. daily (or even later)?

We hope we can work together in getting your student to produce what he is capable of. It may take only a few words from you to get him on the track. Don't hesitate to contact us if you wish.

—————————————
parent's signature

APPENDIX C

GUIDELINE FOR TEACHER PREPARATION IN FOREIGN LANGUAGES

Competence must be demonstrated before the student-teaching experience.

The following checklist defines the preparation of the foreign-language teacher in behavioral terms, that is, in terms of what the student should be able to do <u>before</u> he is accepted for student teaching.

Minimum acceptable competence is given on the left, and additional desirable competence is listed on the right.

Examples are given for French only. Guidelines using this model will be prepared for the other commonly taught languages.

Minimum Preparation	Preferred Preparation

I. Language Skills

_____ 1. The student can speak for three minutes using prepared material and making no more than five phonemic mistakes (including rhythm, intonation, stress, as well as specific sounds). | The student can speak for three minutes on <u>unprepared</u> material making no more than five phonemic or <u>phonetic</u> mistakes.

These tentative guidelines, developed by a subcommittee of the Massachusetts Foreign-Language Association Committee on Teacher Education, were prepared by Rebecca M. Valette (Boston College; subcommittee chairman) with the assistance of Elizabeth Ratté (Boston University; committee chairman), Richard Penta (Belmont Public Schools), and James Powers (Cambridge Public Schools).

Minimum Preparation	Preferred Preparation

_____ 2. Given learner recordings of familiar material, the student can identify nine out of ten phonemic mistakes.

Given learner recordings of <u>un</u>familiar material, the student can identify nine out of ten phonemic and phonetic mistakes.

_____ 3. Within the limitations of *Français Fondamental, premier degré,* the student can do the following in both spoken and written French at a rate of 95 percent accuracy:

Within the limitations of *Français Fondamental, deuxième degré....*

  a. Use all nouns with the appropriate gender markers.

  b. Find mistakes in gender with these nouns.

  c. Use the appropriate forms of the adjectives and determiners.

  d. Find mistakes in adjective and determiner form and agreement.

  e. Conjugate all verbs listed in the tenses included.

  f. Find mistakes in the forms of the verbs above in the tenses above.

  g. Use the grammatical forms and structures listed.

  h. Find mistakes in the grammatical forms and structures above.

_____ 4. The student can read and summarize an unfamiliar article of a general nature taken from a recent newspaper or periodical.

The student can <u>interpret</u> the article.

Minimum Preparation	Preferred Preparation

_____ 5. The student can listen to and summarize the content of an unfamiliar recording taken from commonly used Level Three or Four secondary school materials.

The student can listen to and summarize the content of unfamiliar radio broadcasts.

II. Literature

_____ 6. The student can scan an unfamiliar poem (rhyme scheme, meter, form).

The student can demonstrate familiarity with French literature by identifying authors, works, periods, movements, and so on.

_____ 7. The student can read an unfamiliar short story and identify the point of view, plot development, order of presentation of events.

The student can identify familiar quotations taken from literature.

_____ 8. Given any brief unfamiliar work of literature, the student can identify key words or phrases, relating to theme, character, tone, as appropriate to the passage.

The student can recite a French poem from memory.

III. Culture

_____ 9. Using an accepted reference work, such as Wylie-Bégué's _Les Français_, the student can answer questions about aspects of French culture, including their historical and geographical origins.

The student can answer such questions without a reference work, either because he has studied French culture closely or because he has lived abroad.

_____10. Given a map of France, the student can locate important geographical features (cities, main rivers, mountains, and so on).

Given a map, the student can describe cultural, historical, geographic and linguistic differences by region.

Minimum Preparation	Preferred Preparation

_____11. Given an example of a French cultural pattern, the student can describe the corresponding American pattern, pointing out similarities in the basic needs which the pattern manifests and showing the differences in their outward forms.

Given an example of an American cultural pattern, the student can describe one or more corresponding French patterns.

_____12. On viewing a French film depicting contemporary life, the student can identify at least five cultural patterns (status symbols, gestures, parent-child relations, and so on).

On viewing a French film, the student can identify five <u>linguistic</u> features (change from _vous_ to _tu_, level of language, regional accents, intonation patterns, and so on).

IV. Professional Preparation

_____13. The student can run a standard ditto machine, a tape recorder, an overhead projector, a slide projector, a film-strip projector, and a movie projector.

_____14. The student can prepare a ditto master (by typewriter or photostat technique), and an overhead transparency.

_____15. The student can prepare and splice a tape.

_____16. The student can use a console (language lab, electronic classroom) to monitor, correct, and test students.

_____17. The student can write behavioral objectives for a lesson he intends to teach. These objectives will be accompanied by suggested activities and a sample test.

The student can write behavioral objectives for a <u>variety</u> of different programs.

Minimum Preparation	Preferred Preparation

____18. The student can demonstrate and describe three alternate classroom techniques to be used at Levels One and Two ...

    a. to present and practice a new point of structure (at least one technique must be entirely in French).

    b. to present and practice new vocabulary (at least one technique must be entirely in French).

    c. to present and practice a feature of the sound system.

The student can demonstrate and describe three alternate classroom techniques to be used at Levels Three and Four. ...

____19. The student can demonstrate and describe three classroom techniques for developing student comprehension at Levels One and Two.
a. via listening
b. via reading

The student can demonstrate and describe three classroom techniques for developing student comprehension at Levels Three and Four. ...

____20. The student can demonstrate and describe three classroom techniques for developing student self-expression at Levels One and Two.
a. via speaking
b. via writing

The student can demonstrate and describe three classroom techniques for developing student self-expression at Levels Three and Four. ...

____21. The student can demonstrate and describe three classroom techniques for teaching a cultural concept at Levels One and Two.

The student can demonstrate and describe three classroom techniques for teaching a cultural concept at Levels Three and Four.

____22. The student can demonstrate or describe three ways to adapt modern foreign-lan-

The student can demonstrate or describe three ways to adapt modern foreign-language instruc-

Minimum Preparation	Preferred Preparation

guage instruction to current trends in curriculum development (individualized instruction, multi-media, and so on), at Levels One and Two.

tion to current trends in curriculum development at Levels Three and Four.

V.   The Language-teaching Profession

____23. The student can decribe the functions and the publications of the following regional and national professional groups: MFLA, the Northeast Conference, AATF, ACTFL.

The student can describe the functions and the publications of the following regional and national professional groups: NEMLA, MLA, NALLD, TESOL.

____24. The student has joined at least one of the groups above.

The student has joined two or more professional groups, and attended a professional regional meeting.

____25. In a mock discussion, the student can defend persuasively the values of foreign-language instruction.

____26. The student can informally evaluate his own performance in a micro-teaching situation and suggest two areas for self-improvement.

The student can use a formal self-evaluation technique to analyze his performance as a teacher.

SELECTED BIBLIOGRAPHY

Altman, Howard B. and Robert L. Politzer, eds. *Individualizing Foreign-Language Instruction.* Rowley, Ma.: Newbury House Publishers, 1971.

Fitzgibbons, Nancyanne. "The Open Classroom: A Case-Study," in *Leadership for Continuing Development.* Reports of the Working Committees of the 1971 Northeast Conference on the Teaching of Foreign Languages, pp. 97–107. New York, 1971.

Gougher, Ronald L., ed. *Individualization of Instruction in Foreign Languages: A Practical Guide.* Philadelphia: The Center for Curriculum Development, Inc., 1971.

————. "Individualization of Foreign-Language Learning: What is Being Done," in Dale L. Lange, ed., *Britannica Review of Foreign-Language Education,* vol. 3, pp. 221–45. Chicago: Encyclopaedia Britannica Educational Corp., 1971.

Mager, Robert F. *Developing Attitude Toward Learning.* Belmont, Ca.: Fearon Press, 1968.

Politzer Robert L. "Toward Individualization of Foreign Language Teaching," *Modern Language Journal,* 55 (1971): 207–12.

Popham, W. James. "Probing the Validity of Arguments Against Behavioral Goals," in Robert J. Kibler, *et al,* eds., *Behavioral Objectives and Instruction,* pp. 115–24. Boston: Allyn and Bacon, Inc., 1970.

Reinert, Harry. "Practical Guide to Individualization," *Modern Language Journal*, 55 (1971) : 156–63.

Smith, Alfred N. "Strategies of Instruction for Speaking and Writing," in Dale L. Lange, ed., *Britannica Review of Foreign-Language Education*, vol. 2, pp. 113–31. Chicago: Encyclopaedia Britannica Educational Corp., 1970.

Steiner, Florence A. "Behavioral Objectives and Evaluation," in Dale L. Lange, ed., *Britannica Review of Foreign-Language Education*, vol. 2, pp. 35–78. Chicago: Encyclopaedia Britannica Educational Corp., 1970.

Strasheim, Lorraine A. "A Rationale for the Individualization and Personalization of Foreign-Language Instruction," in Dale L. Lange, ed., *Britannica Review of Foreign-Language Education*, vol. 2, pp. 15–34. Chicago: Encyclopaedia Britannica Educational Corp., 1970.

Valette, Rebecca M. *Modern Language Testing*. New York: Harcourt Brace Jovanovich, Inc., 1967.

————. "Testing," in Emma M. Birkmaier, ed., *Britannica Review of Foreign-Language Education*, vol. 1, pp. 343–74. Chicago: Encyclopaedia Britannica Educational Corp., 1969.

GLOSSARY

AFFECTIVE GOALS Instructional aims relating to student attitudes, feelings, and values to be developed during a course of study.

AFFECTIVE TAXONOMY A hierarchical system of classifying student behaviors related to their attitudes, feelings, and values. It consists of the five stages Receptivity, Responsiveness, Appreciation, Internalization, and Characterization.

ANALYSIS Behavior that involves analysing unfamiliar individual elements, structures, and themes, as well as explanations of words, ideas, or symbols. It is classified as an internal behavior of Stage 5 in the subject-matter taxonomy.

APPLICATION Behavior that involves applying one's knowledge in situations where basic elements are familiar, but their particular order or combination is not. It is classified as the external subcategory of Stage 3 in the subject-matter taxonomy.

APPRECIATION Behavior that involves voluntarily attaching value to experiences related to the foreign language, literature, and culture. It is classified at Stage 3 in the affective taxonomy and includes the subcategories Valuing and Involvement.

ATTENTIVENESS Behavior that involves fulfilling all assignments and obligations of the course. It is classified at Stage 1 of the affective taxonomy.

247

AWARENESS Behavior that involves awareness of differences between one's native language and culture and the foreign language and culture being studied. It is classified at Stage 1 of the affective taxonomy.

BEHAVIORAL OBJECTIVE *See* PERFORMANCE OBJECTIVE.

CHARACTERIZATION Behavior that involves assimilation of the subject matter, attitudes, and values of the foreign language and culture to the point that one is identified by them. It is classified at Stage 5 of the affective taxonomy and includes the subcategories Integration and Leadership.

CIVILIZATION The sum total of a culture's contributions in the realms of art, music, philosophy, literature, natural and social sciences, and so on.

COMMITMENT Behavior that involves dedicating a major portion of one's time and energy toward the pursuit of further learning. It is classified at Stage 4 of the affective taxonomy.

COMMUNICATION Behavior that involves understanding and generating new messages in the foreign language with ease and comprehensibility, if not with absolute accuracy. It is classified at Stage 4 of the subject-matter taxonomy and includes the subcategories Comprehension and Self-Expression.

COMPETENCE An individual's potential for communication based on his foreign-language background.

COMPREHENSION Behavior that involves understanding the main ideas of a foreign-language speech or text that may include unknown words or expressions. It is classified as the internal behavior at Stage 4 of the subject-matter taxonomy.

CONCEPTUALIZATION Behavior that involves development of a personal system of values relating to foreign-language study. It is the internal behavior at Stage 4 of the affective taxonomy.

CONTINUOUS PROGRESS Method of instruction that permits a student to advance in the subject matter as fast as his learning rate will permit.

CRITERION Part of a performance objective that specifies how student behavior will be measured and what the minimum standard of acceptable performance will be. It may include sample test items.

CRITERION-REFERENCED TEST Measure of student achievement of predetermined performance objectives. Its purpose is to diagnose and remedy weaknesses rather than to exclude from further study the students who do not perform well.

CONDITIONS Part of a performance objective that specifies where student performance will take place, how long it will last, what aids or equipment will be available for us during the test, and so on.

CONTRACT Statement of what students will be able to do at the end of a specified period of time. It includes performance objectives, learning activities, and resource lists that ultimately enable students to exhibit the desired performance.

CRITICISM Behavior that involves analyzing, synthesizing, and evaluating foreign-language material. It is Stage 5 behavior in the subject-matter taxonomy and includes the subcategories Analysis, Synthesis, and Evaluation.

EVALUATION Behavior that involves judging the foreign language, literature, or culture. It is classified as an internal behavior at Stage 5 of the subject-matter taxonomy.

EXPRESSIVE OBJECTIVE Open-ended statement of complex student behavior in which the conditions and criteria are expressed in a general rather than specific manner. In some cases, the conditions and critera might be omitted altogether. This type of objective is most appropriate to Stages 4 and 5 of the subject-matter taxonomy and Stages 3, 4, and 5 of the affective taxonomy. Expressive objectives allow for greater freedom in student performances, as well as for more subjective appraisals of them.

EXTERNAL BEHAVIOR Any overt, observable behavior with which a teacher is concerned. In the area of language skills, it refers to speaking and writing.

FAMILIAR MATERIAL *See* RECOMBINED MATERIAL.

FORMATIVE EVALUATION Measurement of student performance at the end of a lesson or unit (quiz, test, unit test). The results are used to help the teacher diagnose student deficiencies.

GESTURE BEHAVIOR Body movement—such as posture, bearing, gestures, and facial expressions—used to convey messages and feelings. (Also called Kinesics.)

INDIVIDUALIZED INSTRUCTION Method of teaching that provides for ability differences among students by varying time, materials, course objectives, and teaching techniques according to individual needs.

INSTRUCTIONAL OBJECTIVES *See* PERFORMANCE OBJECTIVES.

INTEGRATION Behavior that involves the assimilation of values and attitudes relating to foreign languages into one's own personal value system. It is classified at Stage 5 of the affective taxonomy.

INTEREST AND ENJOYMENT Behavior that involves feelings of interest in the various aspects of a course, enjoyment of the class, and satisfaction with one's language progress. It is classified at Stage 2 of the affective taxonomy.

INTERNAL BEHAVIOR Behavior that occurs within the learner. Since it is not directly observable, it must be measured indirectly. For example, listening comprehension may be measured by circling "true" or "false" after each statement heard. In the area of language skills, INTERNAL BEHAVIOR refers to listening and reading.

INTERNAL CONSISTENCY Conditions whereby all parts of a performance objective measure the same stage of behavior.

INTERNALIZATION Behavior that involves decision-making based on attitudes, values, and concepts developed as a result of foreign-language and foreign-culture acquisition. It is Stage 4 behavior in the affective taxonomy and includes the subcategories Conceptualization and Commitment.

INVOLVEMENT Behavior that involves willing participation in extracurricular activities in order to improve one's foreign-language knowledge and skills. It is classified as the external behavior at Stage 3 of the affective taxonomy.

KINESICS *See* GESTURE BEHAVIORS.

KNOWLEDGE Behavior that demonstrates acquisition of facts and data related to the foreign language and culture. It is classified at Stage 2 of the subject-matter taxonomy and includes the subcategories Recognition and Recall.

LEADERSHIP Behavior that involves the assumption of an active role in furthering the development of foreign-language learning and research. It is classified at Stage 5 of the affective taxonomy.

LEARNING ACTIVITY Assignment designed to enable students to accomplish a specific performance objective.

MASTERY High degree of performance accuracy where the standard may vary from objective to objective.

MECHANICAL SKILLS Behavior that involves automatic rote performance without necessarily requiring understanding of the material presented. It is classified at Stage 1 of the subject-matter taxonomy and includes the subcategories Perception and Reproduction.

NORM-REFERENCED TEST Test whose results are used to rank or compare students on the basis of their performance (semester or final exam).

PERCEPTION Behavior that involves perceiving distinctions in oral and written language without necessarily understanding the material presented. It is classified as the internal behavior at Stage 1 of the subject-matter taxonomy.

PERFORMANCE OBJECTIVE Statement of what students will be able to do as a result of the instruction they receive. Formally stated performance objectives include the purpose of the assignment, a description of desired student behavior, the conditions under which this behavior is to occur, and the criterion used to evaluate the behavior. Formal performance objectives are most appropriate for behaviors at Stages 1, 2, and 3 of the subject-matter taxonomy and Stages 1 and 2 of the affective taxonomy.

PURPOSE Part of a performance objective that states why the desired student behavior is to take place.

RECALL Behavior that involves remembering and producing familiar facts, data, words, sentences, and so on. It is classified as the external behavior at Stage 2 of the subject-mater taxonomy.

RECEPTION Behavior that involves understanding of oral or written recombinations of previously learned vocabulary and structure. It is classified as the internal behavior at Stage 3 of the subject-matter taxonomy.

RECEPTIVITY Behavior that involves openness toward foreign-language learning activities. It is classified as Stage 1 of the affective taxonomy and includes the subcategories Awareness and Attentiveness.

RECOGNITION Behavior that involves recognizing and identifying familiar words, sentences, facts, data, and so on. It is classified as the internal behavior at Stage 2 of the subject-matter taxonomy.

RECOMBINED MATERIAL Oral or written sentences or passages consisting solely of familiar vocabulary and structures that are variations of material already presented.

REPRODUCTION Behavior that involves oral or written imitation of material that may or may not be understood. It is classified as the external behavior at Stage 1 of the subject-matter taxonomy.

RESPONSIVENESS Behavior that involves favorable attitudes toward language learning and a sense of satisfaction with one's progress. It is Stage 2 behavior in the affective taxonomy and includes the subcategories Tolerance and Interest and Enjoyment.

SELF-EXPRESSION Behavior that involves oral or written expression of one's own ideas. The message is easily comprehensible, although it may not be entirely accurate grammatically. It is classified as the external behavior at Stage 4 of the subject-matter taxonomy.

STAGE OF BEHAVIOR Class or type of student behavior listed in the affective or subject-matter taxonomy. The behavior may range from simple (Stage 1) to highly complex (Stage 5) student performances.

STUDENT BEHAVIOR Key part of a performance objective that states the task a student is to carry out.

SUBJECT-MATTER GOALS Instructional aims relating to course content and the skills it develops.

SUBJECT-MATTER TAXONOMY System of classifying student behaviors related to course content and skills from the simplest to the most complex. It consists of the five stages Mechanical Skills, Knowledge, Transfer, Communication, and Criticism.

SUMMATIVE EVALUATION Comprehensive measure of student performance at the end of a period of instruction, usually a quarter, semester, or whole year.

SYNTHESIS Behavior that involves native-like production of the foreign language or original research into the foreign language or culture. It is classified as the external behavior at Stage 5 of the subject-matter taxonomy.

TAXONOMY Classification system that ranks subject-matter and affective behaviors from the simplest to the most complex.

TEACHER ACCOUNTABILITY Concept that holds that teachers be accountable for the learning successes or failures of their students.

TERMINAL BEHAVIOR Performance that students are to demonstrate at the end of a given period of instruction.

TOLERANCE   Behavior that involves student toleration of the differences between the foreign language and culture and his own native language and culture. It is classified at Stage 2 of the affective taxonomy.

TRANSFER   Behavior that involves applying one's knowledge in situations that are different from those in the learning situations. Materials used at this stage consist of familiar vocabulary and structure presented in unfamiliar combinations. This behavior is classified at Stage 3 of the subject-matter taxonomy and includes the subcategories Reception and Application.

UNFAMILIAR MATERIAL   Listening or reading passage in the foreign language that is new to the student. The material may contain vocabulary and structures that students have learned, as well as some they have not.

VALUING   Behavior that involves attachment of worth and importance to the study of foreign languages, as well as a preference for related activities. This behavior is classified at Stage 3 of the affective taxonomy.

WAY-OF-LIFE CULTURE   Study of the daily routine and characteristic attitudes and values of natives in the foreign culture.

INDEX

B 3
C 4
D 5
E 6
F 7
G 8
H 9
I 0
J 1